The Language of Light

THE LANGUAGE
OF LIGHT

A HISTORY OF
SILENT VOICES

GERALD SHEA

Yale

UNIVERSITY PRESS

New Haven and London

Published with assistance from the foundation established in memory of James Wesley Cooper of the Class of 1865, Yale College.

Yale University Press books may be purchased in quantity for educational, business, or promotional use. For information, please e-mail sales.press@yale.edu (U.S. office) or sales@yaleup.co.uk (U.K. office).

Set in Gotham and Adobe Garamond types by IDS Infotech Ltd.
Printed in the United States of America.

ISBN 978-0-300-21543-4 (hardcover : alk. paper)

Library of Congress Control Number: 2017931104

A catalogue record for this book is available from the British Library.
This paper meets the requirements of ANSI/NISO Z39.48-1992 (Permanence of Paper).

10 9 8 7 6 5 4 3 2 1

For Claire, Pénélope, Sebastian, and Alexander

The blind are more intelligent than deaf-mutes.

Aristotle, 350 B.C.E.

Never . . . let the mute use sign language.

Juan Pablo Bonet, 1620

It is no longer possible to doubt whether a deaf man may be perfectly restored to society. With the benefit of instruction, he is neither deaf to those who know how to write, nor mute to those who can read. All the treasures of the human mind are placed at his disposal; he no longer has anything to envy in other men.

Auguste Bébian, 1817

We do not speak, it is true; but still do you think us unable to express ourselves as well with our eyes, our hands, our smiles, our lips? Our most beautiful discourse is at the tips of our fingers, and our language is rich in secret beauties that you who speak will never know. And have we not our own art of Phoenicia to paint the words that speak into our eyes?

Ferdinand Berthier, 1840

You, Sir, who have the rare talent of being at once mute and eloquent, please tell your friends . . . that in my eyes the accession of the deaf to civic and intellectual life must be counted among the most magnificent and decisive accomplishments in the history of the progress of humanity.

Victor Hugo (to Berthier), 1850

The practice of . . . sign language . . . makes deaf-mutes associate together in adult life, and . . . thus causes the[ir] intermarriage . . . and the propagation of their physical defect . . . Segregation during education has not only favored the tendency towards the formation of a race of deaf-mutes, but has led to the evolution of a special language adapted for the use of such a race—"the sign-language of the deaf and dumb."

Alexander Graham Bell, 1887

[T]he work [we have] so far accomplished seems to us to substantiate the claim that the communicative activity of persons using [sign] language is truly linguistic and susceptible of micro-linguistic analysis of the most rigorous kind.

William C. Stokoe, 1960

Technology has decisively shifted the balance of power in the oralists' favor . . . The signing deaf community will last another generation or two, but already it is seeing the signs on the wall and setting its house in order. Going gentle, with diminishing rage.

Michael Chorost, 2006

Contents

Preface   xi

Acknowledgments   xv

1   In the Beginning Was the Word   1

2   Language in Air, Language of Light   7

3   The Age of Darkness   12

4   The Enlightenment: The Age of Bébian   22

5   France Comes to America   50

6   The Banquets of the Deaf   58

7   The Congress of Milan: The Hundred Years' War   83

8   The Debate in England: Bell v. Gallaudet   92

9   Helen Keller: A False Symbol   116

10   Bébian Reborn: The Arrival of William Stokoe   144

11   To Sign Is to Speak   162

12   Milan Is Still, and Always, Today   170

13   Language in Electrons   179

14   Picture a Classroom   195

CONTENTS

Appendix 1: A Mortal Trinity   202

Appendix 2: The Handshapes of American Sign
Language   216

Notes   219

Bibliography   235

Index   251

Preface

This book is an intellectual history, an exploration of certain ideas about language. Everyone needs—it is a universal need—to be able to use his or her own tongue, the one he or she is at home in. The attribute that distinguishes us from other creatures is our capacity, through language, to express and explain our ideas and to receive and understand those of others. Language gives us, all of us, whether Deaf or hearing, a modern soul in the age of science, and underpins our rights as individuals. Take that away, and you have nothing.

I have been partially deaf since the age of six due to a childhood illness. The words that others speak to me are not my language: *lyricals* are the language I perceive and interpret, as I write in my earlier book, *Song Without Words*. They are what I call the transitional words, wrong words, and often non-words that, in lieu of those actually spoken, register in the minds of the partially deaf. Many of the hearing cells in our inner ears are dead or moribund, and the surviving cells deliver incomplete signals to the brain. Thus when others speak we hear only the contours of an elusive language to which, with our imperfect ears, and eyes that desperately search the lips of others, we endeavor to give meaning.

Children who are born Deaf, however, hear virtually nothing at all. They are also unable to speak because their ears cannot transmit to the brain the information it needs to shape the imitative speaking patterns of the voice. These children thus turn instinctively to gestures in order to communicate with others. They do so extraordinarily efficiently once they are exposed to a signed language, which they learn quickly and naturally. The discourse of the Deaf is not, as in the case of spoken languages, configured by the tongue and other organs of speech arranging molecules in the air, but by the motion of hands and other gestures that are transmitted by light to the eyes of their interlocutors. (When I capitalize the term *Deaf* in this history, I generally mean a deaf person whose tongue is a signed language. The term may also be said to embrace all those born deaf, or become so soon thereafter, notably because sign is the only language that comes immediately, fully, and naturally to them.)

Deaf people, like the hearing, have their own national or regional signed languages, shaped by tribe, nation, boundaries, culture, and history. French and Italian sign language or British and Dutch sign language, for example, are no more a common tongue than spoken German and Spanish or Russian and Danish. Occasionally in the book I will refer to "sign language," but the term should normally be understood as a reference to the signed language of the specific country in question.

Signed languages are as sophisticated as our spoken tongues. They have their own linguistic units, just as our oral languages do. When Deaf individuals render or interpret signs, they use regions of the brain that the hearing do when they speak and listen to speech. The neural pathways to the brain are those of the inner ear and the auditory nerve for the hearing, and of the retina and the optic nerve for the Deaf. Like other children, Deaf children develop mature language systems far beyond what they are exposed to. They very soon become able, exactly like their hearing counterparts, to express a limitless number of ideas in well-formed sentences with impeccable syntax.

I love my own language, my language of lyricals, my second tongue. I treasure its false phrases that stir the imagination with their nonexistent places and imaginary people. My imperfect ears may remodel "what will happen after Nora leaves," as *water happens after coral reefs*, or transform "her way of speaking gently" into *arrays of seas she sent me*. Lyricals have an intrinsic unconscious beauty, one that writers of our spoken tongues purposefully seek in their own prose or poetry. My lyricals are the reverse of those in poetic prose such as James Joyce's "the berginsoff, bergamoors, bergagambols, bergincellies, and country-bossed bergones," in which the lyricals are planned.

There is a common grace at the artist's end and our beginning. We start with our lyricals, and Joyce leads us to his. Each of us has or is given his ultimate tongue; the poet's words become fixed as poetry, and our lyricals are transformed into everyday discourse. But I envy Joyce and other writers the luxury of their deliberate wordplay, for the lyricals of the partially deaf are not a conscious poetry, and when they arise in the commerce of necessity they can be a hellish experience. They make of our lives a constant unscrambling of language, punctuated by masquerades of understanding.

I have no fluent understanding of the languages of the Deaf, but the grace and visual clarity of those who communicate in signed languages, which I call in this history the language of light, are to me a wonder, and I feel a close affinity to it and to them. Theirs is not an unplanned but a natural, visual poetry, at once both the speech and the music of the Deaf. Though I live in the realm of the hearing, a part of my life, in the form of my search for communicative grace and clarity, is quartered in my understanding of the world of the Deaf, and I feel as if a part of it.

This history, then, born of that affinity, is the story of the struggle of the Deaf across the centuries, along with their hearing allies, to preserve the grace and clarity of their own humanity through their perseverant insistence on being taught in their unspoken tongue—the only language that renders them complete, fully communicative human beings. We have always understood the critical importance of language. It is the precious faculty that forms the gentlest knot of society. Words and signs bind us together, both in the way we arbitrarily but collectively devise them through the ages and in the manner in which we express and say and sing them, with voice or hand, whether they be spoken in Spanish or German or Setswana or Sioux, or signed in American or Polish or Greek or Turkish sign language, or in the language of any other group or tribe or nation.

The differences between signed and spoken languages are readily observable and thus superficial, like other cultural distinctions, and they bring us all—or should bring us all—back to a better understanding of ourselves and in turn to a greater empathy for others. I am hopeful that this history will lead to a deeper understanding of the Deaf, their remarkable language, and their dramatic history.

Paris, Spring 2017

Acknowledgments

As one of my distinguished mentors in law school has elegantly written, upon the completion of a work a final and pleasurable duty is the tender of thanks to the many who have given aid and comfort. I extend my deep thanks and appreciation to Professor Stephen R. Anderson of Yale University for encouraging me to write the book, for reviewing the manuscript, and for his perceptive thoughts and advice on many issues, notably in the field of linguistics, an area to which I have come (and for the most part have emerged) as a stranger. To Professor Harlan Lane for reading the manuscript and providing invaluable guidance, from the very beginning, on the history of the Deaf and other central questions addressed in the book.

To Florence Encrevé, for reviewing portions of the manuscript and for her invaluable insights on Deaf and social history in France in the nineteenth century; to Dr. A. James Hudspeth of Rockefeller University for improving and correcting my layman's account of the physiology of the ear and the cochlea; to Dr. Richard H. Masland and other members of the staff of the Massachusetts Eye and Ear Infirmary for their generous time in interviews relating to hearing, the ear, and cochlear implants.

To Bertrand Duplantier of the Institute of Theoretical Physics (Saclay) and to Dr. Nicholas C. Spitzer of the University of California, San Diego (UCSD) for their advice on issues concerning the physics of sound. To Dr. John M. Evans for his generous advice on questions of physics from the outset. The inevitable errors in the book are and remain, of course, mine alone.

My deep thanks as well to Alexandra Masbou, the director of the documentary film about my life entitled *L'Art de la déduction* (The Art of deduction), for helping me to know more both about the Deaf and about myself; and to her talented co-editor and cameraman, Jean-Philippe Urbach. To Emmanuelle Laborit, the celebrated Deaf actress, for her remarkable book, *Le cri de la mouette*, and for her empathetic understanding of my previous book, *Song Without Words,* and its depiction of the world of the partially deaf. Also to Tom Humphries of UCSD for reading significant parts of the manuscript and for his advice on signed languages, on teaching at Gallaudet, and on how signed languages have generally been viewed over the years by Deaf people since the Congress of Milan.

Un grand merci to Michelle Balle, chief librarian at the Institut national de jeunes sourds in Paris, for her constant and invaluable guidance throughout the period of my research; to the faculty at Gallaudet University, including Professor William T. Ennis, Dennis Berrigan of Gallaudet's Kendall School; and to Christopher Shea of the Gallaudet library; as well as, for their patience with and tolerance of a poor student, to my sign language teachers at Gallaudet and at the school of the International Visual Theatre in Paris. To Jennifer Arnott, Jennifer Hale, and Jan Seymour Ford, of the Hayes Research Library at the Perkins School for the Blind, for their help with my research at the Perkins archives relating to Helen Keller. And to Patricia Rogers and Jonathan Randolph of the Abbot Public Library in Marblehead, Massachusetts, for their invaluable help over the summer months with respect to both *Song Without Words* and this book.

Thanks are due as well to my illustrious teachers and mentors of earlier years for their personal guidance and support, including Joshua L. Miner III, Robert W. Sides, and Stephen S. Sorota at Phillips Academy, Andover; to Dudley Fitts, also of Phillips Academy, for teaching me how to write (any grace in the writing is his, the clumsiness mine); to Professors Jacques Guicharnaud and Victor Brombert, and to Franklin L. Baumer, of the French and History Departments, respectively, of Yale University; and to Professors Julius Goebel Jr., John N. Hazard, Willis L. M. Reese, and Maurice Rosenberg of Columbia Law School. My thanks as well to Edward A. Perell and Robert J. Gibbons for their invaluable guidance during my years of law practice with Debevoise & Plimpton in Eastern Europe, and to Lucio A. Noto and J. Edward Fowler, my highly talented mentors and colleagues during my years as a lawyer with Mobil Corporation in the United States and in the Middle East.

I am especially grateful to Jean Thomson Black, my editor at Yale University Press, for the extraordinary talent she has brought to bear in shaping the book and improving the quality of the writing; to my able copy editor at Yale, Julie Carlson, for her remarkable ability to focus both on matters of general style and clarity and on minute but critical details; to Merloyd Lawrence, the editor and publisher of *Song Without Words*, for her general advice and guidance with respect to this new book; to my literary agent, Markus Hoffmann, for his customary and valuable guidance, practical and editorial; and to Brigid Williams, a talented architect but also an effective and voluntary literary scout. Warm thanks as well to Rémy Pujol and his Association NeurOreille, for graciously permitting us to reproduce his illustrations of the inner ear; to Bill Nelson for his skillful adaptation of most of NeurOreille's images; and to the Institut national de jeunes sourds, Gallaudet University, and the Mayo Clinic for permitting us to reproduce their images.

Foremost and finally, I express my deepest thanks to and affection for my wife, Claire, for her unfaltering love and support, and for tolerating my long labors over this book; and, for their unremitting filial affection, our sons, Sebastian and Alexander, and my stepdaughter, Pénélope. I also extend my warmest thanks to her husband, Theo Stewart-Stand, for guiding me through the mysteries of documents and images in today's virtual world.

The Language of Light

1

In the Beginning Was the Word

There is little historical record of the Deaf, or of their language, before the sixteenth century.[1] Signed languages in various forms and degrees of sophistication may have existed for at least a hundred thousand years—for as long as has mankind and thus have Deaf people. Sign may even be more ancient than speech. An early prelingual ancestor, like a Deaf person in our own time, could have brought news of a birth by sliding one hand under the other, palms down; of a battle by tapping his open fingertips together; of an invasion by bringing both hands forward, palms in, fingers closed; of resistance by moving his facing fists downward; or of love by pressing both arms with clenched hands to his breast.

It is clear that through the ages isolated Deaf individuals have developed limited inventories of what we today call "home signs," but signed languages require something more. According to one theory, it was only with the rise of the city that Deaf people came together in sufficient numbers to support the emergence of complete languages. We do know that in Nicaragua, for instance, the emergence of a signed language was a direct consequence of the gathering together in a school for the Deaf of enough people (each bringing along his or her own home signs) to form a communicating community.[2]

Plato wrote that if the hearing had no use of voice and tongue, they would want to explain things to each other, just as "mutes" do, with the movement of their hands, head, trunk, and limbs. Aristotle wrote that sight was the more important sense as a practical matter because it enables us to fulfill our primary needs, like getting from one place to another. But hearing took precedence as an intellectual sense because—or so he thought—all rational discourse had to be audible. He thus considered the blind "more intelligent" than the Deaf because the blind could hear.[3]

Saint Augustine in the fifth century recognized the existence of signed languages, but thought Deaf people could never learn to read. Nevertheless, he believed that it didn't matter, as a person grew up, whether he spoke or made gestures, "since both pertain to the soul." Augustine's contemporary Saint Jerome wrote that "by signs and . . . by eloquent gestures of the whole body, the deaf can understand the Gospel." In the sixth century the Council of Orange authorized the baptism of the Deaf if they requested the sacraments by signs. It never occurred to any of these philosophers that if they were to engage the Deaf and study these "movements"— or, for Augustine, these gestures pertaining (like speech) to the soul—they could translate them into the language in which the hearing wrote and thus teach the Deaf to read and write. Augustine may have come close, though he claimed he didn't have the time to learn a signed language, and that it would be difficult for a hearing person to have a signed language explained to him.[4]

Hearing people were not only long ignorant of the nature of the language of the Deaf, but they took careful steps to circumscribe their rights, notwithstanding their eligibility to receive the sacraments. The code promulgated by the Byzantine emperor Justinian in 522 classified deaf people with meticulous precision:

- If a person was deaf from birth and could not speak, he had virtually no rights.

- If through an accident a person became deaf but could still speak, or lost his voice but could still hear, or lost both his hearing and voice but could (still) read and write, he enjoyed the same rights as a person who could both hear and speak.
- If a person were deaf from birth but could nevertheless speak, he would enjoy similar rights.[5]

Though the code calls the last case "rare . . . according to the jurists," it offered a challenging opportunity for teachers willing to give it a try. Presumably a person Deaf from birth who could read and write would enjoy similar rights, though in the sixth century such cases may have been considered too rare, even for the jurists.

In the New Testament, Christ cures a Deaf man, and the event is illustrated in the eleventh-century prayer book of Saint Hildegarde of Bingen.[6] Such events were rare, perhaps because any miraculous healing of the inner ear would lack the dramatic effect of the physical transformation of a leper, a cripple, or a blind man. During the Middle Ages the Deaf were not allowed to marry because, it was feared, they were unable to understand the primary purpose of marriage— producing more souls for heaven and thus the greater glory of God. Guillaume de Mende, a twelfth-century bishop, thought the Deaf were "refusing" to hear the word of God, and as mutes were "unwilling" to speak it, though they were able to do both.[7] Christ himself was at the beginning of the creation a Word—who was *with* God, and *was* God, and was *later* made flesh, and dwelt among us. Though an unfortunate phrase for the Deaf, these words were an imaginative exercise in lexical legerdemain, reconciling as they did the temporal birth of Christ with his timeless nature as the Second Person of the Trinity.

"Ephphatha." Christ curing a Deaf man, from the prayerbook of Saint Hildegarde of Bingen. (Hildegard von Bingen, Gebetbuch. Bayerische Staatsbibliothek München, Clm 935, fol. 30v.)

In Haydn's *Creation* the Word "resounds in all the land . . . never unperceivèd, ever understood"—ever spoken, never unheard or misunderstood. What then was a man or woman who couldn't speak, understand, or even perceive the Word—the Bible, the gospels, Christ himself? Who was this individual who lacked the critical human characteristic that distinguished other men and women, made wholly in God's image, from animals? These dogmatic perceptions of the Deaf served the civil interests of medieval governments as well, because of the fear that the married Deaf would have Deaf offspring. *Healthy* issue served both God and the state, not children whose intelligence was so impaired that they had little or nothing to contribute to the economy and who, despite their normal outward appearance, seemed more closely related to animals than to human beings.

In the sixteenth century, Montaigne nevertheless wrote that "the deaf argue, disagree and tell stories by signs. I've seen some so supple and knowledgeable that, in fact, they are nothing less than perfect in their ability to make themselves understood." Diderot, however, thought that to teach the Deaf abstractions was virtually an insurmountable task, as it was to have them learn tenses, that is, the difference between *I do, I have done, I was doing, I would have done.* No doubt he would have thought the proper use of the *passé simple*, a high threshold for most human beings, the ultimate impossibility for the Deaf.[8]

Diderot compared the Deaf to primitive man, who communicated only (or so he imagined) in the present tense or through the use of infinitives. Of this observation Ferdinand Berthier, the great Deaf French teacher, wrote in 1840: "I prefer to leave the opportunity to refute the great philosopher to those who have seen our students apprehending and happily applying with lightning speed these distinctions he purports to be so difficult."[9] Diderot had no knowledge of French sign language. He felt quite at home with spoken French, however, praising it in 1751 as "the most polished, the most exact and the most estimable of all languages."[10] This was only because, happily for those of us who read him, French was his first language. Had he been raised speaking Chinese, or as a German, a Pole, or a Russian, he would, of course, have held those tongues in equal esteem.

It seems clear that these writers and philosophers were observing individuals communicating with each other with considerable facility, explaining things in "eloquent gestures" and arguing, telling stories, and making themselves "perfectly" understood. They were, in effect, communicating in signed languages cultivated across the ages among the Deaf in local communities, towns, and regions. Pierre Desloges, a leading Deaf thinker and writer in the eighteenth century, describes the phenomenon. Deaf people would meet others more fluent than they, and would learn how to integrate and perfect their signed language. They would quickly acquire, through interaction with others, "the art, *purported* to be so difficult, of depicting and expressing all of their thoughts, even the most abstract, by means of natural signs, with an order and precision worthy of a grammarian."[11] Desloges observed that he often found himself getting together with workers in Paris, Deaf from birth, who though they couldn't read or write were able to express themselves on every conceivable subject. They did so at such a rapid pace that made it seem as if everyone were speaking and listening. In fact, these people were functioning just as we all do in our own first languages.

Desloges was generally well aware of how well the Deaf "spoke" because he was Deaf himself. But Western philosophers could have caught on to things much earlier simply by thinking about what they were looking at. You needn't be a neurologist or a modern linguist, nor even to understand a language, to recognize that the people using a signed language are expressing and understanding complex ideas— that they're engaged in conversation. But it was not until the middle of the eighteenth century that a hearing contemporary of Desloges would seize upon the idea and put it to use. It was a flash of genius that was to lead to immeasurable progress in the education of the Deaf. Before his time, however, beginning in the sixteenth century, others had set themselves an impossible task that was at least partially rooted in the Justinian Code: to teach the Deaf how to hear and speak. Before exploring how they tried to do it, we will examine the indispensable roles that light and air play in what perhaps the greatest teacher of the Deaf has called the commerce of souls.

2

Language in Air, Language of Light

The voice of Caruso, a flute in the distance, the wind in the willows—
these and the infinite numbers and types of the oscillations of our
physical world produce vibrations in the air, which we call sound. It is
the medium through which those of us who hear express our thoughts
to others and they to us, enabling our souls to touch and our hearts to
mingle. Even if we could somehow live and not breathe, without air
we would hear nothing, and our screams, our tears, our laughter, our
music, would be silent, our words nonexistent. From birth to death
we breathe in and out, conscious every moment of our waking lives
that we can't live without air. But we are less aware that air is also our
means of communication with other hearing beings, and the rest of
the world around us.

Air is elastic, and the vibrations of objects temporarily alter its
form. The vibrations don't move the air's molecules from one point to
another; instead the molecules move back and forth about an average
resting place, like the vibrating object itself. When Caruso's vocal
cords or the reeds of a flute or a willow oscillate, they cause the adjacent air molecules to vibrate in the same fashion, creating a zone of
compression and rarefaction as the molecules push together and then
draw apart. The pattern is repeated as successive adjacent air particles
are nudged by their predecessors. The pattern in the air reflects that of
the oscillating object. Not to hear the pattern is devastating. To hear

it, as Rat put it in *The Wind in the Willows*—*O, Mole! The beauty of it! The merry bubble and joy*—can be the measure of a man's happiness.

It is our ears, of course, that make all this possible, by capturing the voices that travel to them through the air. The molecules of air that arrive at the ear of the listener have been shaped by the configurations and movements of the organs of speech (larynx, vocal cords, mouth, tongue, palate, teeth, nose) of the speaker.

From the Hush of a Whisper to the Roar of a Jet Engine

The normal ear is able to hear sounds that differ dramatically in intensity, within a range so great that it is measured on a logarithmic scale. The basic unit of measurement was originally the "bel," named for Alexander Graham Bell a year after his death in 1922 by engineers at Bell Telephone. Zero bels is the level of sound at the threshold of hearing. One bel is ten times that level, two bels is ten times ten or one hundred times the threshold, and so forth. Today the standard unit of measurement is the "decibel" (dB), adopted to denote the tenfold increases in intensity from each bel to the next. Ten decibels are thus one bel, twenty decibels two bels, and so forth.

The loudest sounds we can hear without injuring our ears are at about 140 decibels—equivalent, for example, to the sound of an accelerating jet engine a hundred yards away. This means that the jet engine's sound pressure level is 10^{14} (ten times ten times ten . . . fourteen times in all) relative to that produced by the faint whisper we hear at our hearing threshold at just above atmospheric pressure. In other words, the loudest sounds we hear have 100 trillion times more energy than the faintest. And yet both the loudest and the softest sounds involve almost an infinitesimal displacement of air molecules and of the eardrum—about one-seventh the thickness of this page for the most intense sounds, and one-tenth the radius of an atom for the softest. The "louder" a sound is, the greater is its temporary displacement of air, the more intense the air's compression, the more attenuated its rarefaction.

The ear is a wonder of nature, as the details in Appendix 1 show. To many of us it is just the ear we see. But its most critical components lie inside the head.[1] Our outer, visible ear funnels sound to the eardrum and middle ear, where the three tiniest bones (ossicles) in our body—the hammer, the anvil, and the stirrup—amplify them and send them on to our inner ear and its cochlea. The hair cells in the cochlea convert the sounds to electrical signals and transmit them to the auditory nerve which conveys them to the brain. The middle and inner ear are a miracle of miniaturization. The middle ear cavity, first opened up for us by our marine ancestors (see Appendix 1), is three-tenths of a centimeter wide and 1.5 centimeters high and has roughly the volume of a sugar cube. The cochlea, which contains our critical auditory receptor cells, is even smaller—less than one centimeter in diameter at its widest point at the base and only a half a centimeter tall.

We take our ears for granted, though their mechanical and electronic structures, and their developmental history, are highly complex. What does our knowledge of the complexities of the ear and of hearing signify to the deaf or partially deaf? For those profoundly deafened after they have learned to speak, we know that their cochleae are no longer sending any signals to the brain. Their ability to speak generally survives, but the sound waves they used to hear die in the nerve center of the cochlea, the organ of Corti, among the withered cells, untuned to their respective optimal frequencies, or to any other. At the bottom of the cochlea's lower chamber, figuratively drowned in perilymph, lie millions and millions, logarithms of millions, of phonemes and words and phrases and people and places, and every imaginable orally transmitted thought, emotion, and idea that have gone unheard.

I have been partially deaf since the age of six, and thus have long lived in, and have a certain understanding of, both worlds, that of the hearing and that of the Deaf. For us, the partially deaf, a grasp of the ear's complexity accords us a more profound appreciation of how we communicate. The surviving hair cells in our cochleae receive signals from our middle ear and deliver to the brain incomplete messages, what I call my *lyricals*, from the surviving cells. The brain strives to complete these messages by racing through the possible alternatives, tossing life rafts to our drowning words.

The brain can call upon no other evolved anatomical structure to do so. Its neurons explore the choices by plunging into our acquired treasury of language. The brain then struggles to make sense of the information, and more often than not manages to do so by constructing and moving through the alternatives. And we hear sufficiently well (particularly if the cochlear damage has been suffered after we have learned to speak), to develop precisely the same sophisticated spoken language system as that of other speakers.

In the case of the Deaf, as in the case of those deafened after learning to speak, the cochleae generally house inanimate or moribund cellular life at all frequencies, and are thus unable to transmit to the brain the information sent to it by the configured molecules of air striking the eardrum. Children born Deaf are also unable to speak because the cochlea is unable to transmit to the auditory nerve the information that would have enabled the listener's brain to shape the patterns of his or her voice. Speech unheard will be speech unspoken. But the children will turn instinctively to their eyes and hands in order to communicate with their interlocutors. They will thus convey and receive ideas, to and from other signing children or adults, much as we all might have in a hypothetical world in which our ears had not evolved into the wonder they are.

Deaf children do so in the signed language to which they are exposed, which they will learn immediately and naturally, languages as sophisticated and complex as any spoken tongue. Their languages are not configured, as in the case of speech, by the shape, location, and movement of the tongue and other organs of speech arranging molecules in the air, but by the movements of hands, arms, eyes, and facial expression transmitted by light to the eyes of their Deaf interlocutors. In both cases, for both the hearing and the Deaf, the message is interpreted by the mind. Whether the message is sent as speech through the air to the ear or as a signed language to the eye, the hearing and the Deaf practice both the interpretation and formulation of language in comparable centers of our brains.

Throughout most of this book, references to the historical capacities of people, born Deaf, to hear and to speak are not meant to encompass the complex effects of cochlear implants, which were introduced in the late twentieth century. Deaf infants are now being implanted extensively throughout Europe and the United States, sometimes at ages as young as six months. The cochlear implants' electrodes are threaded into the cochlea in order to send electronic signals directly to the auditory nerve, bypassing the cochlea's hearing cells. In spite of repeated efforts to overcome their limitations, however, the implants lack the breathtaking complexity and precision of the natural system of the inner ear.

3

The Age of Darkness

Beginning in sixteenth-century Europe, substantial efforts were made to teach the Deaf to speak. The goal was not so much to educate them as to enable them to perform the mechanical function of uttering words, whether or not they understood them. A central problem for aristocratic families in Europe, as in Byzantium, was that Deaf offspring had to be able to speak in order to inherit. These and other considerations led to the growth and influence of teachers of speech and lipreading.

These teachers first appeared in Spain, at the pinnacle of its power in the sixteenth and seventeenth centuries (Pedro Ponce de Leon and Juan Pablo Bonet), then in England and Holland in the seventeenth century (John Wallis and Conrad Amman); and later in France and Germany in the eighteenth century (Jacob-Rodrigues Pereire and Samuel Heinicke). These men were the early proponents of the "oralist" movement, which contended that Deaf people should abjure their "signs" and learn how to speak and to read lips. Like many of their successors in the nineteenth and twentieth centuries, the oralists were either charlatans or incompetents. Ponce went so far as to claim that he taught Christian doctrine orally to his Deaf students and enabled them to confess their sins vocally.[1] Signed languages would not be regarded as true languages for almost two hundred years, but to establish and protect their positions as instructors in speech, these teachers generally turned a blind eye to the possibilities.

In 1620, Juan Pablo Bonet published the first known work on teaching the Deaf and dedicated the book to his sovereign, Philip III of Spain. In his introduction, Bonet observes that the Deaf were generally regarded as "inferior beings, monsters of nature and human only in form" (*no parece sirven de mas que de piadossos monstruos de la naturaleza que imitan nuestra forma*). His goal was to "cure" them with his "scientific art."[2] What *was* that art? First, he observed that consonants were given names that were too complex in that they conveyed more than their simple sounds. In the name *Francisco*, for example, the names of the letters are eff, are, ay, enn, see, eye, ess, see, oh. But no one leaves his heart in *San Effarayennseeeyeessseeoh*.

Bonet's first step was thus to teach the Deaf how to make the simple sounds the letters represent, disregarding what we call them. He adds a curious analysis of the origin of Roman letters, showing how each letter represents the shape of the mouth as it makes the sound. The two loops in the letter B, for example, depict our convex lips as we puff on them just before releasing the voiced air. The C shows the shape made by our open mouth and a throat blocked by an arched tongue curved at the back to touch the edges of the soft palate. P has only a single loop because the expiration of (unvoiced) air acts primarily on the upper lip. G is like C, but with the jaw a bit extended, giving us the shelf at the base of the G's opening. The A, turned ninety degrees, is the mouth forming a trumpet as it makes the sound. The A's transversal is there to emphasize that, just like at the dentist's office, the mouth has to stay open.[3]

With this imaginative introduction, Bonet then tells us all that needs to be done. First the teacher shows the Deaf student how to make the simple sounds of letters by shining a light on the teacher's own mouth as he utters them, using a leather replica of a tongue to help illustrate its movements, thus avoiding the messy business of "put[ting] one's fingers into the student's mouth." Some letters, Bonet tells us, are quite simple. To form the letter F, for example, the "mute" blows out air while keeping the upper teeth pressed on the lower lip, holding the tongue immobile. For the letter M, the lips have to stay closed to let the breath escape by the nose. Bonet had some difficulty, sounding a bit like a dentist himself, in describing what his mute had to do to pronounce the letter D: "The tip of the tongue presses against the teeth and the upper gums, as if to close the mouth and hold one's breath, but the tongue releases as soon as the aspirated air strikes this point. To enable the mute to understand that the tongue shouldn't cling to the palate, but releases the moment the aspirated air arrives, one can again make use of the leather tongue. Taking it in your hand and raising it to an elevated point, you blow on it so that the breath makes it fall. In this way the student will understand that he should drop his own tongue the moment his breath strikes this point of his organ."[4]

Bonet did understand that the Deaf couldn't speak because they were unable to hear, not because of any defect in the voice or the tongue. The key to teaching them to speak was thus simply to show them the position of the mouth, the lips, the teeth, and his hand-held leather tongue, in making the sound each letter called for. He compared his mute to a guitar—all you had to do was press the right frets and the proper sounds would be played, no matter who was strumming. Slowly, the mute would move from letters to syllables to words. He could then be taught to read aloud, and to master the pauses represented by punctuation.[5] He couldn't understand what he was saying or reading, of course, but Bonet's principal objective was to be sure that others understood *him*, or at least that he was, in fact, speaking, when he tried to speak.

Bonet did not entirely ignore the need to teach his students to understand the words they were speaking. Once "reading" aloud was mastered, the student could be taught the words for objects by pointing them out—chair, table, nail, hat. As for emotions, the teacher could either wait for the student to exhibit them or (in view of the unpredictable timetable) "provide circumstances that would give rise to inoffensive passions appropriate for his age."[6]

To his credit, Bonet was refreshingly frank about lipreading, considering it his task only to teach the Deaf how to speak (or to simulate speech), not how to understand others, for speech alone was enough to qualify a Deaf child for inheritance in Spain, as in Byzantium. Bonet found lipreading, and its teaching, virtually impossible: "To read upon the mouth of a speaker, the mute will need to see the formation of each letter . . . But it would be too demanding to obligate everyone who speaks to the mute to speak with his mouth wide open, since this isn't the way we do it—in ordinary conversation we don't open our mouths to show the different movements of the tongue. But the mute won't understand if he *doesn't* see them, because they take the place of letters . . . Moreover, he will begin to grimace as he speaks himself, an uncommonly ugly habit" (*que en el y en ellos fuera notable fealdad*).[7] Like eating with your mouth open.

So lips alone won't do, Bonet correctly concludes—there are too many unseen variables to "teach" lipreading to the Deaf. Though lipreading is an indispensable exercise for the partially deaf, and a necessary lifeline for the unraveling of our lyricals, it is virtually impossible without at least some residual hearing. If there is a Deaf student here and there who succeeds, he added, it's a kind of sixth sense, a rarity (according to the jurists and everyone else) not due to anything he can be taught by a teacher. The spy movies we see with Deaf people reading lips with binoculars or through hermetically sealed windows can be fun, but of course in those cases the enemy's secret plans are being unveiled by an actor reciting a script.

All of Bonet's nonsense about teaching "speech," though, was a recipe for disaster. Trying to imagine being a Deaf student and going through the "D" exercise for Juan Pablo makes the thing clear enough. Your tongue is pressed against your upper gum and your teeth; you prepare to breathe out, looking at Bonet shaping his leather tongue; you breathe out hard, precisely at the moment he does, trying to drop your tongue—but you have to push it harder against your palate, too, just before you release it; you must voice the sound by vibrating the inside of your throat (though Bonet doesn't expressly say so), for it's not a T; you aspirate into a void, perhaps with a *dih* or *duh*, to learn later that you must immediately make the vowel sound that follows, and the sounds that follow it.

You can't hear the sounds, so many things can go wrong. You may breathe incorrectly through the nose, as for an N or an M; you may aspirate at the wrong time; if you don't push your tongue against your palate before dropping it, you may make a sound like the I in "it," not a D; if you don't voice the sound, it will be a T; if your tongue touches the palate too far back, it will be a K or a G; and you will not be able, of course, to hear any difference, but you must look alone for the frowns or smiles of your teacher and the serpentine movements of the leather tongue he holds in his hand.

But what *follows* the "D"? If the word is *dawn* you must finish the D with the open trumpet of A, diminishing that transversal to master the closed A sound, being careful not to confuse the word with *down*; the tongue must then come back to the palate, not against the teeth, and, for the N, the vibrations made by the voice must come out through the nose, not the mouth. And one promising day next week, next month, or next year, Señor Bonet might wake you up early, take you outside, show you a sunrise, have you say the word, and behold what it means. "Dawn!" You might then show him in an instant, were you not forbidden to, and were he prepared to pay attention, the sign for sunrise in Spanish sign language.

Unsurprisingly, we have no record of Bonet's accomplishments as a teacher. He conceded that the mute should be taught the manual alphabet, which he borrowed from Ponce and illustrated in his book, in order to assist in the effort at spelling and pronunciation. His true teaching tool was, of course, right before his eyes. Though it never fully dawned on him, he saw it, even recognized it—if you "place two deaf mutes in each other's presence, meeting for the first time," he wrote, "they can communicate because they use the same signs." But he wasn't interested in trying to understand these signs, or to ask himself what the Deaf were saying to each other, or whether these "communications" might be at least a form of language. And because he didn't understand it, he found it critically important, like his successors, "never to let the mute use it."[8]

In Holland in 1692 Conrad Amman published *Surdus loquens* (Deaf man talking), which purported to reject the use of any signs or alphabet. He would first have his students make sounds with breath and larynx to "get the machine going." He would then shape various openings of the student's mouth and positions of his tongue to modify the guttural sounds of the larynx. Astutely observing that the vocal organs of the Deaf were intact, he used a mirror to coax the lips of the student into becoming "the lips of the master." Inevitably, their ears and voices remained their own.

Despite their preoccupation with vocal cords, the shape of the mouth, the position of the tongue and the teeth, and their claims that they avoided signs, these teachers had to rely on at least a few signs in their effort to teach the Deaf to speak. Some used their own hand alphabet representing phonetic sounds to help the deaf who had lost their hearing to recover their speech. Ponce's manual alphabet, first

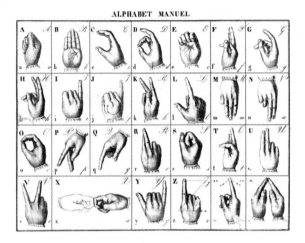

The French manual alphabet in the nineteenth century
(Collection INJS de Paris.)

formalized by Saint Bonaventure in the thirteenth century, is widely used by the Deaf today to spell exotic proper names (Kuala Lumpur) and unfamiliar terms or the first use of new ideas (*toxic* bonds).

As shown in Appendix 2, the handshapes of the manual alphabet and related shapes (for example, Baby O, Bent L) are also used to this day to illustrate the shapes of the hands in communicating in signed languages generally. The handshapes don't represent letters, but are a convention used to show the phonemic elements of signed language, as we shall see in Chapter 10.

But these early teachers did not learn any signed language. They used the limited signs they were able to pick up while observing the Deaf as a crude tool to get through to their students. The elemental problem, suggested by Bonet and readily understood by the abbé de l'Épée in the eighteenth century, is that the cochlea not only contains our vital hearing cells, but as a result, as we have seen, is itself an indispensable organ of speech. Lungs and larynx, the shaping of the mouth, leather tongues, getting the (silent) "machine" going, fretting the guitar, the *lips of the master*, were not enough. It was virtually impossible for a person to speak distinctly if, since birth or early infancy, he or she had not been able to hear. While these early practitioners of speech-teaching were unaware of the biophysical characteristics of the ear, they knew enough about hearing and speaking to realize that as a practical matter they were unable to teach the Deaf this skill to any level of accomplishment.

Nevertheless, efforts to teach the Deaf to speak continued into the eighteenth century and beyond. In Paris, Jacob Rodrigues Pereire claimed as his own a student who was in fact taught in French sign language by an erudite Deaf monk, Étienne de Fay. Pereire's accomplished students, the ones he brought out to demonstrate his speech-teaching talents, had some residual hearing, which was often true for the students of oralists who preceded and would succeed him. Pereire pretended to teach Deaf children to lipread (which Bonet found an impossibility) by having them touch his neck at the larynx to distinguish F from V, B from P, S from Z, ZH from SH (A*s*ia from A*sh*es), though the B could be M, the S could be T, and with no other auditory clues the possible meanings of a phrase are virtually limitless. In order to give the false impression that he was succeeding, he put his partially hearing students on display, and, when all else failed, resorted to surreptitious and rapid fingerspelling.

In Germany, Samuel Heinicke was a teacher of "speech" as was Amman in Holland. Like others, the German kept his methods "secret," although they were revealed in his will as involving an "association" between taste and the shape of the mouth—pure water for IE, water and sugar for O, olive oil for OU, absinthe for E, and vinegar for A.[9] As Pereire ultimately admitted himself (and in their waning years most of these luminaries admitted or abandoned their claims), it was virtually impossible for a person who had been Deaf from birth to read lips in a manner that would enable him or her to understand or actively participate in a conversation.

As Bonet had correctly observed, teaching the Deaf to understand speech through lipreading was a path strewn with insurmountable hurdles. This was the case even for those who had become profoundly deaf as adults. With painstaking effort some words could be taught, as I have just described, by showing the shape of the lips and the position of the tongue, pressing the subject's hand against the larynx, and illustrating the meaning of spoken words through signs. The editor of a preeminent Deaf writer in the eighteenth century put the matter clearly: "As for the art of lipreading, it may doubtless have some utility; we should not ignore it in the education of the deaf, but we would be unwise to put too much reliance on its help. In talking to a deaf person, one must have the habit of speaking in a certain way to make oneself understood; even so, this is practicable only for short and common phrases; for fairly long and quickly articulated phrases, I have yet to come across a deaf person who could follow and understand them."[10]

Lipreading is useful for the partially deaf, like myself, who still hear speech, particularly with hearing aids, and have learned and continue to speak ourselves, but it is not of significant help to the Deaf, except perhaps in the most simplistic contexts (over a farmyard fence, *that* is a cow). It is very difficult for me, for example, to lipread French (except for *ça, c'est une vache*), though I speak French and I hear many of its sounds with my hearing aids. In asking the Deaf to lipread a spoken tongue, these teachers were asking them to understand the meaning of the movement of lips to form the words of a language not their own, that they had never learned to speak, had never heard, and that to a substantial extent is expressed invisibly, inside the mouth.

During the Middle Ages the treatments for deafness, the "medical" efforts to cure the Deaf, were no more successful. The experiments amounted to trials by ordeal, yielding considerable suffering, illness, and sometimes death. Hot coals, for example, were forced into the mouths of the Deaf to enable them to speak "by the force of the burning."[11] These violent experiments continued into the eighteenth century and beyond, and included inserting catheters through the nostrils, twisting them through the nasal cavity and into the Eustachian tubes, and injecting burning liquids. It was thought that air entering and leaving the middle ear through the Eustachian tube would reinforce the action of the eardrum in sending sound to the cochlea's round window (which in fact is the cochlea's "end point" for sound waves).[12]

Other practices included drilling wide holes in the crown of the skull to enable a young Deaf girl to "hear" through the openings (trepanation); introducing ether or electric current into the auditory canal; perforating the eardrum and injecting burning agents into the middle ear cavity, leaving it permanently scarred; applying severe blistering agents to the neck, scorching it from nape to chin with a hot cylinder full of supposedly magical burning leaves; applying adhesive cotton and setting it afire; using vomitories and purgative agents; and injecting hot needles into or removing the mastoids. One French "doctor" threaded the necks of Deaf students with seton needles, and with a hammer fractured the skulls of a number of Deaf children just behind the ear.[13] All of these practices appear to have been based on the premise that drilling, cutting, fracturing, scorching, or poisoning would "open up" the ear, the brain, and the body to the world of sound.

4

The Enlightenment: The Age of Bébian

The Montagne Sainte Geneviève, named after the fifth-century patron Saint of Paris, enemy of the Huns and ally of Clovis, looks out over much of the city. It was here that Louis XV decided to build a great neoclassical church to thank heaven for his recovery from a serious illness. He laid the cornerstone in 1764 and the church, dedicated to Saint Geneviève, was finally completed in 1790.

In 1791 the French revolutionary government decided to recast it as the Pantheon, dedicated neither to God nor saint but to the great men of France. It remains so today after an alternating set of reconsecrations during the eighteenth and nineteenth centuries. The inscription above its sixteen Corinthian columns reads: "Aux Grands Hommes La Patrie Reconnaissante" (To its great men a thankful nation). Jean-Jacques Rousseau, Voltaire, Victor Hugo, Pierre and Marie Curie, Jean Moulin, and many other notables are buried there. Saint Jacques, the eminent French school for Deaf children established on the rue Saint Jacques in 1794, lies just around the corner.

But at least for the moment it is not the gods or great men of France who interest us. It is a house situated, in 1755, on a narrow street just behind this future burial site of the great. In the house, an aging priest had been trying to teach religion to two young Deaf girls, twin sisters, by showing them encaptioned engravings of scenes from the New Testament. He wasn't having much success, for words and

22

images would have been difficult even with lithographs showing everyday scenes of Paris life. Teaching miracles in the *right* medium is difficult enough.

In the midst of these efforts, the priest died. No one would take up his work with the twins who were considered hopeless. But they came to the attention of another priest who, as he put it, was touched by compassion and the unhappy prospect of their living in ignorance of their faith. He agreed to try to find a way to teach them. He didn't know anything about signed languages, but he had little confidence, from what he could see, in his predecessor's engravings. He knew nothing of the history of the Deaf, but he was about to make it.

Observing the girls, the new teacher recalled a notion suggested to him when he was a sixteen-year-old high school student—that ideas have no more natural connection to the sounds we make to express them than they do to the characters we trace to represent those sounds. The priest watched the girls signing to each other and suspected that their signs were mutually recognizable representations of ideas. Going a step further, he wondered whether, just as hearing children are taught to write what they hear, so these children might learn to write what they see. The first thing he had to do was to learn their language.

The idea was at once simple and profound, a natural step, but one that had taken centuries. The teacher's name was Charles-Michel de l'Épée, and his discovery would become the foundation of a revolution. L'Épée was the first to favor teaching the written rather than the spoken word to the Deaf, and he knew it could be taught only if the teacher (in the first instance himself) understood the signed language of his students. He devised a new, reciprocal world in which student and teacher would each naturally become the teacher and student of the other. The bad breath and the imperium of the oralists would be over. His discovery, for the Deaf, was as revolutionary as the work of Copernicus. Signed languages would be their sun, properly centered—illuminating both a path to the written tongue of the hearing and the way of the hearing to the minds of the Deaf.

Before l'Épée, no individual or institution had sought, with this idea in mind, to teach the Deaf in the language that could succeed in bringing them into full discourse with all others. L'Épée established his school for the Deaf in Paris in 1755 at 14 rue des Moulins, a few blocks west of the Comédie Française. Louis XVI gave l'Épée's school a national home in 1785 in a Celestine monastery near the place de la Bastille, and granted him a substantial annual stipend to run it.

In 1794 the French revolutionary government gave the school its imposing home in an ancient seminary on the rue Saint Jacques. The

Saint Jacques, The National Institute for Deaf Children (l'Institut national de jeunes sourds) (Collection INJS de Paris.)

school, named the National Institute for Deaf Children (and known as Saint Jacques) was to become the beacon of an age of enlightenment, awakening the minds of countless Deaf people in Europe and America for the coming half-century. The institute is cherished by the many Deaf Americans who come to France each year to visit, along with numerous historians, linguists, and teachers.

Without l'Épée, his fortuitous meeting with the twins, and what he was able to learn from it, it seems possible that this enlightenment, sometimes called the golden age or *l'âge d'or* of Deaf education, would not have come about. The oralist movement remained strong throughout his time and that of his successors, swimming just under the surface of the accommodating, navigable waters of the hearing world. It is true that, for the deaf who retain material amounts of hearing, and thus generally speak as well as those who hear well, "oralism"—the unflagging belief in communication by speech and lipreading—is not a blind doctrine, but the path that such people, like myself, quite naturally take. Periodic lipreading sessions with teachers make sense, as does the use of hearing aids and other devices to enable us to hear more than we can without them. We can function more or less in the world of our hearing peers, though often we regard them with a fast-beating heart as their language passes us by. We need help in deciphering the words of the hearing, but those words are an integral part of our own spoken vocabulary, and more often than not our lyricals lead us to them.

Those who hear virtually nothing, however, with or without hearing aids, have languages as beautiful, and as precise in every respect, as our own can be. As l'Épée's accomplished successor observed, it is impossible to make a sign known and understood by a simple written description—it could take pages to describe a sign executed in the wink of an eye. For all his perceptiveness, however, l'Épée didn't become fluent in French sign language and never thoroughly understood it. He turned to French (and even more impractically to its etymology and Latin roots), for which he developed his own "methodical" signs, to fill in what he thought were the blanks. He gave his students his own "complementary" signs, rather than learning from them and mastering their own integral tongue.

L'Épée used his artificial signs to recite *dictées* (dictated passages) to his Deaf students, having them write down in French what he rendered in methodical sign. But there was madness in his method, which disfigured French sign language to the point of rendering it unintelligible. The approach sowed considerable confusion, and ultimately benefited the abbé's oralist opponents, who took advantage of the opportunity to confound the resulting mess with signed languages themselves, pointing to this hopeless combination as further reason to extol the superiority of speech.

The sign for *surprise*, for example, in LSF (Langue des Signes Française, or modern French sign language) begins with both hands in front, fingers closed in an S shape (see Appendix 2), palms out. The hands then come toward the speaker (signer), and abruptly open up (to the handshape for the number five, but palms in) and partly cross below the chin. The speaker's wide open eyes, *showing* surprise, behold the opening hands. In American Sign Language (ASL), *surprise* begins with both hands in a Baby O shape, fingertips touching, just below the eyes. The hands move apart, and both index fingers flick up into the shape of the American number one as the head tilts back and the eyes show surprise—simple and easy to remember.[1]

L'Épée's "complements" to French sign language resulted in an unintelligible system. He expressed the verb *surprise* (*surprendre* in French) using two signs. The first was the sign for *take* (*prendre*), an open hand rising, palm down, and closing into an S shape (clenched).

The second was the sign for *sur* or *on*, the right hand in a B shape (fingers together, palm facing left) with the fingertips of the left hand, flat and palm down, touching the bottom of the right. The right hand then falls down upon the left.[2] This combined or methodical sign was contrived and not a part of any language; it never entered the lexicon of the Deaf.

The problem permeated the abbé's system. The word *comprendre* (understand) was given in similar fashion, by adding the sign for *with* to the above sign for *take,* rather than the simple LSF sign of a closing hand coming toward and touching the right side of the temple. Compounding the mystery, l'Épée used Latin roots to devise his methodical sign, for example, *intus legere,* a reading within (oneself) for *intelligence,* rather than using the sign in LSF, a circular movement of the index finger in front of the right side of the forehead.[3]

The term *teacher* (*professeur*) is expressed in LSF by twisting the right hand toward the breast, palm down and then facing in, shaped in an open five. In ASL it is expressed by flattened O's of both hands, palms down, the hands bouncing forward twice from near the head. In l'Épée's system, or more precisely that of his successor, Roch-Ambroise Sicard, the methodical sign for teacher, illustrating perhaps Sicard's own sense of self-importance, had three components: (1) the sign for a school, followed by (2) the sign for a variety of academic subjects (grammar, logic, metaphysics, history), and (3) gestures in pantomime (not sign) showing an individual gathering young people together and lecturing them. All this for a single sign in the students' own language.

L'Épée's *tree* also required three methodical signs: (1) the planting of something in the earth, (2) its growth, and (3) branches moving in the wind. In both LSF and ASL the third sign is sufficient, with the left arm held out pointing right and palm down, the right elbow resting on the left hand, right hand pointing upward in a B shape, still or in half rotation. The words *try to understand me* in French or English require only two signs, one for *try* and the other for *understand me*. In l'Épée's methodical sign they require ten signs.[4]

L'Épée's methodical system added cases, articles, gender (of nouns), and other elements of the French language that are wholly unnecessary in French or any other signed language. The cases of the nouns of French grammar (taught in methodical sign solely for purposes of the *dictées*) were taught by rolling the right index finger around the left, descending the hands from the first roll (the nominative case), to the second (genitive), to the third (dative), and so forth. The numerous articles in French (*le, la, les, du, des*) were "signed" by indicating joints of the fingers, wrists, elbows, and shoulders, which, in a simile that had nothing to do with a signed language, showed how articles were *adjoined* to nouns just as appendages were attached to people.

Articles in general were expressed by a hooked index finger—the letter X in fingerspelling but here a metaphor for the article as being "hooked" to the noun it denotes. The gender of a word in French, *la* or *le, un* or *une*, was indicated by a touch of the hand to the top of the head (indicating a man's hat) or to just below the ear (the edge of a woman's bonnet, or of her hair). These and other elements we are familiar with in spoken languages are not missing from signed languages, but are often expressed in a different way. Given the spatial character of signed languages there is generally only one signifier for the phrase *going to*. The preposition is present in the sign, but has no separate signifier of its own.[5]

To sign the phrase *to look up with extreme pleasure*, l'Épée required thirteen or fourteen methodical signs, including an article and two prepositions:

1. The sign for *look* [a bent V moving forward from the eyes] plus a methodical sign for the infinitive and for the present;
2. A complex methodical sign for the preposition *up,* drawing a horizontal circle in the air and placing a finger through it in several places;
3. The sign for *high* [an index finger pointed and moving upward];
4. The sign for *with* [fists coming together, thumbs up];
5. A methodical sign for the article (*un* in French), and for its masculine gender;
6. Three methodical signs for *extreme*, including the methodical signs for adjective and superlative; and
7. The sign for *pleasure* [a hand circling at the breast, showing the adjective (pleased or content)], followed by a methodical sign for *noun.*[6]

Signs like this could (and must have) put Deaf children to *sleep* with extreme pleasure. While, as noted earlier, the body of a signed language is not recognizably iconic, in French sign language in this case the idea is given by a single sign, the facial expression itself, as the hands signal (simultaneously) the causes or effects of the pleasure. The exercises in methodical signs were all painful ones for the students. They could eventually impress visitors by demonstrating their ability to take dictation word for word, but they understood little of what was "signed" or what they wrote down. Baffled, the students were unable to express even the simplest of their own thoughts in writing. And there was no need for any of this obfuscation—an idea could instead have been expressed in French sign language and then taught and given in written French.

L'Épée was nevertheless a monumental figure (indeed there is a movement in France, and a website, promoting the transfer of *his* ashes to the Pantheon) because of his attempt to learn French sign language and his insistence on employing it as the medium of instruction. Ferdinand Berthier, a celebrated Deaf teacher writing of l'Épée in 1840 (a half century after his death in 1789), summarized l'Épée's singular accomplishment: "Simply by reasoning that it was possible to teach the deaf with the help of signs the way we educate other men with the sounds of the voice, and that with the help of one or the other one can acquire written language, the indefatigable ecclesiastic brought about a new world, an entire generation."[7]

The Parisian Deaf community was hopeful that the work of l'Épée would continue after he died. But things didn't look promising. He had no heir apparent, and his "methodical" signs were proving to

Jean Massieu (1772–1846)
(Collection INJS de Paris.)

be a pedagogical failure. Twenty-five children had been sent home from l'Épée's school after his death, and another teacher spent most of his time trying to find the money to feed and clothe the forty-five students who had stayed.[8] The school was saved, however, by an alliance of two very different men: Jean Massieu, one of the world's first Deaf teachers, and Sicard himself, who was, first and foremost, a showman.

Massieu was born in 1772 in the Gironde region of France, not far from Bordeaux. One of six Deaf children, he was raised as a shepherd. He had no early formal education, though he communicated with his siblings using signs they had devised together. Massieu wrote in his autobiography that hearing children his own age refused to play with him. "They looked down upon me; I was like a dog." When his father forced him to pray he dropped to his knees, folded his hands together and moved his lips, imitating hearing people he had seen in church. I had a similar experience in church as a child, though I could half-hear the prayers of those around me. I began to pray with them, repeating the lyrical *pissa pissa too* (which I mistook for the words of a prayer, "blessed is the fruit") over and over again until persuaded to stop by the disapproving glares of the faithful.

Massieu tells us that he worshipped the sky, not God. Not an illogical deduction, of course, for the sky was all he could see up there. He prayed to it "to make the night come down to earth so the plants I had planted would grow." Massieu had no idea whether he had been created, or he had created himself. Finally, in 1785, at the age of thirteen, he was admitted to a new school for the Deaf in Bordeaux, which was beginning to put aside l'Épée's methodical French and to focus more profitably on the structural and grammatical differences between the spoken and signed languages of France. The young shepherd was to become their most promising student.[9]

In a sense Massieu did create himself—and others as well. He moved to Paris in 1790 and went on to become a member of the faculty of Saint Jacques as its first Deaf instructor. He would teach there for thirty-two years. As a Deaf man, he was able to grasp that sign was a language and not something less—not some kind of stunted system that needed to be completed or expanded into a simulacrum of French or another spoken language. Thus as a teacher he was able to avoid the confusions imposed by methodical sign, though he knew it well.

The second member of this improbable couple, despite his lamentable skills as a teacher, was Roch-Ambroise Sicard. Born in 1742 in the south of France, Sicard studied for the priesthood, joined the same

Roch-Ambroise Cucurron Sicard (1742–1822)
(Collection INJS de Paris.)

order as l'Épée, and was ordained when he was twenty-eight years old. When the archbishop of Bordeaux, impressed in 1786 by what he saw of l'Épée's school in Paris, decided to form a similar school in his own city, he asked Sicard to run it. Sicard himself interviewed the young shepherd Massieu before he was admitted. When he realized how talented Massieu was, he began showing off Massieu's interpreting and signing talents at public exhibitions in Bordeaux and Paris.

Though Massieu's education was left to others at the Bordeaux school, Sicard promptly saw himself as the ideal candidate to succeed l'Épée in Paris. In 1790 he entered a competition for the position by displaying the star pupil, and got the job easily. Massieu's account of some of his signed exchanges with Sicard or the public (interpreted by Sicard) in the late 1780s is intriguing:

What is a sense?
—An idea-carrier.

What is hearing?
—Auricular sight.

What is gratitude?
—The memory of the heart.

What is God?
—The necessary Being—the sun of eternity.

What is eternity?
—A day without yesterday or tomorrow.[10]

While deficient as an educator, Sicard's great skill was his ability to attract talented people to Deaf education (including Massieu) and to get public support for it. As Bébian not very generously put it, Sicard "never understood the language of his students." He had at best only a rudimentary knowledge of French sign language. In his public exercises with his students, it required all the mental skill he could muster to hide the "confusion and awkwardness" of what Bébian called Sicard's "pantomime."[11]

Sicard was also a lax administrator and unable to manage even his own personal finances. Massieu entrusted to him his life savings, which Sicard promptly used to pay his own debts, misappropriating all (and never repaying any) of Massieu's money. But Sicard remains a major figure in the history of Deaf education because of his magnetic enthusiasm for the cause (and for himself). As to the memory of l'Épée, Ferdinand Berthier was delightfully ironic about the teaching skills of the abbé, and by implication, those of his successor. "No one was capable," Berthier wrote, "of grasping the whole of l'Épée's thought and making it fruitful." Not even, his admirer might have added, l'Épée himself, and certainly not Sicard, who made even more of a mess of methodical signs. "But eventually," Berthier continued, "that man appeared."[12]

"That man" was Roch-Ambroise Auguste Bébian, born in Guadeloupe in 1789, the year l'Épée died. Bébian had excellent hearing throughout his short life (he died when he was forty-nine). He was a gifted student, and his father sent him to Paris at the age of thirteen (shortly after his father's second marriage) to study at the lycée Charlemagne, one of France's leading secondary schools, where he stood at the top of his class.[13] Bébian's parents were friends of Sicard, who was both the boy's godfather and his namesake, and Sicard offered to find a place for him.

Auguste Bébian (he used his third name) lived at first at a teacher's house near Saint Jacques. During his vacations he was almost always at the school, joining the Deaf students in their classes, workshops,

Auguste Bébian (1789–1839) (Collection INJS de Paris.)

and games. Before long he had become fluent in French sign language.[14] Although able to hear well, he made friends with several of the Deaf students and, thanks to Massieu, learned to sign as well as those who were Deaf from birth, an unprecedented accomplishment. His skill was comparable to that of hearing children of Deaf parents (awkwardly called "hearing children of Deaf adults" or CODA, in the United States). Destined to become the preeminent teacher at Saint Jacques, Bébian has been called (by Laurent Clerc, his formal teacher) history's greatest hearing friend of the Deaf. Berthier gave Bébian a certificate conferring upon him the distinction of being an *honorary* Deaf man, and called him the "decisive spark" that lighted the path of the Deaf to the future, though he proved unable to take part in it himself. The Deaf scholar Fabrice Bertin, a biographer of Bébian, writes that the little we know of him is "inversely proportional to his energy, reflections and actions, which led to the emancipation of the deaf and the development of their consciousness of themselves as speakers of a complete language."[15]

Bébian was the first to observe that the history of the education of the Deaf and their language was an intellectual history, a history of ideas. And indeed an understanding of Bébian's own ideas provides enormous insight into the man himself, his perceptive and powerful ideas on language and teaching, and his central role in this history. His writings and teaching were the cornerstone of the education of the Deaf in Europe and the United States during the age of the enlightenment. As Berthier wrote, "among the men devoted to our education, there is one, Monsieur Bébian, the most distinguished of all, who has extended the boundaries of this beneficent art in which he has no equal. His works, now become classics, serve to guide our teachers both in France and abroad." Bébian was offering not just another set of ideas, but "a veritable change in paradigm, a profound rupture; thanks to [Bébian], the deaf became Deaf. This change in paradigm wasn't confined to education and teaching; it was of an anthropological order."[16]

Treading as lightly as Berthier, Bébian wrote that l'Épée didn't have sufficient confidence in what he'd so brilliantly begun. Bébian accused Sicard of making matters worse, and made it obvious that methodical signs were no more than the representation of deconstructed French words—the syllabic additions of a foreign language by artificial gestures that were not a part of any language. Signed languages and speech are endowed with syntaxes that reflect their respective gestural and oral origins. Forcing the forms of French sign language to work with and around the syntax, suffixes, and parts of speech of a spoken tongue resulted in nonsense. As a result the system squared the sign with the word rather than the idea.

As Fabrice Bertin notes, "to speak and sign simultaneously is physiologically possible (given the dual instruments of communication) but cognitively it is not."[17] What was needed was the immediate translation of the students' own thoughts and images, as expressed in their own language, into the corresponding written words in French. Central to Bébian's thought and teaching is the reality that words are but the expression of preexisting ideas: an idea (whether the conception of a material object or an abstract thought) necessarily precedes the spoken word interpreting it. Unlike l'Épée, Bébian fully understood and applied the meaning of John Locke's observations on the nature of language:

> Man, though he have great variety of thoughts, and such from which others as well as himself might receive profit and delight; yet they are all within his own breast, invisible and hidden from others, nor can of themselves be made to appear. The comfort and advantage of society not being to be had without communication of thoughts, it was necessary that man should find out some external sensible signs, whereof those invisible ideas, which his thoughts are made up of, might be made known to others. For this purpose nothing was so fit, either for plenty or quickness, as those articulate sounds, which with so much ease and variety he found himself able to make.
>
> Thus we may conceive how words, which were by nature so well adapted to that purpose, came to be made use of by men as the signs of their ideas; not by any natural connexion that there is between particular articulate sounds and certain

ideas, for then there would be but one language amongst all men; but by a voluntary imposition, whereby such a word is made arbitrarily the mark of such an idea. The use, then, of words, is to be sensible marks of ideas; and the ideas they stand for are their proper and immediate signification.[18]

It is thus the idea, wrote Bébian, that must give the word meaning before the word can, in turn, become an effective interpreter of the idea, or what Locke interestingly called the *sign* of the idea. The hearing ordinarily convey their thoughts by speaking, or by writing down words made of letters that are depictions of the sounds we make with our voices, what Bébian eloquently called the painting of our speech. The convention of speech led people to believe that the spoken word was indispensable to the exercise of thought; for the hearing were almost universally unaware until l'Épée that signed languages were even a developed system for the expression of ideas. *Obviously* the Deaf couldn't think, for they couldn't speak. They were therefore regarded as "almost . . . being[s] of a different species."[19]

Flirting with this general prejudice, Sicard had written that until educated (by the hearing, notably himself), his Deaf students were worthless automatons, walking machines limited to physical movements, devoid of practical instincts, less well organized than animals, and unresponsive to maternal affection. Bébian wrote that "among all the admirers of his accomplishments, perhaps none was more sincere than Sicard himself."[20] Sicard offered this absurd portrayal of the Deaf not because it was accurate (he later retracted his words) but in order to vaunt his own supposed achievements as an educator and to mask his ignorance of the language of his charges. Sicard was "completely ignorant" of French sign language, and couldn't make himself easily understood by his students except in writing or fingerspelling or by using l'Épée's or his own methodical signs.[21] Until they learned to communicate that way (thanks to their Deaf teachers), Sicard's students seemed to him no more than "unopened envelopes."[22] At times Sicard seemed to think that the Deaf were not only "less well organized than" animals, but indistinguishable from them, writing that "speech constitutes the irreducible trait distinguishing animal from man, who alone is capable of progress."

Bébian scoffed at Sicard's portrait of the Deaf. He knew that the goal in what I have called the dark ages, and continuing to his own day, had been to give to the Deaf the mechanical faculty of "speech" without enabling them to attach a precise idea to its components, leaving them in the dark not only as to the absolute value of words, but also their relative value and the influence they have over each other in the composition of a phrase. In short, the Deaf were not being introduced to the meaning of our language. The practice brought scant relief to their misfortune and overworked their memories with no benefit to their intelligence. The oralist method was fundamentally flawed—designed neither to enlighten the mind of the Deaf student nor to enable him to express even his simplest thoughts.[23]

Again, for Bébian, for the Deaf, for the hearing—the *idea* is the thing. Letters of the alphabet, for the Deaf, *prima facie*, represent nothing at all. They consist of lines or strokes forming meaningless characters—more complex than their painting of sounds for the hearing, and far more removed from the underlying idea than its expression in their native language. And in trying to "read" lips the Deaf are not receiving any idea, but are forced to observe obscure lip movements in order to guess sounds they cannot hear so that they may infer the other sounds the lips fail to show at all. This was the mental torture of the dark ages: "If the deaf student is brought to a standstill to begin with by the singular difficulty of pronouncing sounds of which the signs fixed on paper lie stationary before his eyes—How is he going to understand the rapid signs that slip through the lips?"[24]

It is with their own language that the education of the Deaf must begin, not with the spoken word, or with l'Épée's artificial, "methodical" French, or with Sicard's meaningless repetition of written words for his students as if (here Sicard wholly ignored l'Épée) they bore some intrinsic relationship to the thoughts they represented. Consistently misguided, Sicard taught his students the written words for trees, vegetables, animals, minerals, almost everything under the sun without, as Bébian put it, enabling them "to form the simplest judgment, express the simplest thought, or compose the simplest sentence."[25] Massieu himself couldn't even read children's stories when Bébian arrived at Saint Jacques.

Sicard had his students skipping from noun to noun, adjective to adjective, and verb to verb, without understanding the relationship among the three. He would draw the word *ball* in solid capitals with *thing* in lower case between the letters—

t B h A i L n L g

or an *animal* with capitals and *being* in lower case—

A b N e I i M n A g L

and then extract the small letters from the capitals to show that the ball was an object, the animal a being.[26] He failed to explore the differences between the two, such as by giving extensive examples, because of his inability to communicate in French sign language. So he began by stitching two words together, in a system that was less than babble for the hearing, that bore no resemblance even to an obscure lyrical for the partially deaf, and that was more meaningless than words for the Deaf (tbhailnlg, abneiimnagl)—then split up those words without being able to explain precisely why.

To designate an inanimate object in French sign language, Bébian noted, the right hand with an extended index finger moved twice outward over the left extended index finger (the face in a neutral expression); for a living being, the index and middle fingers of both hands were pointed outward, palms up, with a double movement upward (and a lively expression). Communicating with the child in his own first language was the key: "We know that the deaf have a language one doesn't teach them, although with art and exercise one can offer it the happiest development. It is in a way the reflection of their sensations, the relief of their impressions. We carry the same timeless and limitless principle within all of us: that of the first language of any human being, which gives immediate expression to his thought and is not a translation of any other language, but expresses his intimate connection with ideas. One never looks to his first language with difficulty for the expression of an idea. The thought, born in the brain, bursts forth like a flame sparkling in crystal."[27]

While students arriving at Saint Jacques would have at least the rudiments of French sign language, Bébian in his practical teaching manual hypothesized the case of a new student at Saint Jacques in order to illustrate, for parents and teachers, that education should begin with the thought, not the written word. The teacher might show the picture of a saber in a book, and then, exaggerating the iconic aspect of the sign, move his dominant hand from opposite waist to shoulder height as if drawing a saber from a sheath; the student would invariably do the same. The sign follows the thought, step by step, he wrote, like a shadow assuming all of its shapes.[28] Bébian would unsheathe the imaginary saber again and have the student show him its picture in the book, whereupon Bébian would point to the written word beneath the picture. He would then have the student fingerspell the word (if he knew fingerspelling) and ask him in sign language what the word meant (*what?*—eyebrows raised to indicate a question, palms up, fingers open, hands moving quickly, laterally, toward and away from each other). The student would then repeat the gesture and, before long, would understand that this written word and others were a kind of conventional drawing of the idea first expressed in sign language.

Bébian also stressed that French *grammar*, what he referred to in his critique of Sicard as the relationship between words in our spoken languages, had to be taught through the medium of sign language: "The deaf student must be able to write the word in order to read it, and to be able to read it he has to understand it; and he'll be able to understand it only if he understands the whole sentence . . . To do that, his instruction must begin in sign."[29]

There was no need for abstruse "method." An idea could be expressed in sign language and then given in written French. Again and again, it is the *idea* that is central. He observed, for example, that in contemporary French sign language one would normally sign *this table I strike*, for the French phrase *I strike this table*. Signed languages may often start with the purpose or goal of an action and then specify the actor and the action itself. Bébian would require the student to follow the normal construction of the sentence in sign language, and to show that he understood the proposition, before being shown and, *on his own*, showing that he understood, making the written (and peculiar—*this is the odd way those hearing people do it!*) inversion required by French grammar in this and in similar sentences (this door I open; that ball I throw; these girls I kiss).[30]

A Deaf student learning to write *there is some paper in the office* or *there are some pens in the drawer* would, influenced by sign, usually begin by writing *some paper is in the office* and *some pens are in the drawer*. Bébian would note in sign that only "very small children" would express themselves that way (the difference is sharper in French than in English), and suggest to the student in sign language that he place the verb first, *is some paper in the office* and *are some pens in the drawer*, and complete the exercise by showing in sign the need for the nonreferential pronoun with the verb: *there is some paper in the office* and *there are some pens in the drawer*.[31] In insisting on this as the only efficient way to teach the written language of the hearing, Bébian rejected, a century and a half before they first appeared, the systems of our own day such as signed French or English, which with disastrous results have tried to mimic, in gestures not constituting any language at all, the grammatical structure of spoken tongues.

Unlike the early philosophers and the speech teachers who knew the Deaf could communicate fluently with each other, the abbé de l'Épée had taken it upon himself to try to learn their language. He never wholly succeeded as a teacher because he was unable to learn it. Unlike l'Épée, Auguste Bébian did master the language: he analyzed it, taught it, and used it to teach his Deaf students how to think about signed and written languages, their own ideas, and the ideas of others; how to read; how to write; and how to become members of a larger human community. He was the first both to observe and reflect, and to act effectively as a philosopher—an early linguist, really—and a teacher. Throughout Europe and the United States, the practice of Deaf education, during and well after Bébian's short life, was to follow his thought, step by step, like a shadow assuming all of its shapes.

Ferdinand Berthier (1803–1886) (Collection INJS de Paris.)

In the early nineteenth century there was vocal opposition to Bébian's precepts, and as we shall see Bébian was unable to fight them. But in his Deaf student Ferdinand Berthier, Bébian had his own disciple. Berthier was born of hearing parents and came to Saint Jacques in 1811 at the age of eight. He became Bébian's star pupil. He taught at Saint Jacques for most of his life and was appointed dean of the faculty. He was fluent in written French, Latin, and Greek, and wrote the definitive biographies of l'Épée and Sicard and an account of Bébian and his work. He is perhaps the preeminent Deaf intellectual and historian and, as we shall see, was the most important leader of the Deaf community in the nineteenth century.

Berthier's first battle was with Joseph-Marie de Gérando, the chairman of the board of Saint Jacques who, after Sicard's death in 1822, installed an oralist crony, Désiré Ordinaire, as director of the school. Together they developed a plan to rid Saint Jacques of its Deaf teachers. Berthier would ultimately outmaneuver Gérando, who was confronted by the reality of the success of Bébian's ideas and teaching. Deaf students were learning the humanities and the sciences in French sign language, but couldn't be taught to speak or to read lips nor, of course, to learn anything in courses given in speech. Yet Gérando's approach would be symptomatic of the conservative undercurrents that persisted throughout Bébian's life and beyond.

The oralists of this era marked an important turning point in the history of ideas about signed languages versus speech. From the classical and medieval periods and throughout the seventeenth century, signed languages were largely ignored, even though Plato, Augustine, and others recognized that the Deaf could communicate with each other. With the arrival of l'Épée and Bébian and their successors, it became clear that the Deaf had a complete language in which they could be taught to read and write. Oralist instructors had been proven unable to teach the Deaf, yet the vast majority of these instructors were unwilling to learn the signed language of their country, and insisted, though it had been proven a failure, upon using speech as the medium of teaching. Beginning with this intransigence, the failure to recognize sign as a language was no longer the result of philosophical or pedagogical inattention, but of a deliberate, ultimately collective, decision to suppress it as an instrument of teaching.

Gérando knew nothing of sign language and, like Sicard (though Gérando meant it), said the Deaf were a primitive people with primitive gestures. His ideas resembled those of Jean-Marc Itard, the physician (and a speech teacher) at Saint Jacques, who knew no sign but throughout much of his professional life blamed the failure of oralist efforts on the use of sign language as the vehicle for teaching. Itard went so far as to suggest at one point that sign language was a source of tuberculosis at Saint Jacques because the use of gestures had caused an excess circulation of "atmosphere" around the students.[32] It was Itard himself who inserted silver probes through the noses and into the Eustachian tubes of both Laurent Clerc and Ferdinand Berthier when they were young students at Saint Jacques.

Although Itard and Gérando were a one-two punch of physical brutality and academic nonsense, they both recanted in later life, as had Pereire and the other oralists before them, when confronted with their accumulation of failures. Gérando finally decided that French sign language should be the principal means of instruction at Saint

Jean-Marc Itard (1774–1838)
(Collection INJS de Paris.)

Jacques. His coadjutor Ordinaire resigned, and the attempted oralist coup lost out to real teaching. Itard himself, after doing considerable harm as a surgeon, ultimately admitted to Bébian, perhaps because of all that fresh air circulating about his own head, that the oral method of instruction had been a failure. The indispensable fertile ground in the education and social development of hearing children, he concluded, was what they heard *around* them. The oral teaching of the Deaf always had to be *direct*, that is, limited to the student's perception of words directly addressed to him. As a result, he noted, Deaf students taught only in the oralist tradition were placed in a state of isolation that made normal conversation inaccessible, leaving them in a passive state whenever not individually engaged.

The advantages of general discourse—of knowing what is going on about you, what others are saying and how they react to what they are being told—Itard now concluded, were abundantly present when classes were conducted in sign language. "No other possible education, in effect, presents a more effective method for [the student's] development; no other is more analogous to that of the speaking child; no other can offer, as does sign language, the benefit of free, easy, continuous, direct and indirect communication, not only between the student and his teachers, but also among classmates. To benefit from all these advantages, the profoundly deaf student needs anything but isolation, but rather an institution with a number of classes, with students of different ages and levels of instruction. It is only then . . . that his intelligence will flourish with the various combinations of these diverse relationships, as he acquires with ease the ability to express his ideas clearly in sign."[33]

Itard was speaking not only of profoundly deaf children, but also of severely deaf students with some residual hearing. Though he knew no sign language he could see it in operation, all around him. After his many years of cracking skulls he had finally come to understand the way out for the Deaf, just by opening his eyes and observing the students at Saint Jacques. He finally used his own ears to listen to Auguste Bébian.

Picture a classroom, Bébian wrote. On one side you have children forced to learn only through speech, constrained to fit all of their ideas into the unbearably cramped quarters of the few words they're beginning to understand; preoccupied by the fruitless "reading" of the mysterious, silent movements of lips. Boredom is the first and the least of the inconveniences for the Deaf subjected to this exercise. On the other side of the room, the students are learning in sign language, engaged in lively conversation, exchanging their ideas in clear and precise form, the play of their expressions reflecting their emotions. Who, he asked, can witness the two scenes and remain wedded to teaching the Deaf by the spoken word?[34] Not even Itard, who put away his hammers, scalpels, and preconceptions for good.

Auguste Bébian, Jean Massieu, Ferdinand Berthier, Laurent Clerc (who was to come to the United States), and their colleagues all taught the natural intricacies of French sign language and used them to teach the Deaf to read with understanding and write with purpose the language of the hearing. They also taught other dedicated individuals, throughout Europe, how to teach. The combination of the two languages would introduce multitudes of those who could not hear to the sciences and the humanities and, in important respects, to themselves.

In 1789, at the time of l'Épée's death, six schools for the Deaf had been established in France thanks to his efforts. By 1866, there were fifty-four such schools in France and sign was the language of instruction in all of them. A significant number of teachers of the Deaf were Deaf themselves. Their students were entering professions typically held by the hearing, and were finding employment in lawyers' offices, banks, trading companies, shipping firms, railroads, government ministries, and large manufacturers. Some were accomplished painters and poets. A number practiced arts that they had learned at school, including drawing and lithographing. Others entered the trades they had been taught, notably printing, tailoring, shoemaking, carpentry, bookbinding, and working as locksmiths.[35]

Teachers came to Saint Jacques from all over Europe to learn from Bébian, Massieu, Berthier, Clerc, and others how to instruct the Deaf, and took their lessons home with them, learning and teaching in the signed languages of their respective countries. The influence of Bébian's insights and accomplishments in Europe and America was to be extraordinary. Though in his time only about 10 percent of the twenty thousand Deaf people in France went to school, his goal was to popularize Deaf education through his new system. In this he was wildly successful. When he began teaching in about 1810, methodical signs (manual French, Russian, Spanish) were used in those institutions, but over the next twenty years they were abandoned everywhere and replaced by Bébian's system of teaching in the natural signed languages of the students' home countries.[36]

Deaf education and literacy were springing up everywhere, with Deaf children reading Racine, Molière, Voltaire, Cervantes, Goethe, and Pushkin, as well as the words of Augustine's *Spiritual Dimensions* proclaiming that the Deaf would never be able to read those words. The potential of the Deaf in the arts and sciences and in commerce was now fully realizable, and signed languages were becoming the motor of their equality.[37] Together, Bébian and his Deaf colleagues and students were changing the world.

5

France Comes to America

For Americans exploring this history, perhaps its most exceptional aspect is the enormous influence a small group of Parisian educators brought to bear on the education, livelihoods, and happiness of the Deaf community in the United States. English immigrants had given us our spoken and written language, but the French, in the person of Laurent Clerc, came to us, and sought out and learned the signed language of our young Deaf citizens.

Clerc was born near Lyons, the son, like Berthier, of a lawyer (*notaire*). He was Deaf from at least the age of one, when he had a serious fall that was thought to be the cause of his deafness. In 1797, when he was twelve years old, he was sent to Saint Jacques, and he would remain there as a student, and then a teacher, until his departure for the United States almost twenty years later. Clerc learned French sign language from Jean Massieu, and his friendship with Auguste Bébian marked a crucial juncture for the future of the Deaf community.[1] Clerc enriched American Sign Language with French sign, and used the new combined language to teach the American Deaf how to read and write in English. The efforts of Clerc, who had to learn English as well, lie at the foundation of Deaf education in the United States. Why did he come?

While on a trip to London with Sicard and Massieu, Clerc met an American with a mission, Thomas Gallaudet. Gallaudet graduated

Laurent Clerc (1785–1869) as a young man at Saint Jacques. His left hand is a symbol of his name and first language, and his right, holding a pen, the mark of his second, written languages, French and, later, English.
(Collection INJS de Paris.)

from Yale College in 1805, the youngest in his class and with highest honors. He tried his hand successively as a law clerk, traveling salesman, and store manager, but hated it all. He finally decided, though probably more out of a sense of vocation than by default, to become a Protestant minister. He enrolled in the Andover Theological Seminary, now in Newton, Massachusetts, but then on the campus of Andover's Phillips Academy. I never sensed his past presence at either

Andover or Yale (although one of his descendants had a navy-blue motorcycle that I would scream at as it raced down Elm Street in New Haven, cutting through the constant buzzing and whirring in my ears of tinnitus, an affliction that often plagues the deaf).

Gallaudet's family lived in Hartford, next door to a doctor, Mason Cogswell. When Gallaudet came home during the summer between his two years at the Andover seminary, he noticed that one of Cogswell's children playing in the garden, Alice, was Deaf, and was conversing with her hearing siblings using signs they had invented together, much like those of Jean Massieu and his Deaf siblings and (as we shall see) Helen Keller. Alice had lost virtually all her hearing to

THOMAS HOPKINS GALLAUDET.
(Founder of the American Asylum for the Education of the Deaf and Dumb.)

Thomas Hopkins Gallaudet (1787–1851) (Collection INJS de Paris.)

spinal meningitis at the age of two and now, eight years old, could no longer speak. With an ear trumpet she could hear a nearby church bell. Gallaudet asked to be her tutor, but made little headway. She was sent to a school with hearing children, where she used a mixture of home signs, pantomime, and fingerspelling, all insufficient for an education.

Alice's father was determined to try to help solve not just her difficulty, but that of the American Deaf generally, of whom he determined there were then about eighty in Connecticut, four hundred in New England, and two thousand in the United States.[2] He raised some money with a group of Hartford businessmen, and they decided to send "a competent person" overseas to learn the European methods of educating the Deaf and bring them back to a school they would open in Hartford. Gallaudet himself was the obvious choice. He sailed for Liverpool in June 1815.

Even during the French Enlightenment or *l'âge d'or*, Britain, though it had its own defenders of British sign language, was a center of oralism, and the British were generally ineffective in educating the Deaf. The members of the Braidwood family, who controlled most of Britain's schools for the Deaf, were defensive and generally unwelcoming to Gallaudet. They claimed, as had many of their predecessors on the Continent, that the methods with which they purported to teach the Deaf to speak and to read lips were "secrets." If Gallaudet wanted to learn them, he could work as an apprentice and pay handsomely for the privilege.

Gallaudet had no time and little money, but was blessed with considerable luck in that London had other visitors at the time, among them the abbé Sicard who had sought refuge there from Napoleon's brief return from exile. As courageous as he was dim, Sicard had been a foe of both the revolution and the emperor. When he came to town he brought along Saint Jacques's star Deaf pupils, Jean Massieu and Laurent Clerc, and decided to show them off to the London public.

Sicard had a taste for theater, and staged frequent performances by his prodigies in Paris, and now in London, a practice he had begun with Massieu when he was a student in Bordeaux. Sicard would begin the show by asking someone in the audience for a copy of the day's newspaper. Massieu would sign to Clerc a chosen text in the paper in manual French (both knew methodical sign), and Clerc would write it word for word on the blackboard. At times Clerc would sign and Massieu would write, or Sicard would question either or both in his methodical signs and they would answer in writing. Toward the end of the performance Sicard would ask for questions from the floor, which he again signed methodically, with Massieu or Clerc answering in writing.

Gallaudet attended and was deeply impressed by one of these performances. He met all three men, and was invited to Paris to audit classes and observe the teaching methods used at Saint Jacques. He jumped at the chance, and spent the spring of 1816 in Paris. In the mornings he attended the students' classes, from the lowest grades through the highest (Clerc's and Massieu's). In the afternoon he learned French sign language from both teachers, and in the evening he studied French. Clerc and Massieu taught their students wholly through the medium of French sign language and by writing, and their classrooms were an awakening for Gallaudet, a way of teaching he had never encountered in the United States or in Britain. Gallaudet's experience was considerably enhanced by the presence of Bébian, who was then twenty-six years old and beginning to put his mark on the school, steering it away from methodical signs to natural French sign language. Both Clerc and Massieu, though older than

Bébian, owed much of their linguistic sophistication to his work, and had spent roughly fourteen years with him at Saint Jacques, six of them as fellow faculty members. Clerc was named an instructor in 1807 and Bébian in 1810. Sicard appointed Bébian director of studies in 1819.[3]

Gallaudet was enchanted by Saint Jacques, but he found Paris bewildering. He was an ordained Episcopal minister whose ancestors, French Huguenots, had fled to the colonies in 1690 after Louis XIV revoked the Edict of Nantes, withdrawing the religious and civil liberties accorded to Protestants at the end of the prior century by Henri IV. Gallaudet wrote at one point to a fellow American minister about Parisians: "Oh! How this poor heathen people want the Bible and the Sabbath! Will my own country ever lose them through its corruption and vice? My heart bleeds at the possibility of this. My dear sir, you read of the depravity of morals here . . . but you don't realize these things; you cannot, without being an eye witness of them . . . I pray God to give me strength to adhere to the prosecution of my object, whatever difficulties may be in the way."[4] Though his lament has the flavor of a repentant sinner's, there is no sign that Gallaudet ever succumbed to the voluptuous temptations offered by the City of Light. He appears to have fled them, morally girding himself with his own stolid sermons at the American chapel on Sunday mornings.

Gallaudet was eager to learn French sign language, but Clerc advised him that it would take at least a year to attain just a "tolerably good knowledge" of the language, in spite of Gallaudet's diligent efforts to learn it throughout the spring. Unable to stay in Paris for that long, Gallaudet promptly invited Clerc to accompany him to the United States. Clerc hesitated at first because of his obligations to Sicard, to Saint Jacques, and to his students, but, as he put it, he "had a great desire to see the world" and to bring the benefits of his teaching to the Deaf across the sea. Sicard allowed him to go on one condition: that Clerc obtain his mother's consent. Then, in an act not wholly out of character, Sicard promptly wrote to Clerc's mother urging her not to give it. But her son ultimately extracted her blessing.[5] Given what we know of Sicard, Clerc may have been relieved to escape him.

On June 18, 1816, Gallaudet set sail for the United States with Clerc in tow. It was a long trip, and each used the time to help the other improve his new language. As he had planned, Clerc brought Bébian's teaching with him to the United States, with which he formed a corps of American teachers for the Deaf. He and Gallaudet toured New England and successfully raised private and public funds to found the American School for the Deaf in Hartford in 1817.[6] Schools were founded in New York and Philadelphia in 1820, in Kentucky in 1829, and in Virginia in 1839. Maryland's was the twenty-seventh state to open, in 1868.

By the 1850s some 250 of the 550 teachers and administrators in the burgeoning national network of schools were themselves Deaf. By the 1860s there were twenty-six schools for the Deaf in America patterned after Hartford—sign was the language of instruction in all.[7] Signed languages had confronted vigorous opponents, both in the United States (the educators Horace Mann and Samuel Gridley Howe) and in Europe (Heinicke in Germany, the Braidwoods in Britain, and Gérando and Ordinaire in France). But time and again the proponents of signed languages had been able to demonstrate the incontestable advantages of teaching the Deaf in their own language.

The emergence and accomplishments of the Deaf in the West in the nineteenth century are perhaps best exemplified in a speech given in French sign language by Ferdinand Berthier on prize day in 1857 to the graduating students of Saint Jacques. Note the warning in his words:

Remember, above all, that although your lot in life has excluded you from partaking of one of man's most precious senses, the one that enriches his mind with the thoughts of others and procures for him the most delicious of life's pleasures; it has, by providential compensation, doubled the vigilance of your eyes and placed a new tongue in your arms and at your fingertips. The only condition it imposes on this immense gift is that you make every effort never to let the fruits of the harvest you have been able to gather in this establishment disappear. Always bear this in mind, to whatever trade or profession your destiny may call you. Never let the demands of difficult work make you neglect the cultivation, ever indispensable, of your maternal tongue. Your instinctive judgment will make you appreciate the reason for this exhortation."[8]

Berthier set himself as the example by devoting virtually his entire life, throughout most of the nineteenth century, to the cultivation of that language among the Deaf and the promotion and exposition of its merits to the hearing. His perseverance would be the fruit of his own instinctive judgment, for he knew the struggle was going to be long, and the outcome uncertain.

6

The Banquets of the Deaf

What were they to do? August Bébian, their most sophisticated ally and the unrivaled master of signed, spoken, and written language, their key ally in the hearing world, had been dismissed in 1821 as the assistant director of Saint Jacques. Bébian was said to have been asked to leave because of his rudeness to the Duchesse de Berry, the widow of a Bourbon heir to the throne. When she had asked to see some students at Saint Jacques, he told her that they had neither shoes nor clothes and were therefore unpresentable. Berthier also tells us that Bébian had fired an employee, protected in high places, who went to communion every Sunday but had "corrupted the children."

But in fact the real reason for Bébian's dismissal had to do with an altercation in Sicard's office with an incompetent hearing teacher, Louis Paulmier, at 11 a.m. on January 3, 1821. Paulmier was an oralist, generally considered an ignorant and conceited fop (*ignorant et fat*), and barely able to write French correctly. As the men began to argue, Bébian should have counted to ten or taken a break and walked around the block. But he didn't: instead he hit Paulmier over the head twice with a trousseau of keys. Itard, so used to drawing the blood of Deaf children, sewed up the cut and, perhaps with some satisfaction (this was prior to his change of heart on signed languages), wrote a detailed report: "At the top of the skull, towards the sagittal suture, I found two small perfectly round cuts, indicating a circular incision, such as might have been caused by a sharp instrument, and which seemed to me to be the result of two blows inflicted by a hand armed with a metal key and keyholder."[1]

This bloodied key would lock the door to Bébian's future. The oralists had it out for him, and this was their chance. Though Bébian remained an adviser to the board, continued to write extensively on the education of the Deaf, and ran for a time his own small school in Paris, he could no longer teach at Saint Jacques. For the Deaf, this was a calamitous turn of events.

Nine years later, in 1830, Berthier, Alphonse Lenoir, and another Deaf teacher and former Bébian student, Claudius Forestier, filed a petition with the new king of the French, Louis-Philippe, to have Bébian returned to Saint Jacques and named head of the school. The students clamored for his return as well, in rather more dramatic terms: the walls of Saint Jacques were covered with graffiti demanding Bébian back. Sixty-one students signed a petition to the Ministry of Interior closing with the words, "Long live Bébian. We want Mr. Bébian as director of the Institute . . . We love him very much." They also wrote anonymous critical letters, including a drawing depicting their hearing teachers as a "windmill of words." One teacher was drawn puffing, not to form a B or a P, but to spin the blades of the windmill. Each blade represented a teacher, one in the image of a chicken, another a bull, a third an ass, and the fourth a little pig.

The controversy marked the first institutional fracture between a hearing director and hearing teachers, on the one hand, and Deaf teachers and students on the other, but it would not be the last—the crisis can be considered a harbinger of the Deaf President Now campaign at Gallaudet University in 1988 and the hunger strike of Deaf students at Saint Jacques in 2005. The response in 1830 was swift. The principal authors of the students' petition and the anonymous letters were dismissed from the school. Their graphic artist was also expelled, and later in life became an accomplished painter.[2] The royal petition of Berthier and his colleagues also failed, and Gérando instead appointed an oralist who, as we have seen, adopted a plan to try to eliminate the Deaf faculty and turn Saint Jacques into a speech-teaching school. Berthier managed to defeat these efforts, but it wasn't the end of them.

In spite of the enormous success of their language as *the* instrument of teaching and learning, Deaf teachers had virtually no voice in the administration of their educational institutions. Throughout the age of Bébian, which included the tenures of the many Deaf teachers he had taught as students, the hearing teachers outnumbered the Deaf. Because they had neither the time nor the inclination or talent to master French sign language, they taught in an early version of *français signé*, signed French (signed English in the United States), a holdover from l'Épée's methodical signs. The hearing teachers were the ones who controlled the language of faculty meetings, and their control was nearly complete because Bébian was no longer there as the bilingual representative and advocate of the Deaf teachers and students.

When Berthier and Alphonse Lenoir asked that the Saint Jacques faculty meetings be conducted in sign language so that they could follow the proceedings, the request was denied and they were sent the minutes instead. Berthier ultimately decided that an independent forum for the Deaf was needed—a committee, a corporate entity, something—at which they could not only deal with issues affecting themselves, Deaf education, and the larger Deaf community, but also bring that community to the attention of the world in general. In 1834 he organized what he called the "Committee of Deaf-Mutes."[3] His hope was that, meeting monthly or more often as required, the committee might serve the Deaf as "their House of Lords, their *own*, their House of Representatives, their Supreme Court, which would address their problems and support their hopes."[4]

Bérthier invited eleven Deaf men to join him on the committee, including Lenoir, Forestier, and Frédéric Peyson, another well-known Deaf painter. They were all in their twenties. Making an implicit reference to the failed Gérando coup, he explained the committee's existence: "The creation of this Committee . . . is necessary because of the critical circumstances into which the deaf have seen themselves thrown following active intrigues against them, and in light of the need to unite their efforts against the attacks of certain men who would take advantage of their infirmity in order to harvest the fruits of their sweat."[5]

But Berthier saw as the committee's most important function its organization of annual dinners of the Deaf to honor the abbé de l'Épée. They would be held every year on the Sunday closest to his birthday (November 25). He had a bust of l'Épée made, which would join them for dinner every year. The formal language of the banquets was to be French sign language. For Berthier, these banquets had a purpose broader than simply celebrating l'Épée; he would invite leading public figures to the dinners to see for themselves what the Deaf had accomplished. His goal was to recruit influential people to the Deaf struggle and thus to extend the debate over signed languages beyond the walls of Saint Jacques and other schools for the Deaf.

Journalists, politicians, writers, lawyers, and others from France and abroad were invited. Hearing participants who signed would render in speech the presentations given in sign language and in sign those that were spoken—showing the French establishment that signed languages were just as nuanced and sophisticated as any spoken tongue. The dinners were held annually over the next thirty-six years, from 1834 to 1869; the publication of their proceedings ended only with the Franco-Prussian War. As Bébian's best student, Berthier was well aware of l'Épée's limitations as a signer, linguist, and teacher, but he saw in the good abbé an irreproachable and disinterested personality, dead for almost half a century, who might serve as a figurehead, a kind of "national" symbol for the Deaf of France and, perhaps, for the Deaf around the world. In short, he hoped to make l'Épée, who had become largely forgotten, the spiritual father of the Deaf community.

The committee raised funds for paintings and statues of l'Épée in Versailles (his birthplace), at Saint Jacques, and in one of Paris's principal churches, Saint-Roch, in the faubourg Saint Honoré where l'Épée was buried, so that the wider world could actually see the image of their hero. Berthier dug up l'Épée's bones from beneath Saint-Roch (from which his coffin had already been taken and melted down to make bullets during the French Revolution).[6] L'Épée was to be toasted endlessly at the banquets as the Deaf community's savior. He was their "glorious apostle," their "immortal abbé," their "common father," their "intellectual Moses who has guided us to our promised land," their "Messiah," and the "God" of their liberty. But l'Épée was a means to an end, a way to rally both the Deaf and the hearing around the language of the Deaf:

It is true that in the time before our immortal founder, a few charitable men devoted themselves to the alleviation of our cruel infirmity; but they wore themselves out in the face of a skeptical public. Their attempts to restore to our brothers the use of speech, which had always been considered the only way to transmit ideas, were too feeble to overcome so many obstacles. Only one man was able to uncover the infallible way, to use it to its best advantage and nourish it to the point of repairing the errors of nature. In his fortunate wisdom he seized upon *language*, the gift of all intelligent beings without exception, upon the language that our ancestors spoke, that our children will continue to speak, a language that is understood equally by inhabitants of the desert and dwellers in the city; that is to say, upon the language of sign.[7]

The dinners were held at a variety of popular restaurants around town throughout the thirty-six-year period, on the place du Châtelet near the Seine, in Saint Germain, in the faubourg Saint Honoré, in Montmartre, in the Marais, and in the garden of the Palais Royal.

Berthier decided to have the proceedings of the banquets published in bound volumes, providing the record that enables us to follow their history today. Members of his committee, but principally Berthier himself and (until 1853) his close and influential hearing friend Eugène de Monglave, who had learned sign language and become a member of the committee, participated in the original recording of the proceedings.[8] Numerous articles about the banquets also appeared in the French press. Sixty graduates of Saint Jacques attended the first banquet. They included teachers, painters, engravers, clerks, printers, and "simple workmen." The proceedings were publicized in more than a dozen French newspapers. Two hearing people were there, one fluent in sign, the other communicating with the Deaf banqueters in writing.

That same night a group from the École des Beaux Arts was honoring Louis Daguerre in the next room, and Daguerre insisted that his group join Berthier's. Berthier writes that the mingled group was "but a single people of intelligent men, working with their pencils, paintbrushes, fingers, and even [in the case of the hearing] their speech." At the same time he made it clear to his colleagues, as he did constantly to his students at Saint Jacques, that the Deaf could not afford to let down their guard: "Remember well, you others, my brothers, my friends, my companions in misfortune, that the fruit of our sacrifices will be lost if we fail to persevere; because nothing here on earth can be obtained without a robust will and a strong faith in the future . . . [So] may this sign I now make burst forth from the depths of the hearts of the deaf who persevere and their devoted friends: To life! Until death!"[9]

With perseverance, writing letter after letter, visiting people at their offices and wherever they lived, Berthier sought out great men to attend his banquets of the Deaf and become their allies. If they could not, he would extract from them letters of support for the banquets to be rendered in sign language for the Deaf and read aloud for the hearing, and then published in the newspapers (and in the bound volumes) along with detailed accounts of the proceedings.

Victor Hugo wrote to the group asking "what matters deafness of the ear, when the mind hears," thus, for Berthier, putting the language of the Deaf on a par with that of France's eminent writer.[10] The lawyer and labor champion Alexandre Ledru-Rollin came to the third banquet in 1836. Alfred de Vigny, invited to the seventh banquet in 1840 but unable to come, sent a well-intentioned but commonplace poem for the banquets observing that the Deaf were better off than Milton and Homer, because at least the Deaf could see. The minutes of the third dinner describe the participants as follows: "The deaf from every country were there, Englishmen, Germans, Italians, whom sign language, this universal language so vainly sought [by the hearing] over the centuries, united as one people. They understood each other as if they had first seen the light of day in the same land. There were teachers, men of letters, painters, sculptors, engravers, typographers, a host of artisans from various trades; and in the company of men of positions so diverse, the scale of social distinctions had vanished: a common link brought them together: they were deaf."

Berthier's reference to a "universal language" is, of course, hyperbole. As previously discussed, the signed language of each country is not in general recognizably iconic and is just as distinct (without any general correlation) as each country's spoken language.[11] But the syntaxes of signed languages can be similar, and the great facility of the Deaf with hands and facial expression is conducive to communication in pantomime (principally) and in the few recognizably iconic signs. For example, in the sign for *house* in both ASL and LSF, both hands, in a B configuration (see Appendix 2), form the shape of a pointed roof.

Berthier invited Lamartine and Chateaubriand to the sixth banquet in 1839, but neither could make it. John Carlin, a Deaf American painter and poet and a former student of Laurent Clerc, attended that banquet and reported in his signed presentation that, until Clerc's arrival in the United States, "there prevailed in my native country a melancholy darkness of ignorance over the unfortunate [Deaf]. There were no bright rays of reason penetrating the total obscurity of their souls. Their agonized parents wept over their misfortune. The good hearts pitied them deeply. The wicked laughed and pronounced them *dogs without a soul.* [But with the arrival of Laurent Clerc,] parents ceased weeping; good hearts rejoiced and praised God; and the wicked hid their heads from the indignant eyes of contempt."[12]

Present at the fifth banquet was John O'Connell, a lawyer and member of the British Parliament and the son of Daniel O'Connell, called the "Liberator" for his championing the Catholic Emancipation Act in 1829 and his early support of Irish independence. Berthier hailed O'Connell in French sign language as "the son of the liberator of Ireland, that oppressed country," and was then himself saluted by the banqueters as the man considered, like O'Connell, to be "the defender and savior of his country."[13] André Dupin, president of the French National Assembly, also attended. A member of the committee, a hearing physician fluent in sign language, stood beside Dupin and signed his improvised speech praising the language of the Deaf and the Paris school: "I am speaking to you, it is true, in a foreign language; but you have faithful interpreters among you, men who are skillful at translating the expressed thoughts of others into your own language . . . It is in France that the Institute of the Deaf [Saint Jacques] has been so gloriously born. It is from here at home that it will spread successively to all peoples who honor civic life, true philosophy and humanity."[14]

Berthier described the dinners as the "Olympics" of the Deaf, "four times more frequent than those of Greece, and a hundred times more curious and engaging." In fact they were demonstrations of the success of Bébian's teaching, of the accomplishment of the goals that he had set for himself and his students, as he had described them five years before his death: "I unveiled to the deaf the richness, the energy, the elegance, the flexibility of sign language, and thanks to this powerful instrument, seconded by the underlying philosophy of language, there was no longer any difficulty that could stop the deaf, there was no author, whether in poetry or prose, not easily within their reach."[15]

Indeed, they became poets themselves. Pierre Pélissier, a Deaf teacher at Saint Jacques, delivered a number of poems at the banquets and published a book of poetry as well as books on French sign language and Deaf history. Pélissier carried on a correspondence with Lamartine, to whom he wrote—

Let your poetry fall into the heart of the mute
to dry the source of its tears
and your melodious voice answer its wonder
and cradle its sorrows.

Lamartine answered Pélissier by giving life to the light of his language—

It is through the senses
that light descends upon us;
but I see in the strains of your verse,
in your captive heart it enters first,
thwarting nature,
and making sense of itself.

And later wrote again to Pélissier—

You pour into my heart,
unfortunate poet,
a mystery of love and tenderness.
To charm your cares,
breathe out your songs,
as sweet as friendship, from
your secret lyre.[16]

Ever the student of Bébian, and now as the most articulate representative of the Deaf, Berthier constantly focused the hearing banqueters on the fact that the signed language they were witnessing and hearing translated at these celebrations was as accurate and complete a language as was mathematics with its system of numbers: "All I can say about sign language is that very few of the hearing, even today, know what it is or are aware of its particular genius. Far from being as complex in the expression of thought as one might imagine, it is made up of only a small number of constituent elements, capable of infinite combination and animated and enlivened by the play of facial expression. Sign requires no more than that to present, in and of itself, all the ideas that crowd the mind, and all the affections that move the heart. In a word, it embodies the simplicity and universality of that most perfect of sciences with its 10 characters, mathematics."[17]

Berthier made sure through speaking signers that the hearing banqueters were kept abreast of what the Deaf were saying, and that his agenda and players came as close as they could to drowning their guests in a flood of eloquence, often poetic, often Pélissier's, but sometimes his own:

> When I see assembled in this spacious hall
> those to whom calamity joins me from the cradle,
> children bereft of the gift of speech,
> ill-treated children of a cruel stepmother nature:
> I walk not alone; my brother comes with me
> and the road is not so long when traveled by two.
>
> We do not speak, it is true; but still
> do you think us unable to express ourselves as well
> with our eyes, our hands, our smiles, our lips?
> Our most beautiful discourse is at the tips of our fingers,
> and our language is rich in secret beauties
> that you who speak will never know.
>
> And have we not our own art of Phoenicia
> to paint the words that speak into our eyes?
> Your arts and sciences, save for sound,
> are they not open to our ardent minds?
>
> Show us the heavens, ambitious heirs of Icarus,
> that I cannot ascend with you.[18]

Also echoing Bébian, Claudius Forestier spoke of the Deaf and their "brothers who speak," past and present, and the future that they would build together: "Brothers! In other times you wandered lost in the world, you were all but ignored, and you vegetated in sad isolation. You lived only for the sake of living. Your joys and sorrows were locked in your hearts and found no responsive echoes beyond them. Your ill fortune inspired in some a sterile and occasionally disdainful pity; and in others the repugnance and disgust that a worm inspires in a passerby who squashes it. But now, what a change! The stature that belongs of right to the intelligent in our society has been restored to you. You will meet, time and again, among our brothers who speak, men who will hasten to offer you their friendship, their services, to put their talents at your disposal. Why did this great change come about? It has come to you because *you* have become a nation."[19]

Another goal of Berthier's at the banquets was to enable the hearing to see the Deaf together, speaking their language, just as Bébian had at Saint Jacques from the age of thirteen, as philosophers and other thinkers had failed to do prior to l'Épée, and as the American William Stokoe would in the next century. Berthier wanted the French establishment to appreciate the talent and humanity of the Deaf fully, over wine and in a relaxed setting, a place of lively faces and graceful hands:

> You may imagine that seeing an assembly of 60 men deprived of hearing and speech has got to be a sorry sight; but not at all. The human soul so animates their brows, mostly quite handsome ones, is written so vividly in their eyes, and forces its way so rapidly to their very fingertips, that instead of feeling pity you are tempted to envy them. And while at the bar, in the pulpit, in the theatre, out in the world, we so

often hear words without thoughts, it is hardly troubling to see, once a year at least, thoughts without words.

It's not an exaggeration to say that none of our most admired orators could compete with, or even come close to, Berthier, Forestier or Lenoir for grace, dignity, and the precision of their language. To tell the truth, when you *see* speeches like these three young men have given, you almost want to unlearn the ability to speak.[20]

By 1837 it became clear that Auguste Bébian's lively classroom had come to the outside world. This development surprised even the Deaf themselves—"Words fail us as we try to describe the outpouring of joy, unequivocal friendship and great cheer that constantly enlivens the dinner. A message launched in sign from one end of the table is avidly grasped at the other; a thought, a sentiment finds an echo in each heart; and when an electric spark takes hold of these exceptional beings, they gather in one group and then another as if moved by a single mind. Here there's a crossfire of questions, there a medley of stories, anecdotes, adventures, and news of the day."[21]

At the first banquet, one hearing guest, the journalist Bernard Maurice, who knew no sign language, was spoken of in jest as an outcast, lost in a world of tables turned, looked on with pity by the group as a whole: "Monsieur Maurice, a man incomplete according to these people, an unfortunate deprived of gestural speech, a *pariah* of society, was obliged to resort to a pencil in order to converse with the heroes of the evening. An ineffable pity could be read on the features of those he approached. *The poor man*, they said, *he can't make himself understood.*"[22]

After being dismissed from Saint Jacques in 1821, Auguste Bébian had briefly run two other schools for the Deaf in France and, of course, written extensively on the education of the Deaf. But he was gravely disappointed in the failed effort to bring him back as director of Saint Jacques in 1830. He became ill and ultimately returned to his native Guadeloupe, where he founded the island's first school for indigenous children. Bébian never recovered his health and, shortly before he died in 1839, lost his own young son. Alphonse Lenoir toasted his late teacher at the banquet following Bébian's death and praised the bond between the Deaf and the hearing who understood them:

> To the deaf! May they be no longer a separate species of the earth. May they display their intellects, the seal of their education. And to the hearing who are deaf at heart. May they glory in having understood us so well that they have bundled our interests up together with their own.
>
> In this solemn ceremony, resounding with joy, we cannot refrain from making a sacred homage to the memory of one of our great and accomplished men who, after having regenerated the instruction of the deaf throughout Europe, having shredded the veil of prejudice and ignorance in the shadow of which the deaf had wandered so long, left us to end his days, weary and full of tribulations, beyond the seas. May the name of Bébian never fade from our grateful hearts. May he live unceasingly in our memory and in that of our future generations, as a beautiful model of boundless devotion and selflessness.[23]

Frédéric Peyson praised Bébian as well, albeit as the "disciple" of Berthier's figurehead: "To the eternal recognition of Bébian! To this great man whom ingratitude has allowed to die on a distant Atlantic island. To the friend we mourn. To the most distinguished disciple of the abbé de l'Épée who sacrificed all, fortune, a life of ease, and personal ambition, for the rehabilitation of the deaf. To the man who single-handedly brought the teaching of the deaf to a level to which no one has brought it since. The living proof of the fruit of his learned instruction surrounds us here today. Look about you, and behold with pride his worthy students, the Berthiers, the Lenoirs, the Forestiers, and on, and on, and on."[24]

Pélissier spoke often of the most intimate connection between the Deaf and the hearing—the fact that about 95 percent of Deaf children are born of hearing parents. At the eighth banquet in 1841 his "agile fingers" signed the lament of such a mother:

> They said to me: "Soon, happy mother,
> his gentle voice will repeat your name.
> and when a stranger sits nearby
> of his words she'll hear the sound.
>
> When your man come home from war
> of his love at last on his knees
> shall hold the prize, the child of his entrails
> will say to him, 'Soldier, I am your son.'
>
> But, oh, sorrow! To his feeble lip
> in vain my lip revealed its accents;
> of not a word in his immobile eye
> did my sad eyes see the sense.
>
> Never his voice enhanced his grace
> by answering the guests he charmed;
> and when my love his son to his breastplate drew
> he never cried out, 'Soldier, I am your son.' "[25]

The child in Pélissier's poem is later abandoned by a careless guide and disappears, voiceless and signless. Years later, the mother learns that he is found with a bloodstained hand, and put to death for an unmentioned crime. But in 1856 Pélissier signs the story of another mother who—

Lovingly cradles her child, covers him with kisses, speaks to him still, but he does not hear her. She draws her ear closer and the child remains voiceless. He is deaf, he is mute; the mother cries. The dear creature will never know what tenderness the soul of a mother can put into her words, he will never share with her who gave him life the delicious babbling that is the eloquence of infants, he will grow up without becoming a man, he will never know what the mouths of men teach, he will never converse with them, his tongue will be chained, and that will suffice to make him a pariah, an exile wandering beyond the walls of the city.

The poor mother comes near to wishing his death. But a friend is there to relieve and console her. He says to her—as joy returns to her brow—he says to her that this prisoner will be set free, that his soul will cast off the distress of his senses, that he will be recalled to human company, that he will receive the second life of intelligence, and the mother moves from tears to the fullness of happiness, knowing that her child will live again, and will come to know her name.[26]

In the nineteenth century, however, women, whether Deaf or hearing, were not invited to the banquets, and played as limited a role among the Deaf as they did in the polity of the hearing. The Deaf painter Joseph de Widerkehr reminded the group of their "devoted" existence in a tribute to them he delivered in sign language at the banquet in 1839, placing Deaf women squarely at the hearth:

> I would like to be the intermediary today for our [absent] deaf women, whose hearts are no strangers to the sentiments that animate us here. They join in our noisy celebration with their silent prayers in devoted blessing of the creative genius of the abbé de l'Épée. As you know it was with two girls that he began his divine mission.
>
> May they give no thought to their infirmity amid the tender care and marks of devotion of which they are so deserving. May they taste, in the bosom of their families, the true happiness and the gentle pleasures that reward the virtues of the heart and the culture of the spirit. May they have their turn to be the pride and joy of their parents, and be admired by the world as the image of their pure and gentle souls, and of their spirits formed by their impeccable upbringing.[27]

The Deaf didn't enlist women in their struggle during these years; had they done so they would have been ahead of their time. Deaf men and women did begin to mix at public gatherings in the 1860s, notably at a conference sponsored by the Deaf school in Lyons in 1861, which was duly acknowledged at the thirty-first banquet of the Deaf (men) in Paris in 1864. But as stated by a leading French historian of the Deaf, Florence Encrevé: "The Civil Code of 1804 . . . included married women among those who lacked the capacity to act on their own behalf. As a result, deaf women were not spared the *a priori* of their time regarding women in general. They were wholly identified with their reproductive function and considered inherently unsuited to intellectual pursuits. Even Berthier, however committed he was to the principle of equality, failed to escape this way of thinking."[28]

In defending the rights of the Deaf community as a whole, including their "devoted" women, Berthier was highly attuned to the fluid political movements of his time. Though certainly not as influential politically as a Talleyrand, Berthier was equally shrewd. He was solicitous of each government—the July Monarchy of Louis-Philippe (1830), the short-lived Second Republic (1848–1852), and the Second Empire of Louis-Napoleon Bonaparte (1852–1870). Saint Jacques was successively called the Royal, the National, and the Imperial Institute, though of course it remained the Institute of the Deaf, whichever government claimed it as its own. Toasts at the banquets were given, depending on the season, to the king of the French, to the Republic, to the Emperor, but always and above all to l'Épée, to the Deaf, and to their language, their struggle, and their future. Berthier was given the Legion of Honor in 1849 by Louis-Napoleon himself, and the Deaf were given the statutory right to vote in 1850 (American women were not given that right until 1920; French women had to wait until 1945).

Berthier was careful to invite to his banquets members of the government who served on the committees supervising Saint Jacques, as well as officials whose help he had solicited in building the monuments to l'Épée in Paris and Versailles. Berthier's copious writings, on l'Épée, Bébian, Sicard, Itard, and the Deaf in general received wide attention among the Deaf and the hearing and, in a world which until recently had thought of the Deaf as incapable of abstract ideas and learning a written language, became living proof of the sophistication of sign language. As to Bébian, though he died young, the original hopes he expressed in his path-breaking essay of 1817, written when he was twenty-eight years old, were coming to pass: "It is no longer possible to doubt whether a deaf man may be perfectly restored to society. With the benefit of instruction, he is neither deaf to those who know how to write, nor mute to those who can read. All the treasures of the human mind are put at his disposal: he knows how to take pleasure as others do from works of genius, the enlightenment of the sciences, the wonders of the arts; and he no longer has anything to envy in other men."[29]

In 1838, Berthier incorporated his committee as the Central Society of the Deaf-Mutes of Paris.[30] As was the case for the committee, sign was the official language of the society and its meetings, and its by-laws required that the president be Deaf. In 1850 he created a separate organization, the Central Society *for the Education and Assistance* of the Deaf, which actively sought wealthy hearing members who were prepared to make substantial contributions to help the Deaf.[31]

But as Berthier knew only too well, the oralist movement did not die with the defeat of Gérando. He made frequent reference at the banquets to opposing forces. In 1838 the discussion throughout the dinner was focused on the "sad vicissitudes" at Saint Jacques since the loss of Bébian. And in 1840 Berthier stressed the need to fight, emphasizing that "silence" in the face of these oralist attacks would not suffice: "New efforts are being made behind our backs to divide us. All's fair for those who want to prejudice our interests. Should we confine ourselves to turning up our nose at these attacks? No, our inaction would only encourage them; silence won't be enough to foil these schemes. We can win only by fighting them. Let's constantly set against them all the energy that a good cause gives to the conscience; let us employ the little of instruction, of light, that Providence has dispensed to us, in order to repel them, to stagger them, to shatter them. May, in the end, our invincible perseverance in following the path we have traced for ourselves dishearten our enemies and reduce them to shame!"[32]

But the hearing teachers at Saint Jacques, as well as elsewhere in France and throughout Europe, remained in the majority, and generally lacked the signing abilities of Bébian and his highly talented Deaf progeny. In 1837 Claudius Forestier, a signer of the petition to restore Bébian who had been teaching at Saint Jacques for ten years, was forced out of the school by being kept at the low level of teaching assistant when in fact he was one of the leading educators in Europe. He left to run, very ably, a private school for the Deaf in Lyons, where he would do battle with the oralists forty years later in an unsuccessful effort to save that school.

Berthier's Society for Education functioned effectively until the 1860s, when the traditional philanthropists, close to Berthier and more interested in philanthropy than in method, gradually withdrew and were replaced by government officials, merchants, and doctors. Control of this society was slipping from Berthier's hold. In 1854 it organized a competition to determine the best way to educate Deaf children before they entered the first grade. A late entrant, Jean-Jacques Valade-Gabel, who was later to become a teacher at Saint Jacques and director of the Bordeaux school, proposed teaching the children "without recourse to sign language." Though his submission was too late to earn a prize, it received the Society's praise.[33] As early as 1850, Alexandre Blanchet, a surgeon at Saint Jacques who would later succeed the eminent Prosper Menière as chief of medicine there, had written—"What more beautiful task could there be . . . than to restore to society . . . with speech and the ability to read lips, the great number of these unhappy deaf-mutes that the world has too long considered as vile pariahs."[34]

Blanchet's successor as chief of medicine at Saint Jacques, Jules Ladreit de Lacharrière, like both Blanchet and Itard (before his conversion), thought that Deaf people's inability to hear made them intellectually backward: "For the child, deafness prevents the development of language and [if postlingual] makes him forget it. Deafness arrests the progress of intelligence and places the child in a position of inferiority which he will always feel deeply. Though it is true that sight permits us to appreciate everything that has a shape, all of our moral ideas, the conceptions of the mind, are transmitted to us by the sense of hearing."[35]

This is Bébian and Berthier upside down. Lacharrière was a regular at the Deaf banquets, and how he could square that statement with all that he witnessed of the erudition of the Deaf in attendance is inexplicable. Jean-Baptiste Puybonnieux, a hearing teacher at Saint Jacques and also often at Berthier's dinners, urged at the twentieth banquet in 1853 that sign language "be not the rival but the understudy of speech."[36] Several scholars have attempted to provide historical explanations for the change in attitude—or rather, the resurfacing of the undercurrents of antipathy toward the Deaf and their language in the latter half of the century—but, as we shall later see, none of them is satisfactory.

Beginning in the 1850s the ideas of l'Épée's unsuccessful rival, the late Jacob Pereire, were to have their modern champions in his extraordinarily wealthy grandsons, Émile and Isaac Pereire, and Isaac's son Eugène. Together with James de Rothschild and other French industrialists, they invested heavily in banking, real estate, shipping, energy, insurance, and other enterprises and became among the richest men in Europe. The Pereires had always been anxious to rehabilitate the image of their grandfather, and once they had the resources they set out to do so with a vengeance. Signed languages to them were not only the instrument of Jacob's undoing, but a relic of the past and tainted with Catholicism—given the cult of l'Épée and the influence of Catholic teaching orders in the private Deaf schools (only Saint

Jacques and the Bordeaux school were government-run). L'Épée had also, of course, been a significant force in the discrediting of their grandfather's "teaching" of speech and lipreading. They were determined not to let this stand, and to destroy signed languages as instruments of learning, thus restoring Jacob's reputation and enhancing their own already considerable standing in the community.

The Pereires rationalized their position by purporting to promote "equality of opportunity" for the Deaf, but their notion of equality was based on the proposition that the Deaf could achieve it only by learning to speak and lipread, a practical impossibility as even their grandfather had recognized toward the end of his life a hundred years earlier. Their proposals should have been doomed from the beginning, but Bébian was dead, and Berthier was aging and had no successor. In 1875 the J. R. Pereire Society was established "to promote the teaching of speech and lipreading, *by* speech, to the deaf." The Pereires opened a school for that purpose in 1879 and hired a French oralist then teaching in Geneva, Marius Magnat, to run it.[37]

In 1856, at a sermon given at the Church of the Madeleine, for the benefit of the Society for Education, François Le Courtier, a Catholic priest (later an archbishop), expressed the Church's enlightened view of signed languages in terms that were not only reflective of the thinking of Bébian and Berthier, but also, remarkably, anticipated the findings of linguists and biologists in the twentieth century. Speech, Le Courtier said, was "a few molecules of air, altered by the action of the tongue, produc[ing] articulate sounds of convention that contain an idea; that idea, clothed in speech and enveloped in sound, strikes the ear; the ear captures and twirls its vibrations, the mind perceives it and answers it with words that will strike another ear and another mind. Such is conventional communication." When the ear is obstructed, he continued, sound "fades and dies with it."

But God has given the Deaf another language, by which "the ideas depicted thus enter by the eyes and reach the mind; the mind answers them by the hand in the same language, and communications are almost entirely restored. The only difference is, they enter by the window instead of the door, and the commerce of ideas finds a most happy and exceptional way of passage."[38]

Thus we have God, Bébian, air as the medium of speech, the winding pathway of the cochlea, light as the implied medium of signed languages, and a suggestion that common areas of the brain process, respectively, the reception (through the ears or eyes) and utterance (by voice or hands) of sign language and speech. Here were the linguistic worlds of the hearing and the Deaf just as Lenoir had suggested—all bundled up together by a hearing cleric and intellectual in practical and prescient fashion. But almost twenty years later, in 1874, another Catholic bishop, speaking again in honor of the Society for Education, offered quite a different conception of the nature and function of voices in the air, exhuming the specter of the dark ages:

> When God decided to make man his masterpiece, he created him as a speaking being. After having kneaded with his hands the clay that we are, he drew from his breast the breath we breathe and played it like the strings of a lyre with the magic pressure of a living bow, bringing the breath to our lips as the echo of man's soul and testimony to his life.
>
> If God had not done what I have just said, without this thin stream of mobile air which carries our thoughts, our souls would have vegetated in solitude; humankind would have been a multitude of beings with no bond of union among them, all of nature a temple without a voice . . . A mind deprived of the light of speech turns hopelessly around

in circles in a dark prison . . . [Though] in sign and in writing [the Deaf] have a second language, more importantly . . . they have the power to read speech on the lips of others, to detect thoughts without hearing them. In this way, by this patient but fruitful work, society is recovering a part of its own.[39]

God remains, but spoken words, and not signed languages, are the voices in this misguided notion of "light"; gone is the enlightenment, the analysis, the history, the future, and the truth. In 1865 Berthier, Lenoir, and other Deaf notables were still officers or directors of the Society for Education, but they had lost any semblance of influence. Doctors and hearing teachers were gaining control.[40]

The hearing teachers at Saint Jacques and officials of the Ministry of Interior tried to supplant the banquets of the Deaf by holding their own dinners of the *hearing* in honor of the Deaf. Berthier, now retired, was summoned to Saint Jacques by its director, Léon Vaïsse, in November 1865 and told that from that time on, l'Épée's birthday would be celebrated at the school itself and nowhere else. Berthier was invited, of course, as were all others who attended his banquets. A representative of the ministry responsible for the school would preside, however; not the Deaf Berthier. Berthier agreed to attend in his personal capacity, adding that the banquets of his Society of the Deaf would continue and that, as provided in its by-laws, a Deaf person, whether it be he or someone else, would always preside. Vaïsse tried again each of the next two years, holding his third dinner in 1867 on the same evening as that of Berthier's. None of Berthier's guests, of course, defected to Vaïsse's event.

Berthier's Deaf banquets of 1867 and 1868 were held in a house in Montmartre that had been one of l'Épée's two original schools one hundred years earlier. Both Vaïsse and Lacharrière were there to hear the teacher Benjamin Dubois emphasize in sign the significance of the venue, as if to imply that a takeover of Saint Jacques could never destroy their institutional memory:

> This is the second time we find ourselves in this house that served as a school for the students of our intellectual father . . . He gathered his children together here on holidays, too. Why should we prefer this house for our celebration to any other? . . . It is because we have the gentle pleasure of treading on the ground where our elders tread, of touching the walls they touched, of contemplating the traces they have left behind . . . As simple and as modest as this place is, let us consider it with respect and love, and attach ourselves to the memories it preserves for us.[41]

By 1860, the wives of both Émile and Isaac Pereire had joined the board of the Society for Education, and Léon Vaïsse had become its secretary. Lacharrière became secretary-general in 1870. Increasingly, the Deaf were turning inward, to their original Society alone. Before long they would change its name to the "friendly association" of the Deaf.[42] By the late 1870s, the *te deum* that Ferdinand Berthier wanted the banquets to be for his immortal l'Épée and for the Deaf, their language, their culture, and their prosperity was beginning to assume the pale complexion of a long requiem. Berthier believed that the very life or death of Saint Jacques as an institution, and as the model for all schools, was at stake. He predicted that the intellectual future of the Deaf would be lost if, as he feared, the partisans of oralism were to win the day, for signed languages were not a goal of the education of the Deaf, but its indispensable instrument. Take that away, he warned, and you have nothing.[43]

7

The Congress of Milan: The Hundred Years' War

For the Deaf in the latter part of the nineteenth century, Paris was not a happy place. True, by 1869 there were several hundred teachers of the Deaf in Europe and the United States, and 41 percent of the teachers were Deaf themselves. But at the same time others were searching for ways to alter the manner of teaching the Deaf, not only in France but throughout Europe. And the number of schools for the Deaf was growing faster than the number of teachers able to teach in signed languages.[1]

Hearing teachers had always been in the majority, as we have seen, but Deaf education in Europe was once again becoming dominated by those who had little connection to the culture or language of the Deaf and had a vested interest in speech. A hearing instructor attempting to teach speech to a class of signing students would easily lose his authority if he could neither make himself understood nor understand what his students were saying to each other. The proposed solution was a simple one: separate the Deaf students from each other, and abolish their language as the medium of teaching. Fighting for their salaried positions and armed with their voices, these hearing teachers slowly gained preeminence in France, England, Italy, Germany, and, ultimately, the United States.

The Pereires decided to organize a number of conferences or "congresses" on the education of the Deaf, seeking out the hearing educators as their allies. Such gatherings had become popular in the latter half of the century as a way to assemble experts on a variety of subjects who could present and exchange their ideas for progress and scientific advancement. In 1900, no fewer than 242 such gatherings were held in Paris alone.[2] With the help of France's Ministry of Education, the Pereires succeeded in organizing a congress on the "improvement of the condition of the deaf" as part of the 1878 World's Fair in Paris. There were to be a number of scientific displays, including Alexander Graham Bell's telephone and Thomas Edison's phonograph.

The congress was attended by more than fifty hearing teachers and others who, in effect, mounted their first collective assault on signed languages. Attendees included Léon Vaïsse, the speech teacher and former director of Saint Jacques, and its physician, Jules Ladreit de Lacharrière ("all of . . . the conceptions of the mind are transmitted to us by the sense of hearing"), Marius Magnat, the head of the Pereires' school for teaching speech to the Deaf, and the directors of private (primarily Catholic) Deaf schools.[3] Martin Etcheverry, then the head of Saint Jacques, refused to attend, saying that French sign language should continue to serve as the basis of instruction.[4] Serafino Balestra, an Italian priest and the head of an oral school on Lake Como, was there as well, as was an American from the Clarke Institution in Northampton, Massachusetts, the center of the oralist movement in the United States.

The Pereires' congress would prove to be a dress rehearsal for the Congress of Milan two years later. The principal resolution adopted in Paris provided that, while signed languages should be preserved as an "auxiliary teaching tool" and the "first means of communication" between teacher and students, "the goal of the method called 'articulation' and the reading of speech on the lips, is to restore the deaf more fully to society. This method must be preferred resolutely to all others. It is a preference which has justified the increasing use of the method in Europe and even in the United States . . . Nevertheless, [there are Deaf children who because their] intellectual development has been neglected or abandoned [should be taught] by way of the signs common to all deaf-mutes so that they may develop their faculties to the extent possible."[5]

The congress also proposed studies of the intermarriage of the Deaf "and of the deaf [offspring] that could be the result." Boys and girls in Deaf schools should be separated to avoid early contact between themselves, for separation was "preferable to their union." It was agreed, following a proposal by Balestra, that an international conference would be held in Italy two years later, in 1880.[6]

A second congress was held in Lyons just a year later, and paid more deference to signed languages than was given in Paris. A teacher from the Deaf school in Marseilles, the abbé Guérin, pointed out that neither the state nor the country's charities (notably the Church) had the resources to "teach" speech and lipreading to the Deaf because of the very small classes required. He also observed that any enforced prohibition of signed languages cut off the Deaf from one another: "The pure oral method doesn't allow sign language. It raises a barrier so high among the deaf themselves that, when they leave their schools, they won't be able to understand each other."[7]

The importance of the idea of the souls of the Deaf still had strong currency, but for the Pereirists (who controlled the conference), the question was how the Deaf got along with and were able to please the hearing, not one another. Nevertheless the Lyons Congress decided that signed languages should retain "a very large place" in Deaf education, all the while recognizing, as the Paris Congress had, "the advantage of speech over sign language, especially in order fully to restore the deaf to the world."[8] Present at Lyons was a little-known priest from Milan, Giulio Tarra, an uncompromising champion of speech and lipreading, who could not have been happy with the result. The Italian congress was coming, and he was determined to hold it in his city, a center of oralism, and to take control of it.

The Congress of Milan, held in 1880, would prove to be the seminal traumatic event in the modern history of the Deaf. The organizing committee for the congress was Pereirist and French, and included Isaac and Eugène Pereire, Vaïsse, Magnat, and other allies of the industrialists. A total of 256 people attended, of whom 88 percent were either Italian (62 percent) or French (26 percent).[9] There were but a few English, Germans, and Americans. Only four of the 256 people who attended were Deaf, including Claudius Forestier, who had then become the director of his private school for the Deaf in Lyons, Joseph Théobald, a Deaf teacher at Saint Jacques, and Lorenzo del Lupo, an Italian student from Siena. Edward Gallaudet and his brother Thomas (both hearing) were there. James Denison, the Deaf director of the Kendall School (the elementary and preparatory school for the Deaf on Gallaudet's campus), attended as well.

Although the French had organized the congress, the Italians quickly took control. Tarra noted at the outset that he was sure he was expressing the majority view when he said "the most important question here is *method*." Balestra offered a novel scriptural reminder to the assembled group, many of whom were religious teachers of the Deaf, that brought everyone full circle back to the Middle Ages: the true "mission" of the congress was to fulfill the gospel of Saint John: *in principio erat verbum*. Other voices from the podium declared that speech was the expression of the soul and the manifestation of divine thought.[10] What then, as in the twelfth century, was a man or woman who couldn't speak, understand, or even perceive the Word of God?

Giulio Tarra (1832–1889), president of the Congress of Milan, 1880 (Collection INJS de Paris.)

Tarra had decided to present to all the conferees the advantages of oral education by staging demonstrations of talking and lipreading deaf students. For that purpose he had the week-long meeting reduced to daily half-sessions so that the participants could witness these events, which were given at the two (oral) schools in Milan and included spoken public exercises, plays, and classes. Guérin, the French priest who had stressed the importance of sign language in Lyons the previous year, was so impressed by the Italian students that he spoke of his "conversion" to oralism as a result of both the "grace of God" and the skill of the Italian teachers, who in their work were the "instruments of His Providence." He observed that a number of Deaf students could actually sing scales to perfection, except "for one or two slightly missed half-tones."[11]

Edward Gallaudet pointed out, however, that many (probably all) of the children put on display had learned how to speak before losing their hearing, suggesting to the skeptics (there were few) a more temporal interpretation of Balestra's scriptural invocation. An American writer later noted that approximately 70 percent of the students at the Milan schools were partially or post-lingually deaf children, though in the province of Milan such children accounted for only about 15 percent of the deaf population.[12] And even these students gave the answers to questions before they were completed, and were unable to lipread unfamiliar texts read by people they didn't know.[13]

The views expressed at the conference were vestiges of an earlier time, such as statements that signed languages could not express abstract thoughts and were unworthy of "the dignity of man." Italian oralists would cling to this view: two decades later at the Paris conference of 1900 an Italian educator claimed that the Deaf "persist in considering as a natural language their violent and spasmodic miming, which can at best simply establish their kinship with the famous primates."[14] The most important resolution adopted at Milan, by a vote of 160 to 4, provided as follows:

> The *Congress*, taking into consideration
>
> (a) the incontestable superiority of speech over signs in order to restore the deaf to society and to give them a more perfect knowledge of language, and
>
> (b) that the simultaneous use of speech and signs has the disadvantage of being prejudicial to speech, to lipreading, and to the expression of ideas,

Declares that the pure oral method must be preferred to that of sign for the education of the deaf.[15]

For the Deaf, however, speech was a practical impossibility beyond memorized, awkwardly uttered phrases; reading lips was conversationally impossible; and the only way to express and receive ideas was through their own language. Moreover, it was signed languages, and not speech, that "returned the deaf to society" by making reading and writing, and thus the arts and sciences, fully available to them. So the declaration of the Milan Congress was dramatically wrong on all counts. And yet almost everyone, and predominantly teachers of the Deaf, voted for it. Why?

Balestra made the old religious arguments to help win over the clerical educators. Following Christ's example, depicted in the prayerbook of Saint Hildegarde, the priest must "open the mouth of the deaf."[16] Tarra clearly didn't know Italian sign language, or knew it only imperfectly, for he claimed it was incapable of the expression of abstract ideas, including those of religious doctrine. He took the view that to describe a sin required the miming of it, and thus its virtual replication.[17]

This might have been true if you confessed your sins to Tarra, for they could not have been signed given his limitations. They would have to have been mimed using conventional gestures for various offenses. In current ASL, for example, as no doubt in the past in signed languages generally, the signs for sexual behavior are usually subtle ones. The sign for sexual intercourse, though quite often not a sin, may be expressed in ASL, hands facing each other and touching, by moving the dominant hand in a Bent V shape down along the other identically shaped hand as it moves up.[18] But whatever the word or the sign, it comes to represent the *idea* of the sensual behavior involved, and thus (theoretically) presents the risk of stimulation and sin whether recounted in Italian to the hearing or given in a signed language to the Deaf (or to a fluent confessor). The "converted" Guérin, who must have known better, agreed with Tarra as to the incapacity of signed languages to express abstract ideas. "If God is omnipresent, Guérin asked, why does the sign for God "indicate his limits"? The French sign is a D-shaped hand, for *Dieu*, moving upward and thus suggests that God is somewhere "up there," the source of Massieu's confusion, though he was led to worship the sky by the fervent upward glances of the hearing faithful.

Most of the assembly must have been keenly aware, as educators of the Deaf, that their proceedings and conclusions were based on false propositions. Nevertheless, on the continent, as the direct result of Milan, speech became the sole method of instruction. In France, the home of the Deaf enlightenment, and in the other countries of Europe, signed languages were forbidden in Deaf schools, and would remain so throughout most of the twentieth century.[19] In at least one school in France, students were put on a diet of stale bread as a punishment for communicating in sign language. Intellectual skills in schools throughout Europe were confused with degrees of deafness, and students unable to make progress in speech and lipreading were classified as "idiots" or "semi-idiots" and refused admission or expelled. Claudius Forestier refused to adopt the oral method at his school in Lyons, so the school was closed: he died the following year.[20] The Deaf teachers at Saint Jacques, Tessières, Tronc, Théobald, Dusuzeau, Simon, and others, all of them taught by Berthier and Bébian's other students, were summarily dismissed.

The cardinal reason why the Congress of Milan makes the Deaf shudder, and indeed why it should make us all tremble, is that to deprive an individual of language is to appropriate his or her identity.

Next comes the person's culture, then his or her family and friends. We have always understood the central importance of language; it underlies Saint John's speculation, whatever the doctrinal exigencies, as to the nature of Christ before he was born. Words and signs bind people together, the ones we collectively devise and endow with meaning and the manner in which we express and say and sing them, with voice or hand, whether they be French or English, Setswana or Sioux, ASL or LSF, or any other spoken or signed language.

As Christian Cuxac observed more than a hundred years after the events in Milan:

> On a number of occasions I have given historical accounts of the Congress of Milan to a public of deaf people. And at the end of my talk, in the charged atmosphere that arises in the audience almost every time I speak, I've had the curious impression that this buried memory, once awakened, is strangely fresh. Such is the effect of Milan among the deaf—this sorrow, this shudder of anger not far below the surface. And here indeed lies the whole problem: What does this mean, if not that Milan is still, and always, *today*.[21]

A key first step in the elimination of a people is to destroy their language. Such an endeavor often arises out of a visceral contempt for their "difference," and is commonly initiated after a conquest or to root out a minority group. When I confront the harm done by the Congress of Milan, with its effort to drive the Deaf to desolation by destroying their right to be educated in their own language, it is as if a collection of the gravest of human offenses were embodied in that single crime.

8

The Debate in England: Bell v. Gallaudet

In 1886, six years after the Congress of Milan, the British government established and empaneled a Royal Commission to decide the "best way" to teach the Deaf. Each side had its eloquent advocate at the commission's hearings—Edward Gallaudet for signed languages and Alexander Graham Bell for speech. Gallaudet, the world's most prominent hearing advocate of signed languages, had said little at Milan, but the congress had been a prearranged show and offered little opportunity for real debate. Bell was the most articulate and influential opponent of signed languages. Though Gallaudet and Bell each had a Deaf mother and a Deaf wife, the two men could not have been more different. Each man gave extensive testimony, providing the world with a profound insight into both the perceptions that divided the two sides and the character and objectives of the men themselves.

Edward Gallaudet was born in 1837, the son of Thomas Gallaudet, who had brought Laurent Clerc to the United States, and of Sophia Fowler, who had been Thomas's student at the American School for the Deaf in Hartford. Sophia had been Deaf from birth. Like the vast majority of children of the Deaf (including Deaf couples), Edward Gallaudet could hear. Following his father's example, after graduating from Yale he devoted his life to teaching the Deaf. He was not alone, for from 1817 to 1879 all six of the principals of the Hartford School were Yale alumni, as were all of the principals of the New York Institution

Edward Gallaudet (1837–1917), circa 1905 (Image courtesy of Gallaudet University Archives.)

for the Instruction of the Deaf and Dumb, the largest school for the Deaf in the country.[1]

Edward Gallaudet became the first president of Gallaudet College (named for his father), which was organized and is funded by the U.S. government.[2] Abraham Lincoln signed the college's original charter in 1864. At the inauguration ceremony, the college awarded its first degree, an honorary master of arts, to John Carlin, the Deaf American painter and poet who had spoken at Berthier's banquet twenty-five years earlier, in 1839. From its inception, the college based all of its instruction on American Sign Language. In the first three decades of the college's history, it produced fifty-seven teachers, four clergymen, three newspaper editors or publishers, fifteen government civil servants, a nationally known botanist, two architects, and other notables, including a lawyer admitted to practice before the U.S. Supreme Court.[3]

Alexander Graham Bell was born in Edinburgh in 1847, the year of Berthier's fourteenth banquet. He was a Scottish elocutionist, as were his father and grandfather. As an adolescent, Bell made a device resembling the vocal cords and mouth that, when one blew into it, pronounced the word "Mama." Remarkably, he taught his dog to pronounce the word as well, an historical feat never surpassed before or since except perhaps by Lady Blemley's cat, Tobermory, who a half century later and with "studied indifference" called her old automobile "The Envy of Sisyphus, because it goes quite nicely uphill if you push it."[4]

Bell's discovery of the telephone was inspired by his study of the tissue-thin eardrum and how the ossicles of the middle ear move to transmit its vibrations to the inner ear. The telephone uses a diaphragm, a magnet, and electric current to convert the sound waves produced by our voices into electric pulses. The receiving phone converts them back into sound waves by performing the exercise in reverse. He filed for the patent (another claimant filed his own application hours later) and fought off all rivals with the help of his wife's wealthy father. Had he not turned his attention to the telephone, it would have been invented and patented by someone else. That he succeeded was a disaster for the Deaf, for he was to devote a substantial portion of his energy and fortune to attacking their language.

Bell's motives were intricate. Both his mother and his wife, Mabel, had become Deaf as children from scarlet fever. Because their deafness was post-lingual and they retained some hearing, both were able

*Alexander Graham Bell
(1847–1922), circa 1880*
(Photograph by E.A. Holton,
Boston, 1876. Library of Congress,
Prints & Photographs Division,
Gilbert H. Grosvenor Collection of
Photographs of the Alexander
Graham Bell Family,
LC-USZ62-127046.)

to speak, though only their intimates could understand them easily. Bell's mother used an ear trumpet and was able to play and teach the piano, and Mabel could hear a church bell. She had originally been a student of Bell's, but in all their years together he had not been able to improve her speech. After many years of marriage, Bell did say that, when speaking to Mabel directly, he often forgot that she couldn't hear.

While she sounds extraordinarily gifted, Bell must have been particularly attentive when addressing his wife, whom he considered blessed with the "miracle" art of lipreading. But listening to people other than her devoted, nearby, stentorian husband must have been very difficult for her. The forty English consonant and vowel phones produce only sixteen discriminable visual units, and even among them, as we have seen, rapid choices have to be made.[5] Mabel nevertheless, with her memory of sound and the comfort of an occasional church bell, tried to function in a "normal" world, struggling to hide from her own predicament and avoiding the very company of the Deaf: "I have striven in every way to have [my deafness] forgotten and to be so completely normal that I would pass as [normal]. To have anything to do with other deaf people instantly brought this hard-concealed fact into evidence . . . I [therefore] would have no friends among them."[6]

Mabel's attitude is relatively common among the post-lingually Deaf who have retained some ability to speak and as children were steered away from sign language. Jean-Max Coudon, for example, was deafened by antibiotics in 1949 when he was five years old. His parents put him in the hands of a determined speech therapist who, like Bell, was "resolutely opposed to sign language." Though he was trained initially in speech and lipreading, he is difficult to understand and, of course, he can read lips only as Mabel could, with considerable difficulty. In his book, Coudon characterizes sign (which he does not know) as "a language with limited syntax that gives a 'deaf' structure to the mind of the child." Coudon "would never have married a deaf person" for it would have excluded him from the world of the hearing he took so long to "conquer." He leads a normal life, "sheltered from the stares of the curious." He is not "deaf," but has "a real family life" in spite of his "absent looks and vagabond thoughts."[7]

Women smile at him, find him charming, seek his company. He is "a man like others"—that is like men who hear. He finds the spoken language he cannot hear "much more complex" than the sign language he does not know. He is not a man who signs, and his "cognitive thought is . . . like that of the hearing," and thus unlike the minds of those who sign. Yet he cannot hear, cannot sign, and converses as a stranger, often lost, in the language of the hearing. Coudon says he is "normal" and, like Mabel, welcomes no friends among the Deaf—though the two lived their lives largely cut off from the world of the hearing.[8] Bell's own views of the congenitally Deaf arose at least in part out of sympathy and pride, in an effort to distinguish his wife and his mother from what he considered an underclass.

Edward Gallaudet: Of the Heart, the Imagination, the Intellect, and the Affections

Gallaudet was the first to testify in London, and he was an uneven witness. He was at his best when he observed that the greatest value of signed languages was that they afforded the Deaf the ability to engage in free and unrestrained social intercourse throughout their lives. A Deaf child taught in a signed language learned quickly, and soon came to be far better educated than a pupil "orally" educated. As Bébian's foremost American successor would write, in the twentieth century, "though the deaf person may never have heard a sound, such is the power of symbolics and the adaptability of the human mind, he may still have acquired the ability to use the written . . . word with as much symbolic force as any speaker of English can achieve."[9] Gallaudet listed the occupations that his students pursued after graduation, including editing and publishing, journalism, civil service, chemistry, architectural drafting, teaching (the Deaf), and trade.[10] Had he been able to turn back the clock and choose his own mother's form of education, Gallaudet would have changed nothing:

> My mother, as is known, was a deaf-mute, and of course I observed her life, so far as I was able, after I arrived at a sufficient age to be observant, and I have no hesitation in saying

that in my judgment the happiness of a deaf person is greater who may be educated without speech but . . . who uses the manual alphabet and signs, than one (and I hope I shall not be misunderstood) who has the power of speech and lipreading but refuses to use signs . . . I know of such persons, and I am certain that their lives are more isolated, and they have a less degree of happiness in society and among their friends than those who without speech still use freely signs . . . I would not be understood, in giving this answer, to under-value the usefulness of speech to the deaf, but understanding the question as put to me to have reference to the general happiness of the person, I should not hesitate to say that one taught under the manual method would have a great superiority over one taught on the pure oral method, with all that that implies.

In response to a question about the depth of communication in a signed language, posed by an eminent educator of the Deaf on the panel memorably named the Reverend W. Blomefield Sleight, Gallaudet gave his opinion that the heart, the imagination, the soul, and the affections of the Deaf could never be so deeply stirred by speech and lipreading as they are by sign language. In response to another question, he said he doubted whether it would be possible for the Deaf to conduct an oral debate or discussion among themselves. Gallaudet had never seen a congenitally Deaf person, orally taught, capable of participating freely in a general conversation with hearing people sitting around a table. And certainly it was true, and they all knew it, that very few, if any, orally taught pupils could "go into the world" and "converse freely with all with whom they come in contact."

But Milan had been held only a few years earlier and Gallaudet knew that oral education was gaining enormous ground—indeed, it was becoming the general practice throughout Europe. It was to appease the threat of the oralist movement, then, that he spoke of the "usefulness of speech." Although he didn't expressly say so, he was undoubtedly referring to the usefulness of teaching the Deaf a limited number of words—"doctor," "police," "apples," "what time is it?"—to meet their daily or urgent needs in a hearing world. But Gallaudet made it appear as if he welcomed some unspecified general training in "speech" and "lipreading" for the Deaf. At one point he said it "was difficult to answer" the question whether Deaf pupils could rely on articulation and lipreading as their sole means of communication in later life.

Gallaudet even agreed with one questioner that all Deaf children might begin under the oral system, with those who couldn't succeed in speech then switching to sign language. He added, however, that the period of oral training could be relatively short (six months), no doubt because he thought the system would quickly fail, with virtually all the students moving to sign language: "The giving of speech to the deaf, while it is admitted by everyone to be a very valuable thing, occupies a secondary position by the side of the mental development which may be brought about by a course of training which will open up to a deaf person all the stores of literature. Of course oral training is not an essential thing in the education of the deaf—it is an important thing, but by no means a thing of such transcendent importance as some pure oralists would have the world believe. To the mass of the deaf I should not hesitate to say that a knowledge of the use of written language can be best imparted by the use of the manual alphabet, by signs, and by writing."[11]

Gallaudet was up against a formidable and hard-headed opponent, as we shall see, but his lapses did the Deaf a disservice. They remind us of how much Auguste Bébian could have done for the Deaf, in the United States and elsewhere, had he accepted the invitation to run the New York Institution, rather than going home to Guadeloupe.[12]

Alexander Graham Bell: Of Infirmity
and Natural Selection

Bell came to the commission's table in June 1888 as a soldier to battle. He had studied (American) sign language for a year, he said, and readily conceded that "if we have the mental condition of the child alone in view, without reference to language, no language will reach the mind like the language of signs; it is the quickest method of reaching the mind of a deaf child."[13]

Notwithstanding this concession, Bell said that, unlike Gallaudet, he would never have chosen the path of sign language for his own mother or his wife, even if they had been born Deaf.[14] They were not, of course—but reaching the minds of the Deaf generally was as unimportant to Bell as it was primordial for Victor Hugo. He cared little or nothing for Bébian's, Gallaudet's, and Blomefield Sleight's belief in the need to educate the Deaf as complete, conversant, and cultivated human beings. He had been fascinated by speech all his life—its transmission by telephone, good elocution, talking animals, talking machines, the talking Deaf. He had little interest in the goals of Gallaudet or the great French teachers of the eighteenth and nineteenth centuries.

Because Bell's wife and mother could speak (though indistinctly), he thought that all the Deaf should do so, however disagreeably, and even if they had been born Deaf and had never heard nor spoken a word: "I believe that all children should be taught . . . articulation, and taught to use articulation; but I do not think all children should be taught by articulation, that is to say, speech-reading. All who can be successfully and readily taught by speech-reading should be so taught, and those who cannot should be taught manually—by which I mean that written language should be used by the teacher. In all cases, however, the mouth should be used by the pupil as *his* means of communication. In this sense I would use an oral system for all. 'Speech' for all; 'speech-reading' for as many as can readily profit by it. That is my opinion."[15]

Bell conceded that his wife had been able to hear and to speak normally until the age of five—"four and a half" he corrected his questioner.[16] As to the congenitally Deaf, he testified that they could learn to read lips (and presumably to speak) just as well, provided they learned written language first. This whole notion of lipreading by the Deaf, of course, had been discredited by Bébian sixty years earlier and, indeed, by Bonet in the seventeenth century. Bell was being disingenuous, ignoring his own admission that the quickest way to reach the minds of Deaf children was through a signed language. His real goal, as we shall see, was not to educate the Deaf—not even, in fact, to teach them to speak or to read lips—but, ultimately, over time, to eradicate them.

In an ongoing, parallel debate with W. G. Jenkins, an educator of the Deaf in Hartford, Bell's argument came to no more than letting Darwinian principles decide which system of education was the fittest. Jenkins had written that "the children who come to our schools having used signs all their lives before coming, children who know nothing but signs, who have been under their influence from the day they were born until they leave home, whose whole mental life consists of sign thoughts fixed by years of habit, at a time of life when habits become most persistent, these children prove to be our best students. They are the pupils who use the most correct English, think to the best purpose, and show the most sound judgement in all that they do. This is the experience of all whom I have consulted on this question."[17]

Just as students educated in signed languages were reading Molière in France, Cervantes in Spain, Goethe in Germany, and Pushkin in Russia, so American students were becoming scholars: "It has been the constant charge of oralists that [primitive written] English is due to the use of signs, [but] here we are finding it every year in pupils who have been taught in *oral* schools. Someone ought to account for it. Right under my eyes are two irreconcilable things. Pupils sign-bound, sign-grained reading Dickens, Scott, Alcott, and oral pupils unable to read number one and two of our Hartford Readers."[18] Bell refused to reply on the merits, writing instead that "competition is the soul of progress," and that the progress of oralism in Europe and the United States since Milan was proof that "natural selection" was bringing about the "survival" of the oral system as the fitter method, and the "near extinction" of the system of signs.[19]

Bébian had shown that through sign language Deaf students could be taught the relative value of words and the influence they have on each other in making up a sentence. Jean Massieu, like Jenkins's orally educated students in Hartford, couldn't read children's stories until Bébian clarified for him, in sign language, the structure of written French by contrasting it with the grammatical and syntactical structure of Massieu's native language. Bell's sole criterion for educational accomplishment, however, was the ability of the student to utter a few words and to "read" simple messages on familiar lips, letting them "use their vocal organs to render whatever articulation they have . . . be [it] of the most abominable character."[20]

Bell told the Royal Commission that signed languages should not be permitted because they were not the language of the people, of the "communit[ies] in which the deaf lived."[21] He said that signed languages should not even be spoken of in the same breath as speech because sign "is of no use in the hearing world." He also fancifully testified that shouting into a Deaf child's ear could improve his powers of perception by strengthening the muscle that controls the tension of the eardrum.[22]

Bell went so far as to make the false claim that the Deaf student had to "unlearn" sign language, which "got in the way" of his learning English. Since a Deaf child still had his vocal organs, Bell reasoned, he ought to use them to speak.[23] Bébian, by contrast, stressed that it was "absurd, ridiculous, tyrannical . . . to adopt as the principal instrument of a deaf child's instruction the very faculty that the child lacked."[24] Furthermore, Bell made no mention of Bonet's, l'Épée's, and Bébian's implicit recognition that the cochlea, silenced in the case of the Deaf, was an organ of *speech* as well as of hearing. He also ignored Itard's crucial observation, made well before Bell was born, that direct oral "discourse," whatever that meant, left a Deaf child isolated, passive, and without access to normal conversation.

Alphonse Lenoir would undoubtedly have praised Gallaudet, like he did Bébian at the sixth banquet in 1839, as "deaf at heart" and as one who "may . . . glory in having understood us so well." But deafness for Bell was an infirmity, if not a deformity, to be hidden from the rest of the community. "If you had false teeth," he in effect asked the panel, "would you care to exhibit them in public?" He objected to the public spectacle the Deaf made of themselves while communicating in their own language: "Now, I think [not making a scene] is a very proper spirit, and I think the spirit of the oral system is to make the deaf persons feel that they are the same as [hearing] people, to make them object to exhibit their infirmity to the world; whereas on the special [signed] language method they glory in the defect, they glory in being deaf mutes, they glory in being distinct from the world. These two radical tendencies are very important to consider."[25]

Bell was surely aware of all that had been accomplished since the time of Bébian, both in reaching the minds of Deaf children through signed languages (as he admitted), and in educating them first in their own language and then teaching them to read and write. But none of this mattered. He held Laurent Clerc responsible for founding a system that forced the Deaf to stick together: "Is that not what we do in America? These are the two chief elements that produce deaf children in America. First, segregation which itself evolved the sign language; and secondly, the sign language which prevents the acquisition of English as the vernacular which brings the deaf children together in adult life, and forces them to marry one another."[26]

But as we shall see Bell was aware that about 95 percent of congenitally Deaf children were born of hearing parents. He knew as well that it was not practicable to do away with educational institutions for the Deaf, although he blamed them for the development of signed languages—a misrepresentation because it appears they have existed in various forms as long as spoken languages have. But whatever the circumstances, signed languages were the culprit: "The chief cause of the intermarriage I hold to be that special language." He testified that "whatever speech a child has is something in addition to what a child has who has no speech."[27] Bell could not have believed his own assurances that a Deaf person could be taught to lipread. He correctly told the Royal Commission that consonants were important for the understanding of speech, but then suggested that homophonous or invisible sounds could be read by context once the Deaf lipreader developed a facility with the English language. He must have known that vowels were often indistinguishable from each other, and that deriving meaning from "context" except for the occasional short phrase in unambiguous circumstances would be impossible given all the guessing going on.

At one point Bell offered the extraordinary suggestion that the higher education of properly trained Deaf students could be conducted orally in "small classes," with students "ask[ing] for an explanation" when they didn't understand the teacher. The unstated implication is that the students would have to understand not only the teacher but also (1) the other student's question (notwithstanding his or her inability to speak with any clarity, even for the hearing), (2) any requests for clarification of the student's question, and (3) the teacher's explanation of both. When reminded that Gallaudet had testified that such classes would be "useless," Bell said Gallaudet probably never even tried it. Bell was right—Gallaudet never did.[28]

Perhaps the most startling aspect of Bell's testimony is, as I have suggested, its resemblance to the claims of the speech teachers of the seventeenth century. Bell sounded like Juan Pablo Bonet or Conrad Amman. As Bell explained: "I took a number of [Deaf children at the Hartford school] and gave them a looking-glass apiece, and taught them to depress the tongue and control these muscles so that they could approximate the posterior pillars of the soft palate or separate them at will. Their voices became more natural and pleasant in quality the moment the pharyngeal cavity was expanded . . . I have such a control over the mouth that I can make the deaf pupil pronounce foreign sounds."[29]

Étonnant! As we have seen, Amman used a mirror to transform the mouth of the student into "the lips of the master." Like Bonet, all Bell had to do was press the right frets to get the mute to make the sound he wanted. His goal here was to develop a pleasant sound for the hearing, not to educate the Deaf. In the face of all the evidence to the contrary, Bell called speech and lipreading a "bond of union" between the Deaf and the hearing.[30] In reality, as Guérin had correctly warned in Lyons, they were devices to sever the bonds of language—their own—that linked the Deaf to each other.

A Deaf Variety of the Human Race

Likes tend to associate, as is evident from clubs, veterans' groups, political parties, tribes, compatriots. We usually regard the association of people with common ideas or interests, particularly those with a common language, as a normal and acceptable thing. But for the Deaf, Bell was against it. Four years prior to his testimony before the Royal Commission, he had written a paper on what he called the "deaf variety" of the human race. The essay formulated his theory and justification for reducing the numbers of the congenitally Deaf among us and, if possible, to "breed" them out of existence. In Bell's view, it was not at all desirable that they associate with each other: "The practice of . . . sign language . . . makes deaf-mutes associate together in adult life, and . . . thus causes the[ir] intermarriage . . . and the propagation of their physical defect . . . Segregation during education has not only favored the tendency towards the formation of a race of deaf-mutes, but has led to the evolution of a special language adapted for the use of such a race—'the sign-language of the deaf and dumb.' "[31] Bell reaffirmed this thesis in London. If the Deaf were allowed to continue to "congregate" in segregated schools and to use their language, the "establish[ment] of a deaf race [would be] only a question of time." He associated deafness with other "abnormalities" in his testimony, including dwarfism, people with six fingers, and sexual deformity.[32]

It is worth remembering that in the United States in the 1880s, eugenics was in fashion. It was a movement in which Bell was a conspicuous participant, devoted as he was to "improving" the human race through the control of hereditary factors—the promotion of "good genes"—in marriages. Bell explained how his "deaf breed" could come about: "The conditions are these: that large numbers of the congenitally deaf shall marry one another, and that their congenitally deaf children, if they have any, shall again marry congenitally deaf; ultimately after a certain length of time, a true breed or race will be formed." To develop the relevant statistical information, Bell made files of the Deaf community's "gossipy papers, speaking of their marriages, their families and their children."

His pursuit of the mating practices of mutes was relentless: "I have succeeded in making complete files of . . . these deaf-mute journals for preservation; I then took these deaf-mute journals and had copied out on cards . . . all the records of marriages, giving the names of both parties who were married. Generally the journals did not state whether the deaf mutes were born deaf or not, but I have taken these cards and as far as I have been able *I have hunted up the deaf mutes* that have been married in the institution reports; and now I have a collection of marriages from which we can deduce a percentage."[33]

Bébian had explained that before l'Épée the Deaf were generally regarded as "almost a being of a different species," or "of a different nature" from ourselves, because people believed that if they couldn't speak, they were unable to think. Bonet had observed that the Deaf were generally regarded in seventeenth-century Spain as "inferior beings, disgraced of nature and human only in form." In his toast at Berthier's sixth banquet, the Deaf painter John Carlin exclaimed that before the work of Laurent Clerc and Thomas Gallaudet in the United States, the Deaf were considered "dogs without a soul." At the same dinner Alphonse Lenoir expressed his hope that, with the hearing community's growing awareness of the sophistication of signed languages, the Deaf would no longer be considered "a separate species of the earth."[34]

Bell was now, centuries after Bonet, depicting the Deaf as a breed and setting them apart not because they couldn't think, but because they "gloried" in a disagreeable language that was not the language of the larger community. He referred again to Laurent Clerc, this time to cast aspersions on Clerc's own breeding practices: "So far as I can find historically (and I have examined the subject) the first case of inter-marriage of deaf mutes seems to have been the marriage (in 1819) of Laurent Clerc, the teacher whom the elder Gallaudet brought from France to America; and as I look through the literature of the subject, I see evidences that the results of that marriage were watched with very great interest and eagerness by the deaf mutes of the country. There undoubtedly was a feeling before that time that it was wrong for a deaf mute to marry a deaf mute." When asked about "the re-sults" of the marriage, Bell replied that "the children [there were six] all heard." He explained the result by saying that Clerc's wife was not congenitally Deaf and that Clerc himself may not have been. Clerc's name in sign was expressed by drawing two fingers down the cheek, which Bell falsely interpreted in his testimony as meaning "the false deaf mute." In fact, Clerc's name was derived from a scar he bore on his cheek from a childhood accident.[35]

Bell's own statistics showed that about 90 to 95 percent of the congenitally Deaf were born of two hearing parents, as is the case to-day. Hearing people are, of course, far more numerous than the Deaf, and we know now from Mendelian genetics that their having con-genitally Deaf children can come from a number of genetic configura-tions. Bell was unaware of the reasons but he had the statistics. He had also undertaken a study of the marriages of Deaf couples in America, and he knew that Deaf parents had Deaf children only about 10 percent of the time.[36] It does appear to be true that two genetically Deaf parents are more likely to have Deaf children than hearing parents, but to keep Deaf men and women apart in order to deprive them of their language and offspring is unthinkable today and, for many in Bell's own time, was morally unacceptable then.

Bell knew that the congenitally Deaf from birth would never be able to speak with any facility, or to engage in sustained oral discourse, or to read lips beyond simple phrases spoken by people they knew well. He had been unable to improve Mabel's speech, which he conceded was "very defective" even though she had some slight residual hearing and had spoken until she was five (or four and a half). He granted that the speech taught in the "oral" schools was "somewhat defective," though he had "tried to find out the cause of that defect."[37] Bell also spent four years working with George Sanders, the Deaf son of a merchant in Salem. His efforts with the boy failed as well: Sanders never learned to speak (or to read lips), married a Deaf woman, and lived a full life.

Bell's father's "visible speech" was also a failure. It was a method whose "alphabet," like Juan Pablo Bonet's specially formed Roman alphabet in 1620, consisted of characters shaped to "denote the vocal organs that are used in uttering sounds." It never worked. Bell said that only his father and he were able to teach it, and that the telephone took him away from the project.[38] Bell's later promotion, if not exploitation, of Helen Keller as a role model for the Deaf also did the Deaf community a great deal of harm, as I shall explore later. Indeed, none of Bell's efforts to oralize the Deaf succeeded—a failure that stands in stark contrast to his success with the telephone.

The Royal Commission's Verdict: Deaf and Dumb

The Royal Commission was weighted with oralists and there were no Deaf members on the panel. The commission sided with Bell, and recommended that all children be educated orally for the first year of school, and that only the "physically or mentally disqualified" be thereafter transferred to schools "on the sign and manual system." Children taught under the oral system should be known as "deaf"; only the Deaf who did not "speak" should be called the "deaf and dumb." While the commission offered lip service to education in British Sign Language, they considered it a form of education for the unfit, and its fate was sealed. Britain was to return almost exclusively to oralist schools by the early twentieth century.

The Congress of Milan and the proceedings before the Royal Commission in London ultimately had a dramatic impact in the United States as well. In 1867, ASL had been the medium of instruction in all American educational institutions for the Deaf; by 1927, however, it was used in very few. Efforts were undertaken in the United States and elsewhere to prohibit signed languages both within and outside the classroom. The principal of the Wright Oral School in Pennsylvania called for constant supervision of its Deaf students to prevent them from signing with each other, "outside of the classroom, on the playground, in the shop, everywhere . . . morning, noon and night."[39]

There are many theories about what motivated the oralists in the nineteenth century to prohibit signed languages as the medium of teaching. It was no longer "God" or the "Word" or the awakening and baptism of the immortal soul of the Deaf (or enabling them to inherit), as it had been during the Middle Ages and beyond, notwithstanding the clerical pronouncements from the podium at Milan. The historian Florence Encrevé sees the motives of the Pereire group and of the Paris, Lyons, and Milan congresses as stemming from a notion of "progress." But progress connoted advances in the applied sciences and technology—things that worked. Victor Hugo used the term in its true sense in one of his letters to Berthier, which he read "aloud" in sign language at the seventeenth banquet in 1850: "You, Sir, who have the rare talent of being at once mute and eloquent, please tell your friends . . . that in my eyes the accession of the deaf to civic and intellectual life must be counted among the most magnificent and decisive accomplishments in the history of the progress of humanity."[40]

The evidence against speech and lipreading for the Deaf, and for the advantages of signed languages, was overwhelming. Victor-Gomer Chambellan, a teacher at Saint Jacques during the era "was amazed that educators would think there was 'progress' in this oralist pedagogy because the instruction of deaf children was going nowhere."[41] To attempt to educate the Deaf using the very faculty they lacked, Bébian's phrase, was unmistakable retrogression. So it was not "progress" the oralists were after.

For the Pereires, the goal was the rehabilitation of their grandfather's legacy; for the hearing educators, the protection of their jobs. Tarra suggested as much in his opening remarks at Milan when he observed that "no accomplishment of science can be as great as its nourishment and enhancement of the reciprocal affection and esteem of those who teach it."[42] Their mutual protection and advancement was the only key accomplishment at Milan, for the hearing teachers present and for generations of them to come. The teachers rationalized their position by asserting that signed languages, and not deafness itself, were the principal impediment to their students' ability to learn how to speak and read lips. That abolishing those languages entailed not an ounce of "progress" for the Deaf did not matter.

Some have seen the rise of oralism in the nineteenth century as a reflection of bourgeois notions of "accomplishment"—the engagement of the Deaf, notably in Protestant Germany, in a productive society. Others have noted the desire, during the wave of nineteenth-century nationalism, to make the Deaf conform to the society and language of their co-citizens. Still other observers have pointed out that European public schools for the Deaf at the time were mixed (poor and lower middle class) and taught in signed languages, whereas private schools were oral places of learning for the well-off. When the public-school students taught in their own language proved to be academically far ahead of those educated privately, the hearing teachers and their influential allies decided to take their revenge at Milan and at other conferences in Europe.[43]

But the oralist movement can perhaps best be understood through Bell's testimony before the Royal Commission. In the face of his utter lack of success, of which Bell was acutely aware, and his knowledge that most Deaf children were born of two hearing parents, why was Bell waging this battle and making it (in addition to the telephone) a principal part of his life's work? As we have seen, the signing Deaf were the antithesis of the people and mission he loved most in the world: his mother, his wife, and the articulation of speech, which was the life's work of his father and grandfather. He was driven by his own intimate concerns combined with the prejudices and public sentiments of his time. This mixture of motive, in the end, amounted to little more than a visceral prejudice against a people who were "different"; who were the "other"; who were not, like his speaking, lipreading wife and mother, Deaf in a "normal" way; who were ignorant of speech; who were undignified exhibitionists; and who "gloried" in their defect as they exhibited a language that was antithetical to that of the community as a whole. "The production of [such] a defective race of human beings," he wrote, "would be a great calamity to the world."[44]

Bell's motivations reflected those of the oralist community generally—the priests, the nationalists, the advocates of the Protestant

This painting at Saint Jacques by the Dutch painter Hendricus Jacobus Bürgers
captures a visit by the French president, Félix Faure, to Saint Jacques in 1889.
The painting is an ironic depiction of the teaching of the Deaf after the Congress
of Milan in 1880. While the teacher is demonstrating how he teaches speech to a
Deaf student, the other Deaf students (on the front bench) are communicating
with each other in sign language, as the light from the window illuminates
both them and the bust of l'Épée (above right), which (in the painting)
replaces the traditional bust of Marianne (the symbol of the French Republic).
(Collection INJS de Paris.)

ethic, the wealthy, and the "teachers" of speech and lipreading. If you
abolish signed languages, the pride, the exhibitions, the "other" will
be gone. The Deaf, like Mabel and so many others who live in relative
isolation, will then "feel the same as" the hearing and lock their deformity and gesticulations in the closet where they belong. They will

become, as Giulio Tarra put it at Milan, more "physiologically human."[45] That they cannot hear, cannot speak, cannot read lips, cannot understand, and won't be educated, matters little. Moreover, given their inability to communicate, they'll marry less, will have fewer children, and their number among us will diminish. That is what matters.

A French study of the results of Milan and the oral method conducted a quarter century later, in 1907, challenged the entire system by examining the lives of France's graduates: "It is said that speech is a form of communication beneficial to someone who is deaf. This is not true; he can't engage in a conversation with a stranger; he can't even communicate his immediate needs to those who are close to him except by a combination of gestures or signs he needs to provide meaning to his speech; the 'demutisation' of the deaf is of no social, professional or practical usefulness."[46]

Deaf students in Europe and the United States, who since the time of Bébian had become readers of Pushkin and Dickens, were now to graduate from these schools as functional illiterates in both their own natural languages and in the written language of their native countries. Deaf teachers at Saint Jacques and Gallaudet College, the world's most highly regarded institutions of learning for the Deaf in the earlier part of the century, were to become relatively marginalized, though courses in French and American signed languages survived at both institutions. By the middle of the twentieth century, 80 percent of Deaf children in the world would have no schooling of any kind. In France itself in the late twentieth century, 80 percent of the Deaf would be illiterate, and only 5 percent would reach high school.

Like England's forays into France in the fourteenth and fifteenth centuries, the oralists wrought havoc in their hundred years' war. The educational realm of the Deaf, which had been painstakingly built, step by step, from the time of l'Épée, was no more. Deaf people knew they were losing it, as reflected in the declaration of the World's Congress of the Deaf held in Saint Louis in 1904. The congress formally resolved that the "champions of the oral method [were] carrying on a warfare, both overt and covert, against the use of the language of signs" and were "rob[bing deaf] children of their birthright."[47]

If you lose your language, you shall have nothing, Ferdinand Berthier had in effect warned his Deaf students and peers in 1857. A half century later, and for the century yet to come, in the halls of the very institution where he signaled his warning, and indeed everywhere else, Berthier's prophesy had, and would, come true.

9

Helen Keller: A False Symbol

From the time of the Congress of Milan and the Royal Commission's hearings, the Deaf were losing ground on all fronts. Bell urged the hearing parents of Deaf children to enroll them in oral schools, leading almost universally to a poor education. When the grandmother of an American Sign Language teacher I know at Gallaudet, Deaf from birth, was brought as a young girl to Alexander Graham Bell and was introduced to Helen Keller, he recommended an oral school. She was sent to a school where, after other methods failed, her hands were tied behind her back to prevent her from signing. She finally resorted, hands bound, to banging her head against her desk, and in doing so won passage to a Deaf school, where she found her language and her life.

Helen Keller herself, who lived from 1880 until 1968, was in significant respects a creature of Bell's and a symbol of the benefits of an oral education. Helen's father brought Helen to Bell when she was six years old, Deaf and blind from an illness (scarlet fever or meningitis) that she had contracted when she was nineteen months old. Bell recommended her to the Perkins Institute for the Blind in Boston, where administrators found for Helen a young (hearing) graduate, Anne Sullivan, who had impaired vision from trachoma as a child but had surgically regained much of her sight. Anne made the long trip to the Keller family place in Tuscumbia, Alabama, in order to take Helen under her wing as her teacher. Thanks to Anne's tireless and constant presence, Helen developed a facility to understand and express herself to others through fingerspelling by touch, though with Anne as her almost exclusive intermediary. Anne became her eyes, her voice, and her ears. Helen could fingerspell with just a few others, notably Anne's husband, John Macy, and Anne's successors Polly Thomson and Nella Henney.

Before long, Helen became an emblematic figure. Bell persuaded her, always accompanied by Anne, to attend oral schools in Massachusetts and New York, then claimed that Helen could speak. Anne and Bell also asserted that Helen could read lips with the help of fingers on the lips and nose and a thumb on the larynx of her interlocutor, the same failed maneuver that Jacob Pereire had used in the eighteenth century with his sighted Deaf students. Bell induced Helen to make an effort to speak at conventions of his American Association to Promote the Teaching of Speech to the Deaf. If Deaf and blind Helen can do it, he would argue, then why not the Deaf who can see? He was clear about his goal: "Helen's presence would inspire the teachers of the deaf and send them back to their schools with the conviction and belief that if such results could be obtained in the case of a child who had been blind as well as deaf from infancy, they can surely do more for their own pupils than they have yet accomplished."[1]

Helen was extraordinary. She graduated from Radcliffe in 1904 at the age of twenty-four, with Anne as her medium in the classroom and study hall, fingerspelling lectures and books not available in Braille into her hand. During her lifetime she wrote several books, the most acclaimed of which was *The Story of My Life*, published in 1903 and written while she was at Radcliffe. She also wrote several articles and had an extensive published correspondence.[2] But contrary to the general impression that Bell had helped to engender, Helen never developed intelligible speech and could not, without her teacher's ever-present hand touching her own and spelling out the words, read lips by touch.[3] Helen was in an important sense not one person but two, and she and her teacher remained inseparable until Anne died at the age of seventy in 1936, when Helen was fifty-six. They had been together for fifty years. After Anne's death, two others successively took over the task of fingerspelling for her, and the quality of Helen's writing declined.[4]

There is good reason to ask whether Helen's celebrated work was her own. As Roger Shattuck has gently put it, "Since Anne attended Helen almost constantly at Radcliffe and since John Macy helped extensively in organizing and assembling the pieces of [Helen's autobiography], one has reason to wonder if to any degree Helen's part of the book was ghostwritten."[5] As surprising as this suggestion may be to most people who know the popular version of Helen's story, questions about what Helen could and could not do emerged long before her autobiography.

The issue first surfaced in "The Frost King," a story purporting to be Helen's that Anne sent to the director of Perkins, Michael Anagnos, on November 4, 1891. Helen was eleven years old. She had been blinded and deafened by illness at the age of nineteen months, and had no memory of sound or light. And yet "The Frost King" is resplendent in its descriptions of sound and color. In fact, Anne Sullivan had plagiarized almost 80 percent of the 1,500-word story, virtually verbatim, from "The Frost Fairies," a story that had been written eighteen years earlier by an American, Margaret Canby, and was no longer in print.[6] Anne's ambition to advance Helen's (and her own) cause came close to destroying them both.

In Canby's story "The Frost Fairies," the master of winter, King Frost, asks his elves to deliver a part of his treasure to Santa Claus in order to assist in helping the poor. But the elves dally in the forest, the sun melts the treasure, and it begins to rain. Here is a typical extract from the story in Canby's hand, marked to show the changes made by Anne:

> They plainly heard the tinkling of many drops falling like rain through the forest, and sliding from leaf to leaf until they reached the ~~bramble~~ little bushes ~~beside them~~ by their side, when, to their ~~great dismay~~ astonishment, they ~~found~~ discovered that the rain drops were melted rubies, which hardened on the leaves, and turned them to ~~bright~~ crimson and gold in a moment. Then, looking around more closely ~~at the trees around~~, they saw that much of the treasure was al~~l~~ready melt~~ing~~ed away, ~~and that much of it was already spread over the leaves of~~ for the oaks ~~trees~~ and maples, ~~which~~ were ~~shining with their~~ arrayed in gorgeous dresses of gold and ~~bronze,~~ crimson and emerald.[7]

Canby's story was never available in Helen's Braille. "Helen's" words are virtually identical to Canby's throughout the story, except at its beginning where Anne inserts the relatively few words of her own or Helen's and, just after the inserted passage, reorders the sequence of seven or eight of Canby's early sentences before going on to copy her story wholesale. This event, together with her collaboration with Anne and others, would cast doubt on Helen's accomplishments for the rest of her life. But more importantly, it takes us to the question of language and the heart of Helen's own dilemma.

Despite close questioning about authorship from Helen's father, Anne sent the story to Anagnos, who had recommended Anne for Helen.[8] "I think you will be pleased," Anne writes in her transmittal letter, "with the little story Helen wrote for your birthday. We think it pretty and original."[9] Helen's letter was enclosed as well, in which she writes, "I shall send you to-day a little story which I wrote for your birthday gift."[10] In her account of the affair, Anne asserts that "the story was written by Helen in Braille, as usual, and copied by her in the same manner; I then interlined the manuscript for the greater convenience of those who desired to read it."[11]

Anagnos, ever effusive in his public praise of Helen and believing the story to be hers, promptly had it published in *The Mentor*, the Perkins alumni magazine. The story made national headlines. But a faculty member at the Virginia School for the Deaf later read it to a friend, who immediately recognized Helen's story as Canby's—and had a copy of the book. When the school published a side-by-side comparison in their *Gazette*, they accused not "little Helen, who has done merely what she was told to do," but Anne Sullivan (though not by name) of "attempted fraud."[12] Deaf educators were incensed.

Anne claimed, falsely, that she had never heard of Canby's story, as did Helen, who had little choice. Anne enlisted Bell's help in finding some sort of explanation. One was invented. "It came out that" Sophia Hopkins, a teacher at Perkins close to Anne and Helen, was said to have had a copy of the book and to have read it (in fingerspelling) to Helen when she visited her on Cape Cod in 1888 at a moment when Anne was not present. Helen (or Anne or Macy) writes in *The Story of My Life:* "Miss Sullivan never heard of "The Frost Fairies" or the book in which it was published. With the assistance of Dr. Alexander Graham Bell, [Anne herself] investigated the matter carefully and at last it came out that Mrs. Sophia C. Hopkins had a copy of [the book] in 1888."[13]

To what extent Bell may have interceded with Sophia Hopkins is not known. She made no public statement about the matter, although

Helen Keller with Anne Sullivan at the Cape
Cod House of Sophia Hopkins, July 1888
(Photograph of Helen Keller with doll and Anne Sullivan,
Thaxter Parks Spencer Papers, Mss 1126, R. Stanton Avery
Special Collections, New England Historic Genealogical
Society. Image courtesy of the New England Historic
Genealogical Society, www.AmericanAncestors.org.)

Anagnos described her (or rather his) position in the Perkins Annual
Report published in early 1892: "Though Mrs. Hopkins does not rec-
ollect [Margaret Canby's] story, I presume it was included among the
selections [that she read by fingerspelling to Helen]. No one can re-
gret the mistake more than I."[14] The explanation itself was implausible
because Helen was only eight years old in 1888, did not have the story

in Braille, and could never from memory, nor without Anne's help (with the book in front of her), have copied the entire 1,500-word story virtually verbatim three years later, in the fall of 1891, when she sent "The Frost King" to Anagnos.

Anagnos's note was printed on an un-numbered page apparently interleaved at the last moment between the printed page on which Anagnos glowingly announced the story in the Annual Report (94) and the page on which the story itself was printed (95). In that announcement, Anagnos had written that "the story gives tangible proof of Helen's extraordinary imagination, as well as of the originality of her thoughts and ideas, the vividness of her descriptions, the elegance of her style and the tenderness of her feelings."[15]

An unidentified teacher then reported that Helen had told her in early 1892 that Anne, and not Mrs. Hopkins, had been reading Helen the story not in 1888 but in the fall of 1891.[16] Helen later said (at Anne's insistence) that she had been misunderstood, but Anagnos felt obligated to hold a formal inquiry, which proved to be an ordeal for Helen.[17] Helen nevertheless stuck to their story: she had never been read or even known of (and thus never copied) Canby's work. By a single casting vote, that of Anagnos himself, Helen was absolved of wrongdoing, as was Anne, the real target of the investigation. In March 1892 Anagnos wrote to the American Annals of the Deaf that "a most rigid examination of the child . . . failed to elicit in the least any testimony convicting either her teacher or anyone else of the intention or the attempt to practice deception."[18]

Anagnos then considered the matter closed until Sophia Hopkins herself finally came forward to tell Anagnos what had happened. John Macy has described Mrs. Hopkins as "like a mother" to Anne.[19] Anagnos writes that "there is an error in the date given as that at which the stories were read to Helen. It was at first said to be 1888, but

Mrs. Hopkins has recently made a positive statement that . . . in May 1890 . . . Helen and Miss Sullivan accompanied [her] to her home in Cape Cod. The book of Miss Canby's stories was taken with them [to Cape Cod] and parts of it were then read to Helen."[20]

Anagnos deduced that Anne and Helen had the book in the summer of 1891 as well. Helen (or Anne) had written him a letter, dated August 8, 1891, freely using phrases (as Helen's) from another story of Canby's in the book. The letter was sent to him from Helen's family house in Alabama, just three months before he was sent "The Frost King."[21] Anagnos concludes: "These facts added to the testimony of one of our teachers to whom the child voluntarily mentioned [that Anne was] the reader of the stories before she was cautioned not to talk about it, explodes [sic] entirely the hypothesis of absolute forgetfulness and leaves no doubt that Helen was induced to assert with pitiful pertinacity that no one read her Miss Canby's book."[22]

Anagnos lost all confidence in Anne, and Helen as well, and their break with him and the Perkins School was permanent. Helen's biographers appear to have overlooked the Anagnos letter. Joseph Lash indicates that "Anagnos left no record of why his views altered, as Helen subsequently asserted that they did."[23] Cynthia Ozick wrote in the New Yorker in 2003 that "Margaret Canby's tale had been spelled to Helen perhaps three years before, and lay dormant in her prodigiously retentive memory; she was entirely oblivious of reproducing phrases not her own."[24] But what was reproduced here was not simply "phrases not her own" but almost all of a 1,500-word story, virtually verbatim.

Helen or Anne describes Anagnos as having said at one point: "Helen Keller is a living lie."[25] One may doubt whether he used such brutal words, but those he did write and speak of Helen were harsh, given her youth, her deafness and blindness, her vulnerability, and her inability to distinguish herself from her teacher. Living without Anne would have been the equivalent of living without herself—and losing Anne would have been the inevitable consequence of her admitting the plagiarism.

Helen is a significant historical figure both because of her own dramatic story and because she became a symbol of oralism in the twentieth century. It is essential to keep in mind Helen's achievements as a Deaf and blind person who learned to fingerspell, to read (in Braille) and to write in Braille, on the typewriter, and in "square hand."[26] But it is also important to remember the thousands of Deaf children whose language was being suppressed and would continue to be throughout the twentieth century, and before whom Helen was being exhibited as an example. Frank Sanborn, a Boston oralist (and the recipient of Helen's letter on Anagnos's final view of her), and someone who had helped Anne early in her life, wrote of the attacks on Helen and Anne as follows:

[Helen] had been taught [at Perkins] to speak, though deaf, dumb and blind when first received there . . . [P]oor Helen [simply] forgot . . . the avenue by which these pretty fancies [Canby's words in "The Frost Fairies"] came into her opening mind . . . [B]ut the Pharisees are not extinct, by any means . . . There are still [deaf mutes] in Boston, but they are a decreasing class, and it is not expedient to increase them. Whatever restores them to their own families, their own churches, and to the general life of the community is for their advantage and for that of others. The schools of articulation do this—the language of signs, though necessary in many cases, is apt to do the contrary . . . Italy and the French republic have exchanged the sign system of de l'Épée and Sicard for the oral system of Germany and Switzerland, which guarantees to parents the inestimable privilege of retaining [*sic*] the speech of their deaf children . . .

[N]ow that teaching by articulation has been made known through its merits it is not likely to be abandoned anywhere—least of all in the city where . . . Helen Keller [has] been educated.[27]

As Helen grew into a young woman, the battle lines were drawn around the notion that her oral accomplishments made her an example for the future and a sign of the "ever decreasing class" of deaf mutes. It was an extraordinary argument, because the wonder of Helen (whatever roles Anne Sullivan, John Macy, and the words of others may have played in her writing) was not that she could "speak" or "read lips" to any extent that enabled her to carry on an oral conversation but that, through fingerspelling and the use of her *hands*, she had learned to read and to write, become educated, and graduated from Radcliffe.

That Bell could make Helen a symbol of his goals was an indication both of his determination and his disingenuousness—he knew what he was doing. Commenting on Helen's and Anne's appearances before his American Association, he claimed that "Pupils . . . oral[ly educated are] superior in their ability to use and understand speech. It cannot be denied that many deaf persons have obtained an excellent education with a good command of English without any recourse to the De l'Épée Language of Signs . . . Helen Keller is a notable case in point."[28] In a presentation she struggled through for the association when she was sixteen, Helen concluded her remarks as follows: "Remember, no effort that we make to attain something beautiful is ever lost. Some time, somewhere, somehow we shall find that which we seek. We shall speak, yes, and sing, too, as God intended we should speak and sing."[29]

Bell insisted not that she take singing lessons (the scales at Milan notwithstanding), but speech lessons at the Clarke Institution in Northampton, and at a similar school in New York. He presented Helen, who lacked *two* senses, as living testimony to the reality that the "language of l'Épée" was not a viable solution for the Deaf. After Helen's graduation from Radcliffe he fingerspelled to her: "You have learned to speak, and I believe you are meant to break down the barriers which separate the deaf from mankind . . . There are unique tasks waiting for you, a unique woman."[30]

When *The Story of My Life* was published in 1903, Helen dedicated it to "Alexander Graham Bell, Who has taught the deaf to speak." But in fact, despite Bell's and Helen's affection for and commitment to each other, Helen's speech was incomprehensible, except to Anne Sullivan and others who knew her well. Anne wrote that "the absence of hearing renders the voice monotonous and often very disagreeable; and such speech is generally unintelligible except to those familiar with the speaker." Helen herself conceded that "it is not always easy for strangers to understand me." Roger Shattuck refers to her "unintelligible speech . . . a skill she never learned despite a lifetime of practice." John Macy tells us that it is "hard to say" whether she is easy to understand . . . I am told that she speaks better than most other deaf people."[31]

There is footage on the internet of Helen Keller speaking— repeating, for example, the words of Anne Sullivan on cue ("I am not dumb now") or uttering short unintelligible passages translated by Anne's successor, Polly Thomson. The films show an endeavor reminiscent of the efforts of Juan Pablo Bonet in the seventeenth century to create eligible Spanish heirs by enabling them to parrot speech, though in Keller's case the purpose was to Promote the Teaching of Speech to the Deaf. They display what Bébian and Edward Gallaudet called examples of speech as an accomplishment ("doctor," "police," "apples," "what time is it?"), and indeed, particularly the longer though incomprehensible passages, a remarkable accomplishment for Helen given her blindness. But speech (by responding to fingerspelling) could never have been a language in which Helen would be able to converse with others.

Joseph Lash tells us that "every word was . . . a battle [for Helen] to enunciate."[32] The daughter of Samuel Gridley Howe (Anagnos's sister-in-law), a Perkins founder, wrote that Helen's voice "was to me the loneliest sound I have ever heard, like waves breaking on the coast of some lonely desert island." Another observer compared her voice to "that of a Pythoness." Thomas Edison reported that it reminded him of "steam exploding." Helen's biographer Dorothy Herrmann writes of Helen's "broken, metallic, and mechanical voice . . . that no one could understand." "Helen's voice," she added, "tinny, robotic and grotesque, was always her nemesis."[33]

Very few Deaf people were able to speak at all, and those who could did so only after painstaking effort and years and years of work by parents, speech therapists, and others. They were able to make their speech understood by the hearing only with great difficulty, and not at all by the Deaf. They could not, of course, read lips themselves. And yet Bell would maintain that he was "perfectly astonished" at Helen's progress, which was "great news for all the deaf." Helen readily repeated the ideas of Bell and the Boston oralists, including Frank Sanborn and Samuel Gridley Howe: "Well, I must confess, I do not like the sign-language, and I do not think it would be of much use to the deaf-blind. I find it very difficult to follow the rapid

Helen Keller, Anne Sullivan, and Alexander Graham Bell in Chautauqua, New York, at the time of the meeting there of Bell's American Association to Promote the Teaching of Speech to the Deaf (July 1894) (Library of Congress, Prints & Photographs Division, Gilbert H. Grosvenor Collection of Photographs of the Alexander Graham Bell Family, LC-G9-Z1–137,816-A.)

motions made by the deaf-mutes, and besides, signs seem a great hindrance to them in acquiring the power of using language easily and freely. Why, I find it hard to understand them sometimes when they spell on their fingers. On the whole, if they cannot be taught articulation, the manual alphabet seems the best and most convenient means of communication. At any rate, I am sure the deaf-blind cannot learn to use signs with any degree of facility."[34]

John Macy made his own ideas unmistakably clear in language reminiscent of Giulio Tarra in Milan and of Bell in *Deaf Variety*, describing the Deaf as a race apart, unable to pray in their own language: "At one time it was believed that the best way for the [Deaf] to communicate was through systematized gestures, the sign language invented by the abbé de l'Épée . . . [But] let [the educated man] get language . . . the thought and experience of his race. The language must be one used by a nation, not an artificial thing . . . The deaf child who has only the sign language of de l'Épée is an intellectual Philip Nolan, an alien from all races, and his thoughts are not the thoughts of an Englishman, or a Frenchman, or a Spaniard. The Lord's prayer in signs is not the Lord's prayer in English."[35]

Rich descriptions of sounds and colors became an essential part of Helen's own vocabulary as she grew older. They were images borrowed from Anne or from works that Anne continued to encourage Helen to repeat in her own writing. She wrote in her autobiography of "childish prattle," "everything that could hum, or buzz, or sing," "noisy-throated frogs, katydids and crickets [who] . . . trilled their reedy note," a frog who "made the summer nights musical with his quaint love-song," the "luminous shadows of trees and the blue heavens," a Christmas tree "shimmering in the soft light," horses "with bridles ringing and whips cracking," champion hunters "with hark and whoop and wild halloo!"[36] In 1930 Helen provided what Dorothy Herrmann calls "one of her disturbingly elaborate visual descriptions" in writing about Scotland: "I love it all—the moorland peace and hills of beauty. I love the mountains when they are cloud-capped or when soft veils of mist, spun of wind and dew and flame, are drawn around their shoulders . . . If I am ever born again, I know I shall be a Scot."[37]

Helen was even more elaborate in a letter to Nella Henney about Ireland: "The bluest sky you have ever been under—white, crimson, scarlet, pink, buff, yellow and every shade God has painted on leaf and flower! . . . As if this was not beauty enough, you come out of a mountain pass and gaze, breathless and trembling, upon 'purple peaks that out of ancient woods arise,' and there, in the gorge below, are silver lakes reflecting as in a row of mirrors all the glory that surrounds them!"[38]

Helen could not have understood these words, for trilling crickets, music, ringing bridles, and cracking whips were but silence to her because she had no memory of hearing. The colors of Ireland were similar fictions because of her blindness. Helen's predicament with language, throughout her life, whether her own as largely Anne's voice or that of others, was perhaps best described by a clinical psychologist of the time, Thomas Cutsforth. He himself had been blinded (but not deafened) by illness at the age of eleven. He thought Helen better adjusted to her real world before Anne's arrival. Anne had taught her to express the seeing and hearing world's experiences, including color, sounds, brightness, and perspectives—not her own. As Charles Copeland, who taught Helen the course in Daily Themes at Radcliffe, informed Helen, "We want more of you and less of what you have read."[39]

But good writing, regardless of its lack of content meaningful to Helen (and often regardless of whose it was), was the goal toward which Anne had strived. This goal bore some resemblance to Sicard's when he had used methodical signs to elicit perfectly transcribed sentences from Jean Massieu, who (until Bébian) could not read well and was often less than fully conscious of what he was writing. When Helen was interviewed in 1930 by Robert Coates of the *New Yorker*, he found that her way of saying "I'm having a nice day," was to tell him that "I have the immeasurable fires of the mind for light."[40] Cutsforth writes:

> The average reader will recognize [in Helen's visual and aural words] meanings and situations that are common to him, but . . . from which [Helen] is excluded . . . [Her] own experiential life was rapidly made secondary, and [she] regarded [it] as such . . . In order for one to comprehend this situation, in which one personality capitulated completely to a system of education or another person's values, it is necessary to understand [that] the process was a lifetime, and the capitulation took place on an infantile level, when the personal affection and confidence of the child Helen were given completely to her teacher. From that time on, Helen's world contracted by expanding into that of her teacher. Her teacher's ideals became her ideals, her teacher's likes became her likes, and whatever emotional activity her teacher experienced she experienced . . . It is a birthright sold for a mess of verbiage.[41]

"A lamb," he adds, "is not a snow-white, innocent, gamboling lamb" to the blind, but is "kinky, woolly, bony, and wiggl[y]."[42] The essential problem is that Anne and her fingerspelling forced Helen to think in words first, and then in ideas, not, as Bébian always urged, the other way around. Moreover, the words were those of the sighted and the hearing, with an emphasis on the depiction, for their benefit, of colors and sounds, and distant clouds, mountains, moorlands, and hills—about which, because of her predicament, Helen would never be able to formulate any clear idea. Of Helen's companion, Polly Thomson, Dorothy Herrmann writes: "Most of the time Polly's life was drab and monotonous. Day and night, she was alone with Helen, a woman who could express herself in writing, but who due to the nature of her disability, was dismal at conversation."[43]

Emmanuelle Laborit, the Deaf actress who won the Prix Molière for her role in the French stage production of *Children of a Lesser God*, writes of her encounter with a Deafblind woman at Gallaudet—

> An affecting meeting with a deaf and blind woman. How can I communicate with her? I am told [in sign language] to fingerspell my name in the hollow of her hand. She smiles at me and repeats my first name in mine. I am profoundly troubled by this woman. She is magnificent . . . I ask [through another in sign language] how she manages to speak, because she can't spell all the words in the other person's hand. She answers in sign language:
>
> "You use sign language, and I'll put my hands around yours in order to touch each sign, and I shall understand."
>
> It's a mysterious thing for me; I need my eyes in order to understand a sign, I have to be facing the other person. Does she really understand? Really? I put the question.
>
> "Don't worry, I understand you, there's no problem."
>
> I ask her how she grew up, how she learned. This woman, whose hands gently envelope mine, and follow in space the drawing of each sign, moves me terribly. She has many more difficulties than I, her situation is more difficult than mine, and nevertheless she is speaking to me![44]

Laborit's astonishment was probably due in large part to the fact that yet another sense—touch—could be used, quite naturally, to communicate, or to "speak," as she put it. She focused on the Deafblind woman's "many more difficulties." As we shall see in Chapter 10, William Stokoe did the same when he wanted to "give credit" to certain Deaf children, not previously exposed to sign language, for creating their own visual communications systems with language-like properties. In fact the woman was speaking in the only way possible for her, through touch, in tactile American Sign Language, to which she had been exposed, free of the constraints Helen was forced to live with.

Though he could understand and empathize with Helen's blindness, Cutsforth was not Deaf, and he overlooked the critical element missing from Helen's upbringing and education. By the age of six (and before Anne's arrival), Helen had developed a vocabulary of many dozens of "home" signs that were seen and understood by the Keller family, who signed to her in turn by touch.[45] Like those children, Helen was developing a system of communication with language-like properties without being exposed to an authentic language, either oral or gestural. As Helen's mother wrote to John Macy, "after [Helen's] illness, when [we] were dependent on signs, Helen's tendency to gesture developed. How far she could receive communications is hard to determine, but she knew much that was going on around her."[46]

Anne herself wrote that when she arrived, Helen "made many signs which I did not understand."[47] As we shall see, many of Helen's signs had an iconic origin, although as in signed languages, those origins become quickly unrecognizable. Helen also wrote of her own use of signs, "I do not remember when I first realized that I was different from other people; but I knew it before my teacher came to me. I had noticed that my mother and my friends did not use signs as I did when they wanted anything done, but talked with their mouths." In effect, her own and her family's reciprocal forms of sign were becoming Helen's language. Helen signed "bread" by simulating the cutting of slices and buttering them. The sign for *bread* is similar in both ASL and LSF, but without the buttering. Both hands are in a horizontal B shape (see Appendix 2), palms facing in as the dominant hand moves down, or up and down, as if slicing along the back of the inside hand. To sign *ice cream,* Helen would move her hands and arms as if opening the ice box, and then shiver. To indicate that the family dog had just had puppies, she pointed excitedly to the fingers of one hand and suckled each fingertip.

Helen's mother would sign to her as well by touch. If Helen was asked to get something, she would know where to go and what to get. As we shall see in Chapter 10, signs, like words in spoken languages, have phonological-like elements. A sign has at least three components or visual "aspects," that is, dimensions along which its formative elements can contrast. The first is the location or place where the sign is made; the second the configuration or shape of the hands; and the third the motion or movement of those hands as they compose the sign. Facial expression is also critically important, and a part of its phonetic system, but the blind who sign replace this element with additional signs that are touched (for example the raised eyebrows in sign that indicate that a question is being asked are replaced by a question mark drawn on the listener's hand).

When Helen tried to open Anne Sullivan's bag upon her arrival in Tuscumbia, her mother signed to her not to touch it. When Helen realized that Anne had brought her candy, she told her mother "by means of emphatic signs" that there was candy in the trunk. In signing *small,* Helen would pinch the thin layer of skin on the back of her hand. In ASL the sign for very *small* (or *tiny*), the thumb and index finger close without touching (at face level) as if to pinch, a variation in the location of the sign but, curiously, in configuration and movement the same as Helen's. To sign *big,* Helen would spread her hands apart in a bent B shape, bring them toward each other and then stop as if she were holding a large ball. The sign in ASL is identical to Helen's, except that the hands (also in a B shape) stop to hold the imaginary ball as they move *away* from each other. That is, the place and shape of the sign are the same as Helen's, but the motion is slightly different.

Helen signed her *father* by mimicking his putting on his glasses. In both ASL and LSF the sign for *father* is toward the top of the forehead, and in LSF's sign for *papa* the hand is not unlike the shape of a single hand putting on glasses, giving similar place and shape (in ASL the thumb of an open hand taps the forehead twice). To sign *mother*, Helen would touch her cheek. In ASL and LSF, *mother* is signed by a touch of the chin with an open thumb. To sign *aunt*, Helen would simulate tying bonnet strings under her chin, almost identical to the place, shape, and motion of the sign for *tante* in LSF (both hands forming the fingerspelled letter T move down and in under the chin). In ASL the place is similar, with a single hand moving near the cheek in the shape of the letter A. The places for all of Helen's family signs, for father, mother, aunt, and probably for men and women in general, were similar to their locations in both ASL and LSF, in which *men* are signed at a slightly higher place at or near the forehead (l'Épée tells us this sign originated with the place of a man's hat) than are *women*, with the sign for *women* thought to represent a woman's longer hair or, indeed, the edge of a woman's, in this case Helen's aunt's, bonnet.[48]

Cynthia Ozick has seen Helen's invented system of signs as "intimations of intelligence." They were certainly that, but they were also more than just a hint of Helen's natural capacity to express herself in her own language. The crucial reason that Helen could never find her own voice was not the constant presence of Anne, which was a factor, but the fact that Helen as a child—and for the rest of her life after

Anne took her under her wing—was deprived of her own tongue. Helen wrote and fingerspelled with the voices of others because she had lost her own.

As Bébian stressed, it is the idea that gives a word meaning before the word can, in turn, become an effective interpreter of the idea. The word has to become part of the fabric of the idea. Written and fingerspelled characters, for the Deaf, are significantly more complex than their painting of sounds for the hearing. Those characters are too far removed from, and too cumbersome an expression of, the underlying idea. Helen, like every one of us, carried Bébian's "timeless and limitless principle" within her: that of the first language of any human being, which gives immediate expression to his or her thoughts and is not a translation of any other language, but the expression of the individual's intimate connection with the idea.

As Cutsforth observed (though he missed the underlying cause), when Helen expressed abstract thoughts through the manual alphabet they were a repetition of ideas expressed to her (usually by her teacher) rather than the expression of her own. Helen learned to write not for herself, but to please the sighted and the hearing. Bébian's "precious faculty" of communication was immediate and direct, endowed with what he called a simultaneity of circumstances.[49] As both he and Locke had observed, the ability to use signs that are readily perceivable by the senses—whether audible phones, morphemes, words, and sentences for the ears of the hearing, or hands, fingers, arms, motion, configuration, and orientation for the eyes or the encompassing hands of the Deaf—are critical in unlocking otherwise unperceivable thoughts from our own breasts and thoroughly assimilating the thoughts of others.

The ideas of *bread, small, large, come, go, man, woman, art,* and other concrete concepts were also, of course, conveyable by fingerspelling (just as the Deaf could mechanically be taught to try to "speak" the words and associate them with the concrete concept), and Anne succeeded remarkably in getting these meanings through to Helen. But by compelling Helen to begin with the letters, words, and syntax of spoken language as her means of communication, rather than the natural language she had started with, Anne led Helen, for virtually her entire life, to express herself in a way that was not natural to her. She was deprived of the step, which Bébian identified as so crucial, of learning her own language first and then, through it, mastering the language of the hearing as the vehicle for the written expression of her own.

Anne claimed that Helen was little more than a "wild animal" when Anne arrived in Tuscumbia to teach her, just as Sicard had described his Deaf charges as "animals unresponsive even to maternal affection" when they were placed in his charge at Saint Jacques. Both described their Deaf students this way in order to vaunt their own teaching skills. But their claim was far from the truth, for the children had come to them with their own language. Indeed, Anne tried to destroy two letters that Helen's mother had written in which she claimed that Helen was neither a wild nor an uncouth child before Anne's arrival.[50] Given the sophistication of Helen's signs and her extraordinary native intelligence, this was very probably the case, although there were the inevitable moments of the kicking and screaming of a frustrated child blinded and deafened by illness.

Anne praised her own achievement when she got through to Helen with the spelling of the word *water* as Helen placed her hand under the water pump in the garden at Tuscumbia. But if Helen had signs for such a broad variety of ideas in her own experience—for big, small, come, go, ice cream, bread, butter, mother, father, aunt, don't do that, and for eating, cake, and pouring or drinking—in all likelihood she had a sign for water as well. If so, Anne had her abandon it and all the others in order to adopt as her introduction to formal language the abstract, complex, and cumbersome characters for the Deaf, of painted speech.[51]

As we have seen, in the early nineteenth century Sicard had a taste for vaudeville, and he put Massieu and Clerc on display by "dictating" to them in methodical sign so they could write the words of a newspaper story verbatim on the blackboard. They were also asked philosophical questions, and would respond, in sign language, with ideas that were sometimes their own, sometimes borrowed. Massieu would explain that *eternity* was "a day without yesterday or tomorrow, a line that has no end." A *difficulty* was "a possibility with an obstacle." Clerc was asked, in London, whether he would object to marrying an English lady, and he would respond in sign language, "As much a French as an English one." When asked exactly what he meant, he replied that he wasn't rich enough to support either.[52]

From 1920 to 1924, when Helen was in her early forties and Anne her late fifties, and they were in need of money, Anne, Helen, and Polly Thomson went on the vaudeville circuit. Anne and Helen prepared a list of expected questions, and they would rehearse the answers. When the questions were asked, Anne would fingerspell them, and Helen would try to answer in her broken speech, which Anne would then interpret for the audience. There were serious questions and answers, such as "What do you think is the most serious obstacle to peace?," and its answer, "The human race." Some came close to the question posed to Clerc in 1816—"Does Mrs. Keller think of marriage?" to which the answer was "Yes, are you proposing to me?"

Sicard's purpose was to raise interest in the cause of the Deaf (it was at one of those shows in London that Gallaudet met Clerc), but also to show the wonders of his and l'Épée's methodical sign (though, unlike Sicard, Clerc and Massieu of course knew French sign language as well). He demonstrated this by having the Deaf men write down their account of the newspaper stories not in their own words, but word for word. Anne's motive was one of necessity, but she also wanted to demonstrate how far she had brought Helen from her "primitive state" by teaching her fingerspelling and, ultimately, to "speak" and to "read lips."

Presenting Laurent Clerc, Jean Massieu, and Helen Keller as carnivalesque was, of course, a mistake, the more so because a central purpose of the exercise was to draw attention to the merits of flawed teaching systems. Helen was as true as she could be to a lost self, and was a living victim, for all her talent and achievement, of the system established by Milan, Bell, and the oralist view of the nineteenth and twentieth centuries.

I first witnessed extended conversations in what might have become Helen's natural language a short time ago, on the campus at the University of Paris at Saint Denis. The school was hard to find because the 1960s architects of the university's main buildings drew them all alike, and they looked a lot like the rest of the dismal city save for the ancient royal basilica, where France's monarchs lie in sarcophagal state. I parked in front of a gray building somewhere near the university, and got lost on foot trying to find the entrance.

I spotted a group of a dozen or so people, five of whom were wearing dark glasses, as they were coming out of the metro, about twenty meters away. The right hand of each rested on the left shoulder of the hearing, sighted interpreter beside him. They were blind, and they were Deaf, and they were the ones I had come to see. I asked one of their interpreters where I could find the university's main amphitheater. He began to sign to me, looking at my hearing aids, though I had spoken to him. I couldn't follow, and quickly rotated my index finger, laterally, in front of my mouth, the *American* sign for a hearing (and thus a speaking) person, and he understood. He invited me to follow them.

It was a long way in, lefts, rights, signs, arrows, ellipses, as we moved from building to building in the university's maze of court-yards to find the right one, the interpreters leading the Deaf and blind leading me. Once in the amphitheater they moved to a side aisle, step-ping down every two paces to make the thirty-meter descent, taking their direction and the measure of their steps from the declining path of the shoulders now in front of them. The room was filled to its ca-pacity of about five hundred people.

The front row was empty, so I took a seat there, as I almost always do at lectures, churches, and meetings, because the intensity of speech and other sounds is inversely proportional to the *square* of the distance from its source (here, the speakers). When they arrived at the base of the amphitheater, the people in the group that entered with me excitedly touched and greeted their friends, Deaf, Deafblind, and fluent hearing, their excited eyebrows dancing up and down. They were elated to see, to speak to, to hear from, each other again, particularly now, here, in the amphitheater of the University of Paris, for this was their day.

Sandrine Schwartz, an interpreter become academic, was there to defend her thesis on the language of the Deaf and blind. As she began to speak, those who spoke this language each took a seat, facing the public, and held out their hands to their seated, sighted interpreters, opposite them, their backs to us, who took the hands in theirs. On a raised level behind them, facing us, was a panel of leading authorities on signed languages in general, mostly hearing, all sighted, one Deaf. They were Schwartz's jury.

As Schwartz warmed to her subject, the hands of the Deafblind moved more and more excitedly, smiling, laughing really, as they listened to the academic exchanges between jury and student, about the phonemics, morphology, syntax, and other elements of their own tongue. They were the stars of the show. I could not hear many of the panelists' questions, but I caught many key words and, in any event, kept watching their subjects' expressions and fast-moving hands, as everyone did.

The signed languages of the Deafblind are very close to those of their Deaf compatriots. They are not, of course, visual languages, but tactile ones in which, as we saw in Emmanuel Laborit's experience at Gallaudet, the speaker's hands are enveloped or held by his or her interlocutor. The signed languages of the sighted are modified in a number of respects to reflect facial and bodily expressions in manually tactile form. These languages of the Deafblind are called tactile ASL or TASL in the United States, LSFT in France, and TBSL in Great Britain.

The panel did not go easy on Schwartz, who was new to the academic study of language. She had learned through experience as an interpreter, and her study was limited to the empirical to an extent that made the panelists, all linguists, uncomfortable. "You are giving us the *letters* of the language," signed the Deaf academician on the jury, "not its linguistic structure." But Schwartz defended her method as a practical study of how the Deafblind communicate, one that represented a significant first step (one panelist called her a "pioneer") and a rich resource for future scholars.

Schwartz had filmed and freeze-framed her Deaf and blind subjects as they signed to each other. She started her presentation by covering some familiar ground, such as showing that the blind form a "hook" in the palm of their interlocutor's hand to indicate that a question is being asked (as noted earlier, in ASL and LSF the eyebrows are raised), and noting their practice of using the body (principally the hands) of the listener in lieu of the eyes—making of their language voices in flesh and touch, the equivalent of the voices in air of the hearing and in light of the Deaf.

There was extensive discussion as to whether LSFT was an entire language, since it is rooted in the signed language of the French Deaf who see (LSF), and supplements or alters it to accommodate the interlocutors' lack of sight. Christian Cuxac, also on the panel, said that Schwartz might explore, perhaps in a later paper, the crucial question of what made LSFT a complete language, if it is one. He observed that *le regard* (roughly, the sight and appearance of both interlocutors) was not there—so what new elements does blindness bring to the language of the Deaf to make it another language or, if it is not, to make it whole for the Deafblind? We know that, like visual signed languages, the tactile signed languages that build on them differ from country to country, but what shapes these tactile differences? The underlying sighted language? Culture? Circumstance? We know there are Deafblind people who, when signing in public, as in a lecture hall, sign in the language of the sighted Deaf. How would that person, how would a scholar, how may we, account for the differences when they sign to each other?

A Spanish juror noted that one ought to explore the Deafblind manner of expressing concepts that we who see can't really understand. The Deafblind can't look out a window or into the distance, or imagine themselves walking down the street, among the near and far, amid houses, cars, people, buildings, vendors, shops, dogs and cats. How are their thoughts, visions, or ideas of these things understood and expressed? As his words were spoken into the hands of the Deafblind at the front of the room, two of them broke off from their interpreters to clasp hands and sign to each other. I have no idea what they were saying about the near and far, but it was clear that we would all be learning more about these perspectives and how those who are Deaf and blind understand and express them. The entire session ended with an enthusiastic ovation, the Deaf waving their hands in applause and the hearing clapping, for Schwartz and for the jury, but especially for those at the front of the room, waving their hands to each other, to their interpreters, and to us.

In hearing the Spaniard's words I recalled that Helen Keller, too, was unable to look into the distance, or to imagine herself among the near and far, amid the noisy-throated frogs or silver lakes, or the luminous shadows of trees in a soft light. And I wondered how Helen would have described her sensations sitting against a tree in a garden at home, standing barefoot on a mountain rock in Ireland, or trampling through the heather of the Scottish moorlands. Had she the good fortune to have met at seven years old a Massieu, Bébian, or Clerc, she might have become the Ferdinand Berthier of the twentieth century, a writer with her own voice, a spokeswoman for the Deaf and the Deafblind, a consummate speaker and listener, through touch, of the language of light.

10

Bébian Reborn: The Arrival of William Stokoe

Alexander Graham Bell continued to use his money and substantial influence to wage his battles to require Deaf people to speak and lip-read until the end of his life in 1921. His tactics included the lobbying of Congress to withhold funding from educational programs that used sign language as the medium of teaching. By 1927 sign language had fallen out of favor in the United States. Like Ordinaire and Gérando before him, he had as a primary goal the elimination of Deaf teachers—in Bell's case, in order to avoid the "formation of a deaf variety" of the human species. Gallaudet College itself discouraged its Deaf students from becoming teachers.

The name of the American Association to Promote the Teaching of Speech to the Deaf (AAPTSD) was finally shortened to bear only Bell's name. The change may have been inspired by a speaker at a Deaf convention who marched across the stage (thirty paces over, twenty-nine back) and, step after step, fingerspelled each of the fifty-nine letters of the association's name. The group fights Bell's battles today.

By the early twentieth century, Deaf children were leaving school after twelve years with educational accomplishments far below the national average. Helmer Myklebust, an American psychologist, wrote in 1960 that deafness might preclude a student from reaching his or her true intellectual potential because of "limited language." He wrote that deafness "feminizes the male and masculinizes the female" and leads to "deviant emotional and social behavior."[1]

At Gallaudet itself, ever since its founding in 1864, all of its presidents and virtually all its directors were hearing. A number of classes at Gallaudet, given by Deaf teachers, have always been taught in ASL. But for many of the hearing faculty, sign language had no grammar and wasn't considered a language; it was just the way you talked to Deaf people (if you could), and the way they talked to each other.[2]

It was to this environment that William Stokoe (rhymes with Skokie), an unknown English instructor from Wells College in Aurora, New York, was introduced when Gallaudet hired him as an English teacher in 1955. Stokoe had graduated from Cornell in 1942 and received a doctorate in English there in 1946. He was to shake the doctrines of Bell, Milan, Myklebust, and their kind to their foundations. As Bébian had predicted toward the end of his short life, "I've shown the path; another, abler or with better support, will accomplish the goal."[3] The moment Stokoe arrived on the Gallaudet campus, well over a hundred years after the death of the man whom Berthier called history's greatest teacher of the Deaf, the new Auguste Bébian was born.

Bill Stokoe was a Chaucerian scholar, a student of the evolution of early language, and a master of written lyricals. He studied Old English as it emerged after the invasions of today's British Isles by Anglian, Saxon, and Mercian tribes in the fourth and fifth centuries. He was a scholar as well of written and spoken Middle English, which was a blend of the French and Anglo-Saxon languages that arose following the Norman Conquest.

Stokoe cut his own hair in the shape of an inverted bowl, and looked like a medieval monk himself. He also had an unusual level of perseverance and passion for detail. Jane Maher reports in her biography that while Stokoe was teaching at Wells College he spent a

William C. Stokoe (1919–2000) (Courtesy of
Gallaudet University Archives.)

substantial part of a year-long sabbatical in Scotland trying to figure
out the precise meaning of a single word in a ninth-century translation attributed to King Aelfred (in the king's own Wessex Anglo-
Saxon) of Orosius's Latin *Historiae*, written in Rome in the year 417.
Stokoe also had a passion for playing the bagpipes, forever practicing
on the Gallaudet campus rather than at home, he said, so that neither
his wife and neighbors nor the students would have to hear him.[4]

Stokoe was hired by George Detmold, who had been his friend at
Cornell. Gallaudet had hired Detmold as dean in 1952 amid a host of
problems at the college, in order "to get the place accredited." The
hearing faculty at Gallaudet viewed sign language as simplistic pantomime, a view that, unknown to them, bore witness to Ferdinand

Berthier's apocalyptic vision a hundred years earlier. Many hearing people appeared to think of signed languages as no more than sequences of primitive gestures inferior to speech. Expectations for Gallaudet graduates were low. The men would become typesetters in the Government Printing Office, or teach the trade in vocational schools for the Deaf, or become dormitory supervisors in Deaf residential schools. Women graduates would teach sewing and cooking in those schools.[5]

Upon his arrival at the College, Stokoe was told that the signs the students used among themselves were "inappropriate" for the classroom. Instead, students in classes given by Gallaudet's hearing teachers were taught using what was called "pidgin sign language," in which, as noted earlier, signs were given in English word order. Stokoe took a three-week course in manually coded systems and was told that the ASL signs included in these codes were a "necessary evil, a 'visual aid' to the English we teachers were expected to speak simultaneously with our signs." Lou Fant, a hearing teacher at Gallaudet, writes that "like most children of Deaf parents, I grew up with no conscious awareness that ASL was a language. I thought of ASL as an ungrammatical parody of English."[6]

As we have seen, to speak and sign simultaneously is physiologically but not cognitively possible because of the fundamental differences between spoken and signed languages in form, structure, syntax, and word order (though often words are mouthed by signing interpreters, they do not do so in English-language order). To alter the order of signs in ASL, LSF, or BSL to conform to the word order of English or French is to scramble the meaning, as it would be for French or English if we were to do the reverse.

Ferdinand Berthier had written that signed languages were not the goal of Deaf education, but its indispensable instrument. Stokoe saw the issue as one of control: "Since the middle of the eighteenth century at least some hearing people have recognized, consciously or subconsciously, that educational use of genuine sign language would logically lead to greater and greater deaf control over deaf education; after all, deaf people, as native users, are more frequently fluent in sign than hearing people. Such a development would challenge the dominance of hearing people, a fundamental characteristic of nearly all deaf education. For all these and other reasons, signed languages were kept well outside the language preserve, and professional [hearing] educators termed them substitutes or surrogates for 'real,' that is, spoken, languages."[7]

When Stokoe observed students communicating with each other, whether in or outside the classroom, he noticed that their signing was quite different from what *he* was being taught— something else was going on, as plainly exhibited by the play of their eyes and faces. Stokoe decided to get to the bottom of it. It was a similar experience that led Harlan Lane, when he was visiting the Salk Institute and happened to observe a conversation in sign language in a waiting room, to devote himself to the field and ultimately to become the world's leading scholar and historian of the Deaf.[8] It was the very observation that had generally eluded philosophers and teachers until l'Épée in the eighteenth century and Bébian a few years later, and that hearing academics, teachers, and thinkers in the West had been ignoring since the Congress of Milan.

Stokoe's focus was on the language itself. He was won over not only by his students, but also by a lecture on *Wuthering Heights* given in ASL by Robert Panara, a Deaf teacher at Gallaudet who used fingerspelled symbols (H for Heathcliff with the index and middle finger of the left hand pointing out together, C for Cathy with the right hand curved in a C), and signs moving syntactically, to explain with considerable grace the characters' relationship and their influence upon each other. Stokoe thought he could follow the drift of the lecture because he knew the book, and he was enchanted. His observations of this unknown language were an epiphany. They would mark a quiet rebirth of Bébian's age of reason and the beginning of two major battles, one intellectual, the other practical, of the hundred years' war.

Stokoe, like l'Épée, quickly realized that he would not be able to teach his students English literature unless he learned their language, so he began to take lessons in ASL. Although Panara was the standard to which he aspired, he would never reach it. He ultimately learned to understand ASL, but was a poor signer himself. Moreover, wrote Robin Battison, one of his closest colleagues, "Bill was not essentially a very good teacher . . . He tended to . . . burden his message with complicated metaphors and literary allusions."[9]

Stokoe also became an historian. From 1957 to 1960, in addition to his teaching and his study of sign language itself, he read l'Épée, Sicard, and Bébian. He praised l'Épée's groundbreaking accomplishment: "Though not the first to recognize the existence of a sign language among [the] deaf . . . l'Épée was the first to attempt to learn it, use it, and make it the medium of instruction for teaching French language and culture to the deaf."[10]

But Stokoe was new to the field, and may not have read Bébian's important criticisms of l'Épée's and Sicard's work, nor the accounts of Berthier and others of Bébian's preeminence. Although Bébian had thoroughly discredited l'Épée's methodical signs, Stokoe believed he was seeing substantial evidence of them in modern ASL, which he attributed to Laurent Clerc's early influence. He wrote that l'Épée "realized" that natural sign alone "was insufficient as a medium for teaching [the Deaf] French language and culture," and thought that l'Épée's methodical signs had made their way into American Sign Language.[11]

Bébian, however, had shown that natural sign language was the indispensable medium of instruction. Clerc did, in fact, use methodical signs as a tool to teach English to his students. But they were never used outside the classroom. Stokoe also thought that methodical signs probably "underwent considerable change as they moved from the textbook and the systematic course in French grammar into the colloquial language." But they never broadly entered the LSF or ASL lexicon. Clerc was of course aware of l'Épée's techniques, and had used them himself along with Sicard and Massieu in the celebrated *dictées* to which Thomas Gallaudet was a witness in London in 1815. But in 1817, the very year that Clerc and Gallaudet opened their school for the Deaf in Hartford, Bébian published his "Essay on the Deaf and Their Natural Language," which led to the general abandonment of methodical signs. They were quickly dropped in both the Hartford and New York schools, and indeed in most schools throughout the United States and France.[12]

Stokoe was neither the philosopher nor the writer that Bébian was, but rather the tinkerer, the aspiring young scientist who wanted to apply his scientific mind to other things. He went to Cornell originally to study the physical behavior of minute particles in chemical systems, but had wound up studying Greek, Latin, French, German, and Chaucer. He fully understood the need to teach the Deaf in their own language, but seems not to have given much thought, at least outwardly, to philosophical considerations such as Bébian's central notion that language, whether signed or spoken, is the outward expression of preexisting ideas. Stokoe credited Sicard with being the "direct link" between the "developers" of French sign language and ASL, and thought it was Sicard who had acquainted Thomas Gallaudet with the "methods" of the Paris school.[13]

In fact, as we have seen, Sicard knew little if any sign language, and Gallaudet's instructors were Clerc and Massieu. There were no "developers" of French sign language, as Stokoe later readily acknowledged, for signed languages have probably existed (and evolved) in various forms for as long as human beings have. Stokoe also, unfortunately, gave Bébian little more than passing credit for his "Mimography: An Essay on the Writing of Sign in Order to Standardize the Language of the Deaf." That essay was to be the original foundation for a dictionary in written and signed language, illustrating each sign with a code showing its handshape, movement, configuration, location, and facial expression.[14]

None of these shortcomings, however, prevented Stokoe from becoming a brilliant scientist of the language of the Deaf. His genius, like l'Épée's with his twins, lay in observation: his early recognition at Gallaudet that sign certainly looked like a language and his instinctive conclusion that it was. He then amassed an enormous body of evidence to support this observation that ultimately forced the rest of the world to agree. He was astonished to discover that the works of the great French teachers of the Deaf in the eighteenth and nineteenth centuries were largely unknown at the college: "it was as if l'Épée had never existed."

Such was the measure of success, and longevity, of the doctrines of Milan eighty years earlier that "no one, not even the deaf students and deaf faculty, believed that their signing was a suitable medium of instruction, much less a legitimate language. Many of the hearing faculty could barely use the language and were unaware that their students' grammatical errors resulted from the differences between their language and English."[15] Stokoe put it mildly when he declared: 'It is greatly to be regretted that from l'Épée's day to the present, his grasp of the structure of the situation of the congenitally deaf confronted with a language of hearing persons has escaped so many working in the same field."[16]

Lou Fant of Gallaudet wrote that a kind of "truce" was in effect between the oralists and the Deaf advocates of signed languages, and that the Deaf dared not jeopardize it, lest the war end in a disastrous "Armageddon," with the hearing winding up with all the power. But Deaf people generally did indeed have a sense that they had a language. As Tom Humphries has said, sign is like breathing—you don't notice it until suddenly you do.[17] The Deaf conversed in American Sign Language with ease and sophistication, but had become unaware they could formally call it a language until Stokoe arrived. "We had only the truth," writes Fant, "and we weren't too sure about that." Edward Gallaudet had also spoken of such a "truce" in his testimony before the Royal Commission a hundred years before Fant and Stokoe. But of course there never was any truce, and the advocates of speech and lipreading held sway.[18]

Although Berthier had warned the Deaf against losing their language, even he couldn't foresee how the world would turn against them. Stokoe was not going to let it happen again. That he emerged at all, over a century later, is a wonder. Like Bébian, Stokoe had the practical advantage of being able to hear in a world that was ignoring the Deaf and the benefit of an ally on the faculty. Both Bébian and Stokoe were also men of extraordinary persistence. The American was called "Stubborn Stokoe" in high school; it was an attribute that would serve him well.[19]

In 1957 Gallaudet College received its accreditation, notwithstanding what the Middle States Association of Colleges characterized as the "social and psychological problems" of the Deaf and the "problem of communicating with signs." Detmold was able to tell the association's committee that a member of the faculty (meaning Stokoe) was engaged in a "structural linguistic analysis" of American Sign Language in order to determine whether (he chose his words carefully) it could be "studied as other languages are with a descriptive grammar and lexicon."[20]

But Stokoe knew that he was a teacher of English literature, not a linguist. So he left Washington to spend the following summer taking courses on linguistics in the cooler climate (and his cherished environment) of upstate New York, at the University of Buffalo. The courses were given by two leading linguists of the day, George L. Trager and Henry Lee Smith. It was there that he began to formulate his idea that a system of symbols didn't have to be vocal in order to constitute a language—they could be gestural.

Linguistics is the science of language. When Stokoe began to study linguistics, most scholars in the field, including Trager and Smith, were behavioral scientists engaged in the empirical study of a kind of verbal botany.[21] They would collect and record utterances of a language and develop its "corpus," which became their subject of study. Linguistics did not include, as it soon would, a study of mind or of meaning, of what we all have in common. The field was rather, in Stokoe's time, a study of differences. The corpus of each language would be broken down into its root components: the phone, the phoneme, the morpheme, the word, and the sentence.

The method had a considerable influence on Stokoe, and he would ultimately adapt it to his study of American Sign Language, undeterred by its voicelessness. Speakers signify differences in meaning with interchangeable sounds, as in *ball* versus *hall*, a switch of consonants, or *lack* versus *luck*, a change in vowels. We call these interchangeable sounds *phonemes*. Our *morphemes* are the meaningful units we speak that are not divisible into smaller units with the same meaning—for instance, *dog, mad, clear*. Our *words* are meaningful units of sound consisting of at least one morpheme (for example, *think*), with or without other morphemes preceding or following (*un*think*able*).

When he returned from Buffalo to Gallaudet in the fall, Stokoe promptly asked a teacher at the college, Carl Croneberg, and a student, Dorothy Sueoka (later Casterline), to embark with him upon an intensive study of American Sign Language. Both were Deaf. Croneberg had spent several years in a school for the Deaf in Sweden and nine years at Gallaudet as a student and teacher; Casterline had attended a Deaf school in Hawaii and worked with students there, and had been an undergraduate and graduate at Gallaudet for four years. They set up a movie camera run by a transformer from an old electric train set of Stokoe's, and began to film the signs of Deaf students. They analyzed over five thousand feet of film, at normal and reduced speeds, showing the signing of fourteen Deaf and two hearing (and signing) subjects. They ran the films, sometimes frame by frame, through a moviola, a film-editing machine, and studied their resulting corpus of the language, both still and in motion.[22]

In 1960 Stokoe published his findings in a monograph entitled "Sign Language Structure." His central thesis was that signed languages are indeed languages. He supported that thesis by presenting and analyzing American Sign Language using conventional linguistic terminology. The paper is a bit encumbered by Stokoe's occasionally inelegant prose (at least to my ear) and his penchant for using complex words for simple ideas, including terms he devised to designate the basic components of ASL, which he must have known was itself an unfamiliar topic for most. But it is a work of genius, and marked a paradigmatic change in the social sciences that would permanently alter the way linguists, the Deaf themselves, and the modern world in general would look upon the Deaf community and their language.

"Sign Language Structure" breaks down ASL (and implicitly other signed languages) into three essential components or visual "aspects," dimensions along which the formative elements of signs can contrast. The first aspect is the *place* or location where the sign is made in relation to the signer's body. He calls this element *tab*, short for "tabula" which is Latin for "tablet," although of course the signer is neither Roman nor writing. The second is the *shape* of the hand making the sign (normally, as I have noted, the dominant hand, the right hand for right-handers), which he calls *dez* (short for *designator*). The third aspect of a sign he calls *sig*, short for *signation,* an obsolete word for the *motion* of the hand in giving a blessing. The *sig* is the *motion* of the *dez* in the *tab*. His terms are hard to keep straight, and here we will generally call them *motion, shape,* and *place.*

These three elements—a specific motion and a certain shape of the hands, made in a particular place on or near the body—together with the specific orientation of the hands comprise the central components of the sign. The sign is the smallest meaningful unit and is thus the *morpheme* of a signed language. Stokoe substitutes the unpronounceable term *chereme* for the term *phoneme* used for spoken languages because of the role of the hands in a language.[23] Here, however, although the analogy is imperfect, I will call these units phonemes to suggest the parallels between signed languages and speech. It is important to bear in mind that speech itself is also formed by elements of place, shape, and motion, of the lips, tongue, and other organs of speech, though they are designed to configure molecules of air to be sent to the ear and not (except incidentally, for example, by the movement of the lips) to configure shapes in light for the eye.

Stokoe's paper takes us one by one through each of the phonemes (cheremes) of American Sign Language. To describe handshapes, Stokoe uses the shapes of the hand used in the manual alphabet, the one that can be traced to Saint Bonaventure and the Franciscans in the thirteenth century. The same alphabet was later adopted by Ponce and Bonet in Spain in the sixteenth and seventeenth centuries as a teaching aid in the education of their Deaf students, and was used by Anne Sullivan to fingerspell to Helen Keller (see Appendix 2). Stokoe identified a total of fifteen different shapes based on these finger-spelled letters (combining some similar letter shapes).

The A is thus more or less a fist (as are the letters S and T), the B is a flat hand, the C a curled hand, the D (like G) a pointed index, the H (like N) the extended index *and* middle finger, and so on. These shape-phonemes have no "alphabetical" significance in a signed language, for an alphabet, of course, is a collection of visual symbols used to "paint" the sounds of oral languages. Indeed the handshapes of American Sign Language are different from the fingerspelled letters in a number of ways—but they are an approximation and a convenient system of notation or symbols for the hearing.[24] Some contemporary systems provide additional shape phonemes as derivatives of the fin-gerspelling shapes, for example, the open A and B (thumb out), the flattened O, the bent V, and others shown in Appendix 2.

Stokoe also identified fourteen specific motions that the shaped hand (or at times both hands) may make—vertical, lateral, twisting, separating, and so on. He then named twelve places, including at the level of the brow, the center of the face, the lower face, and the body, shoulders to hips, through which the shaped hand may move. Though there are exceptions, when making a sign, you seldom reach below the waist, above the head, or to the left or right beyond the reach of each arm with the elbow bent. These constraints keep the signs in view and facilitate rapid movement.

Signed languages are generally captured with peripheral vision for, as in the case of the hearing, the eyes connect the speaker and lis-tener, providing critical clues to the idea the signer is expressing, as to "what's on his mind." They also inform the signer as to whether he or she is being understood. The same is true for the partially deaf. We are able with the benefit of sound and experience to lipread much of what people say. But focusing on the lips disjoints the message, forcing us to take in only a word or two at a time and to lose the thread of the larger thought. The speaker's eyes are essential to what he or she is saying, so we lock eyes and read lips peripherally.

When the shaped hand of the signer moves in the appropriate place (or as Stokoe memorably put it, when the *dez* makes a *sig* in the *tab*), a sign is formed. The sign for *know,* for example, is formed by a bent B (shape), palm down, tapping its fingertips (motion) against the forehead (place). The sign *father* in ASL is the open B, palm left, tapping the forehead with its thumb (not unlike, as we have noted, Helen Keller's sign for her father). If the thumb touches the *breast* the sign means *fine.* The set is, of course (or is very close to), a minimal pair, just as *pull* and *bull* and *love* and *live* and other sets are in English.

Stokoe expanded his system of sign-language symbols to include not just handshapes but symbols for motion and place as well. He did so not in order to develop a system of sign writing, but to describe ASL rapidly and consistently and to show its formal structure. He had to prove to the skeptics that signed languages were just what they were called—languages. He was also preparing an ASL dictionary, and set out his full notational system (for specific shapes, places, and motions) in "Sign Language Structure" to lay the groundwork for it.

Auguste Bébian had also developed a system of French sign language symbols in his "Mimography," and the similarities between the two systems are striking, including their respective notations for specific places, shapes, and motions that comprise signs.[25] Bébian also included notations for facial expressions (*points physionomiques*) in his system, because these too can alter the meaning of signs. As he succinctly put it, "Gesture expresses the objective world around us;

physiognomy, how that world affects us." Thus in signing the idea of *counting*, we lift the finger of a hand, palm up, one by one, with a slight pause between each, and the face (*physionomie*) expresses close attention. In the sign for *some* the fingers are raised successively and almost without interruption, with a facial expression showing a degree of uncertainty.[26] Again, these are signs whose origins are iconic but whose meaning and distinction are difficult to recognize for the nonsigner.

We know today that Bébian's *physionomie* is an integral part of the sign. Unlike Bébian, Stokoe did not generally include facial expressions among his symbols, though he noted, for example, the importance of raising the eyebrows when asking a question—indeed if this is not done the sign is usually not a question. He did suspect that facial expressions could be the key to syntactical structure, but thought that more work needed to be done.

Both Bébian's and Stokoe's systems of notation included extensive subnotations showing diagonal motions, dual motions of the hands, quick or abrupt and slow motions, and other characteristics of the complex (French and American) signed languages. In all, Bébian's system included more than twice as many shapes and places as Stokoe's, three times as many motions, as well as numerous orientations (of the hands) and facial expressions of which Stokoe's code showed few. Bébian himself noted, however, and Stokoe would have agreed, that a signed language could never be fully reflected in any true sign-writing system. Moreover, they both understood that the first task for a Deaf student, once he had learned his own language, was to master writing in order to study the broad body of our knowledge of the world generally recorded in writing.

Bébian was first and foremost a teacher of the Deaf, fluent in French sign language and well aware that it was a language, an unusually gifted writer, a philosopher in the mold of Locke and Descartes—someone

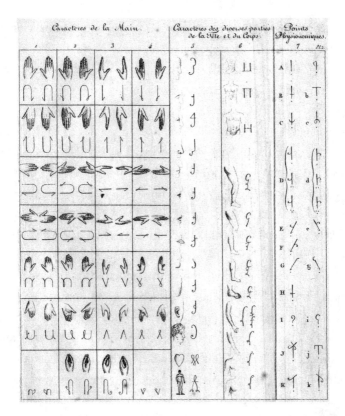

Plate from Bébian's "Mimography" showing his sign-writing codes for the handshapes and locations of signs (Stokoe's "dez" and "tab"), with the added element of facial expressions (Collection INJS de Paris.)

whom Isaiah Berlin would call a *fox*, his metaphor for an individual with many ideas. Stokoe, by contrast, was a poor signer but a dedicated student and scientist of American Sign Language, an unskilled teacher and awkward writer, stubborn, a *hedgehog*, designating, in Berlin's lexicon, a man with a single big idea. In Stokoe's case that idea was that ASL, along with other signed languages, was a complete language and he was going to prove it, to a world that, to his astonishment, had forgotten.

Bébian didn't devise his system of notation to prove anything. He wanted to use it as a pedagogical tool, a way to standardize French sign language, to facilitate its teaching, and to undo the harm done by methodical French. He also thought it might eventually serve as the basis for a French dictionary for the Deaf, keyed to his symbols and to French, a goal that Stokoe ultimately accomplished when he and his colleagues published their *Dictionary of American Sign Language* in 1965. The dictionary provides the sign symbols (specific places, shapes, and motions), and sign and English notations, for almost two thousand signs and words.

One modern scholar of Bébian, Fabrice Bertin, has noted that the age of l'Épée and Bébian could hardly be considered the beginning of an *âge d'or* in a nineteenth century that ended with the Congress of Milan. He sees the ideas ("pedagogical reflections") and accomplishments of Bébian, during the time I have called the "age of Bébian," not so much as the beginning of an age as the opening of an unclosed parenthetical.[27] By this I think Bertin means that those ideas continue to challenge and cultivate our thinking about the Deaf, their signed languages, and their education to this very day, and that they pose an open invitation to delete the parenthesis and to bring Bébian's world back to life. To that invitation, William Stokoe offered a bountiful and enlightening response. Bébian's work had finally come to modern fruition, and Stokoe's achievements have helped to attract large numbers of scholars to the study of signed languages today.

In the closing paragraphs of "Sign Language Structure," Stokoe wrote, in delightfully characteristic form, that "the work [we have] so far accomplished seems to us to substantiate the claim that the communicative activity of persons using this language is truly linguistic and susceptible of micro-linguistic analysis of the most rigorous kind." In scholarly works today as well as in sign/oral language dictionaries in print and online, authors use photographs, pictorial illustrations, and videos of real signers in order to illustrate the vocabulary, grammar, and syntax of signed languages. No system of sign-language symbols or notations has taken hold because of the ready availability of moving images. But Stokoe's rediscovery of Bébian and the appearance of his "Sign Language Structure" and *Dictionary of American Sign Language* marked an intellectual renaissance for the Deaf. His works, considered seminal because Bébian's efforts had lain so long dormant, demonstrated that the Deaf possess the same structural and expressive capacity to transform ideas, whether tangible or abstract, simple or complex, into well-crafted sentences, as do the hearing. Most of the world had fallen asleep as to the linguistic skills of the Deaf and the existence, sophistication, and eloquence of their language.

Bill Stokoe woke them up.

11

To Sign Is to Speak

During the summer of 1957, while Stokoe was studying linguistics in Buffalo with Trager and Smith, Noam Chomsky published *Syntactic Structures,* the "pale blue book" that heralded a revolution in linguistics. As a young boy, Chomsky was given the task of proofreading an obscure medieval text—his father's edition of a medieval Hebrew grammar. He went on to study linguistics at the University of Pennsylvania and wrote his undergraduate and master's theses about the morphophonemics of modern Hebrew. He received a doctorate from Penn in 1955 and joined the faculty of the Massachusetts Institute of Technology that year. He has been at MIT ever since.

Chomsky posits that the observable elements of language are the product of a language-acquisition device that is latent until awakened in us when we are just months old. The device is strongest when we are infants and then diminishes until about age twelve, when our capacity to learn a language with native fluency disappears. This language faculty doesn't just enable us to mimic others. It no more originates from experience, Chomsky writes, "than adaptation of the fin of the fish to the properties of water."[1] Chomsky theorizes that the language faculty is an organic structure, located in the speech-related centers of our brain, although at present we know virtually nothing of its underlying neural substrate—we can neither physically identify the language organ nor observe it in operation.[2]

When Deaf or hearing infants are exposed to a language, they begin to use it and before long to master it, employing rich and complex constructions that go far beyond what the children might form based solely on the "input" or the fragmentary evidence available to them—far beyond what Chomsky calls "the poverty of the stimulus." The device enables the children to master the language they are exposed to, whether signed or spoken, to use and understand it, and to produce sentences they have never heard before, without any grammatical instruction and before even learning to read or write. When they are exposed to Japanese (if raised in Tokyo), or to German (if raised in Berlin), or to Spanish (if raised in Madrid), or if Deaf to the signed language of their country, they will be able to discern and adopt the syntactic elements of the speech or signed language in which they are addressed. As a result, the children will develop a mature language system far beyond what could be expected on the basis of their limited exposure to the language. They will be able to express an infinite number of ideas in well-formed sentences and reject word or signed combinations that are not sentences. What is really at work when the hearing or Deaf speak or sign is the innate capability of human beings, genetically determined and a product of evolution, to express our ideas in a grammatical format.

The heart of this language faculty is syntax, the rules of sentence construction that exist, Chomsky postulates, independent of meaning. Chomsky originally wrote of the "surface structures" of language represented by the spoken word and the "deep structures" or underlying concepts formulated in the brain. The phrase *I like her cooking*, for example, has a surface structure produced by transformational rules that conceal a number of possible deep structures, including "I like her when she cooks," "I like the way she cooks," "I like what she cooks," or even "I like her when she is being cooked." I would regard the last possibility as a disposable lyrical, but the listener chooses among the rational candidates as objects of "like." The sentence is ambiguous because, Chomsky wrote, it has only one surface structure but several deep structures, which must be weighed against each other based on their semantic value—is it *Mary* he likes, is it the *way* she cooks, or is it *what* she cooks? Does he mean all three?

Throughout their lives hearing people keep saying and hearing, and Deaf people keep signing and seeing (linguistically) things we have never before heard or seen. Through recursive devices, which appear early in the utterances of a child, we can express statements within statements, and we could go on forever if we wanted to, whether by using relative pronouns or prepositions or other grammatical tools (or their equivalents in signed languages) to expand a simple sentence. *The man hit the ball* is a sentence consisting of a noun phrase (the man), and a verb phrase (hit the ball). Within the verb phrase is the object, another noun phrase (the ball). We can go on to extend the sentence forever, taking the listener in any direction we wish but always following the rules of arrangement. Adding *into the outfield* gives the sentence a prepositional phrase and expands its verb phrase, creating *hit the ball into the outfield*, and so on. Deaf people can, of course, do exactly the same thing in signed languages, following their rules of arrangement. Chomsky's analysis and the analyses of other linguists have evolved significantly since *Syntactic Structures* was written, but the search for the character and origin of our language faculty, and the study of how the brain formulates the rules governing language production, are as intense and intriguing today as when Chomsky posited the existence of these structures in 1957.[3]

Chomsky's behaviorist predecessors held the view that we learn language and its rules from our mothers, and then from further external observation and education. But Chomsky found their "corpus" of any given language woefully inadequate as a subject of study because all languages offer an infinite variety of sentences. He thinks that the behaviorist approach, which emphasizes the role of the environment in shaping human behavior, is intellectually impoverished. His own work represents a profound break with the mainstream thinking of linguists and anthropologists of the mid-nineteenth century. He invites us to consider whether we are merely creatures shaped by experience or are endowed with a linguistic cognitive structure common to us as human beings, and only to us. His invitation suggests that our language faculty defines us as humans, giving us a soul in the age of science that (though Chomsky does not expressly say so) is an important underpinning of our rights as individuals.

Auguste Bébian, ever before his time, was referring to his own early conception of Chomsky's "linguistic cognitive structure" when he observed that "we all carry the same timeless and limitless principle within us." It is that of our first language, whether spoken or signed. That language is a reflection of our sensations, a relief of our impressions, an intimate connection to our ideas "born in the brain."[4] He meant not so much the first language itself, but the way we all take to it, whether a signed language or English, Dutch, or Seminole—the way Diderot took to French as "the most exact" of all languages.

Chomsky and Stokoe had an opportunity to discuss the language faculty in 1978 while they were attending a lecture together in Chicago. Susan Goldin-Meadow of the University of Chicago was presenting the results of her study of individual Deaf children (from separate, unconnected families) who had never been exposed to a language. Each child was born into a household of hearing parents who, insisting that he or she be raised orally, refused to expose the child to sign language. Each child could understand little of the English spoken to him or her, could produce only a few single words, and could not combine words in sentences.

Goldin-Meadow found, nevertheless, that each of the children had developed his or her own gestural "communications system," just as Helen Keller had done well before meeting Anne Sullivan. Each system had the properties of the early spoken language of hearing children, including consistent ordering of elements ("jar twist blow" [bubbles]), as in Bébian's "this table I strike" (object + subject + verb), an equal proportion of transitive and intransitive sentences, and recursion—which is the expression, as in the case of our ball driven into the outfield of Yankee stadium, of more than one proposition within a single statement. She established that the children were not copying or inferring a system from their parents' natural kinesic movements (gestures accompanying speech), and concluded that a child has the power to develop a system of communication with language-like properties without being exposed to authentic language systems, whether oral or gestural.[5]

During the lecture Chomsky and Stokoe scribbled their thoughts to each other in an exchange that (unsurprisingly) displays MIT's celebrated linguist as an unsparing interlocutor:

STOKOE: The . . . children got zero language input but a great deal of face-to-face interaction [with the interviewers] who attended to their gestures and [were] willing to learn their system.

CHOMSKY: This is a standard fallacy. The fact that a certain condition C [Communication] is necessary for some function F [the language faculty] to develop tells one [virtually] nothing at all about the biological determinants of F.

STOKOE: Right, but most deaf children of such parents get no credit at all for making sense . . .

CHOMSKY: It doesn't seem to me that the question is one of "giving credit," but of finding out what in fact is innate—i.e., what is the genotype, i.e. what is the function that maps experience into

steady state attained . . . Surely no one doubts that deaf children
are genotypical = [equal] in relevant respects to hearing children.

STOKOE: [True, there is] a complex kind of stimulation that allows
the innate pattern to unfold in behavior . . .

CHOMSKY: Exactly. It seems to me that this is suggestive support for
the assumption that the human language faculty is a species-spe-
cific genetically determined organ, much like [for example] the
cat's visual system.[6]

The "structures" that Stokoe had in mind in "Sign Language
Structure" and that Chomsky posited in *Syntactic Structures* were, of
course, not at all the same. Stokoe studied the structure of American
Sign Language much as an anthropologist would empirically explore
the components of a language that he sensed, and came to know and
to demonstrate, was one the hearing world had forgotten. While most
of the discoveries of the complex rules of signed-language syntax were
to be made by his successors, Stokoe had no doubt they existed.

Chomsky's "structures" included both the structure of the brain's
syntactical faculty and the structure of language that this faculty pro-
duces and interprets. But what is central here, and Stokoe was acutely
aware of this, is the importance, for the Deaf, of Chomsky's fundamental
theories for the Deaf. They provided the Deaf with a level playing field
or, as Stokoe put it, were "making it possible for modern linguists to see
both spoken and signed languages as coming from the brain."[7] Victor
Hugo had touched on the point in 1845 when, as we have seen, he wrote
to Berthier, "what matters deafness of the ear, when the mind hears," as
had Lamartine when he wrote in his poem to Pierre Pélissier that light
for the Deaf makes sense (or senses) of itself, enabling the eye to hear
and the hand to speak. Augustine advanced the same suggestion
when he wrote that both speech and gesture "pertain to the soul." Stokoe

was no doubt certain when he began his work that the language centers of the brain function in comparable fashion in the hearing and the Deaf, but with the help of Chomsky's thought and his own perseverance (Berthier's term), Stokoe and others were able to seize upon the idea, and ultimately to prove it, just as Berthier had predicted in 1840 (though he was referring to the advancement of the groundwork laid by Bébian): "Surely this interesting work will, sooner or later, stimulate a general competition of essays and investigations, throwing a powerful light on the study of human understanding as well as on a host of questions hitherto regarded as insuperably difficult."[8]

Stokoe's work has been accompanied by a large body of scholarship by both linguists and experimental neuroscientists. The late Edward Klima of the University of California and his wife, Ursula Bellugi of the Salk Institute, became pioneers in the study of the neural activity of the brains of the Deaf while they are addressing each other. Their work and that of many others have shaped our current way of thinking about and understanding language.

It is now relatively clear, as observed earlier, that when Deaf people render or interpret signed languages, they are using regions of the brain comparable to those the hearing do when they speak and listen to speech. For years linguists and others have been unable to come to terms with what signed languages really are, because their signal is not sound. They have been circuitously called a "manual-visual delivery system for language," a means of communication "fully comparable to speech," the "manifestation of language in the visual modality," a "truly linguistic communicative activity" (Stokoe's words), a "gestural-visual system . . . in a modality different from . . . spoken languages," and a "speech-like cerebral activity."[9]

Following a 1965 lecture in which Noam Chomsky defined language as "a specific sound-meaning correspondence," Klima and

Bellugi, who were in the audience, asked him where that left "the sign languages of the deaf." With scarcely a moment's reflection, Chomsky said that sound was not an essential ingredient of language, and revised his definition of language on the spot, calling it "a specific *signal*-meaning correspondence."[10] Just as a system of symbols doesn't have to be vocal in order to constitute a language, so it needn't be vocal in order to be speech. The word is currently defined in Webster's as meaning "uttered by the voice," and is derived, of course, from the Latin *vox, vocis*. The word *language* is itself derived from *lingus*, tongue, in Latin, and every signed language is itself a tongue. Computers are said to "speak" without human voices, and eyes can be said to "speak" volumes.

A Deaf child raised with a signed language is not simply learning a "gestural" language, but is learning to speak and listen to his own tongue. Both the hearing and the Deaf use bodily or oral gestures to speak: in the case of the Deaf, these consist of configurations made with gestures and expressions, and in the case of the hearing, they comprise movements of the mouth, tongue, teeth, and vocal cords. But the fact that one language is heard and the other seen should not be a distinction that renders one speech and the other not. Though Stokoe and his successors never explicitly said so, signed languages are not simply "linguistic communicative activities." They are speech itself. Deaf people themselves have often expressly said so. Berthier, for example, praised "the language that our ancestors spoke, that our children will continue to speak."[11] And Emmanuelle Laborit exclaimed of a Deafblind woman signing to her, "She is speaking to me!"[12] We are all participants in a single commerce of souls, regardless of whether the ideas we speak and hear are the offspring of the air we breathe or of the light we see.

12

Milan Is Still, and Always, Today

In spite of the advances in linguistics and neuroscience in the mid- to late twentieth century, proponents of teaching in oral languages remained in control of Deaf education throughout the period, as they had in the preceding century. We may call signed languages "speech" or what we will, but they continue to be unwelcome as the instrument of instruction for the Deaf.

If you go to the Visitors Center at Gallaudet University, which serves principally applicants and their families, you will find a pictorial history of Deaf people, but not a single photograph of or word about William Stokoe. As Lou Fant of Gallaudet has written, "I don't think Gallaudet [University] has ever appreciated what Bill did. They shoved him around, cut off funds for his research, and breathed a sigh of relief when he retired. Oh, they pay him lip service, but look at it . . . Gallaudet still does not require ASL fluency from its faculty . . . Why should the college demand that students be fluent in English, yet not hold the faculty to the same standard with regard to fluency in ASL? . . . Whatever prestige resulted from Bill's work must go to him, not to the university . . . People do not look to Gallaudet anymore for new information or research on ASL. There is no marker or monument on campus extolling Bill and his work. Gallaudet . . . didn't and still doesn't deserve Bill."[1] Stokoe of course became a notable among linguists and others, had tenure and remained at Gallaudet until his retirement, but at times he must have been tempted, like Bébian with his ancient trousseau of keys, to hit someone over the head with his moviola.

With advances throughout the twentieth century in the quality of hearing aids, designed to amplify speech, most Deaf children were still being forced to wear them despite their inability to hear virtually anything. During this period the methods of Ponce and Pereire resurfaced in the guise of what the Americans and British call *speech therapy*, the French refer to as *orthophonie*, and the Belgians and the French Swiss call *logopédie*. The methods were wholly unsuccessful, and the language faculties of these young Deaf children, at an age when they would have been most receptive to the language that came to the children naturally, lay dormant.

Moreover, as we have seen from William Stokoe's experience at Gallaudet, new techniques appeared in the 1960s and 1970s that were reminiscent of the "methodical" signs of the abbé de l'Épée in the eighteenth century. Signed English and its cousins abroad (in France it is called *français signé*), as well as a variety of other domestic and foreign signing systems, were born of the unwillingness or inability of teachers of the Deaf, who were often required by law to be able to hear, to learn signed languages themselves. These systems, which are not languages, use the root signs of ASL, LSF, BSL, and so on, place them in spoken word order, and add invented symbols for features of speech like tense, number, pronouns, prepositions, and conjunctions. One scholar has correctly observed that signed French is nothing more than a later version of l'Épée's methodical signs, which were debunked by Bébian a century and a half ago.[2]

In 1975, for example, fifteen years after Stokoe's "Sign Language Structure" appeared, a conference of French teachers of the Deaf adopted a resolution refusing "as a point of honor" to learn French sign language. Ignorant of its morphology and syntax, they announced that they were unwilling to use a language that would make them feel "like little negro children saying 'Candy Mammy give.' " Indeed, the systems these teachers prefer are little more than speech accompanied by manually coded signals to fortify lipreading (or so they say), but in fact they reinforce their own way of looking at things and allow them to avoid having to learn another, better method.[3]

The grammar and syntax of signed languages are born of their gestural character. To attempt to borrow their vocabulary and place them in spoken or mouthed English or French (or any other oral system) results in gibberish. The signs are there, but context are meaning they of lose out they their because. They lose their meaning because they are out of context. Even Virgil's elegant phrases become primitive in strictly literal translation: "To become all still and intent and now they held"; or "arms of a man and I sing of Troy who first from the coasts to Italy, by fate driven, Lavinia and came to the shore."[4] While one might love to fall into the arms of fate-driven Lavinia, she is not what she seems. Proust becomes almost unrecognizable: "Longtime I me am to bed of good hour. By time at pain my candle out, my eyes them closed so quickly that I not had no the time to me to say, 'I me in sleep.' "[5]

The problem of Deaf education in the twentieth century—and it had been a problem since at least 1880—has perhaps best been explained by Emmanuelle Laborit. Speech therapists insisted that Emmanuelle as a young child, born Deaf, be allowed neither to sign nor to meet children or adults who did. She was sent to an oral school, where for hours she formed the lip movements of the same word, over and over again "like a little monkey." In 1979, when she was six years old, her father, a psychiatrist, could see that she wasn't learning anything. He brought her to two Americans he had seen on French television, Alfredo Corrado who was Deaf, and William Moody who was hearing; they both signed ASL and LSF fluently. They had managed to rekindle French interest in signed languages and in the Deaf theater in France, although, like Stokoe and others, they had been unable to make any dent in the French teaching system. When Emmanuelle met Corrado, he seemed to her an impossibility:

> —The man is deaf.
> —He has no hearing aid.
> —He's *alive*.[6]

"It took me some time," she writes, "to understand this triple peculiarity." The only Deaf human beings she had seen until that time were her peers, since she was not allowed to see Deaf adults. In fact she had concluded that she and all of her Deaf schoolmates were going to die before growing up, a common belief among orally educated Deaf children. Her astonishment was twofold: "I was nothing less than stupefied when I saw that my father could understand what one man's hands were saying in the other's mouth. I didn't know that day that I was going to have a language thanks to them. But I came away with the formidable revelation that Emmanuelle was going to live to grow up! That, I could see with my own eyes."[7]

When Corrado gave Emmanuelle her first class in LSF, with other Deaf students, she was astonished. First came the signs, *house, eat, drink, sleep, table, Papa, Maman, daughter*. A miming of *You are the daughter of Papa*, followed by the phrase in sign. A search for someone, a crouch, a hand at the forehead as if shielding the sun, followed by the sign—the question *Where?*, palm up, hand cupped and moving rapidly sideways, back and forth, lips pursed. *Maman*, Helen's sign as a young untutored child, a single hand, a touch of the cheek. Then, *Maman, where?* The hand forms both signs at once, the phrase

Emmanuelle Laborit, born in 1971 (Photograph by
Arnaud Baumann. Courtesy of SIPA Press.)

in a small single swoop in space, subject, adverb, verb understood.
And who was Emmanuelle?—"I became aware for the first time that
you give names to people. This was fantastic. I had no idea anyone in
my family had a name, apart from Papa and Maman. I would meet
people, friends of my parents, members of the family, none of whom,
for me, had a name; they remained undefined. I was surprised to discover that one was called Alfredo, the other one Bill.—And I, especially, I, Emmanuelle. I understood at last that I had an identity. I:
Emmanuelle."

She taught her younger (hearing) sister sign language, and her
sister learned to switch "with astonishing facility" from oral French to
LSF, giving Emmanuelle immense pleasure and a sense of pride. She

came to know herself and to develop her own voice—"My voice, I do not know it . . . [Nor do I know] my mother's voice. One can't miss what one doesn't know. I don't know the song of birds or the sound of waves . . . or the sound of a frying egg! What is the sound of a frying egg? I can try to imagine it, in my own way, the sizzling is something that undulates, it is hot. Hot, yellow and white, undulating. I don't miss the sound. My eyes do the work. My mind is surely more fertile, though I am a child, than that of others. Just a bit disorganized . . . I am not handicapped. I am deaf. I have a language, I have friends who speak it, and I have parents who speak it."

Helen Keller, too, despite her almost unimaginable double difficulty, could, with her intellect and imagination, have had such a voice. With sign language teachers she would not have written of the colors and sounds of abstract pastoral scenes observed and heard through Anne's eyes and ears—instead she would have wondered about the same fried egg. Hot, spraying droplets on a hand held over it. Soft and greasy, two different tastes and textures. No yellow, no white, no undulation. But sizzling, as Helen could have tried to imagine it, in her own way.

Laborit had to continue her oral classes in order to obtain her French baccalaureate, but Moody and Corrado took her under their wing, and she learned LSF fluently. Once she learned it, she was able to express her ideas in written French, and in the French she had been forced to speak, far more easily. She later became one of France's leading actresses. When I saw her as Cordelia one night in Paris in *King Lear*, Laborit held the public spellbound as she approached her father and her hands moved effortlessly, gracefully, signing no longer *where is Maman, Maman is at home* but uttering Cordelia's ill-fated declaration of measured love for her father, "You have begot me, bred me, loved me: I return those duties back as are right fit, obey you, love you, and most honor you. Why have my sisters husbands if they say they love you all? When I shall wed, that lord whose hand must take my plight shall carry half my love with him, half my care and duty."[8]

Laborit would be among the first to say that very few Deaf children have had her own good fortune in being rescued by a father, a Corrado, a Moody. I have known some, notably the daughter of an American diplomat, Deaf from birth and raised in her own language, whose hearing parents and siblings have helped to weave her into what Bébian calls the gentlest knot of society by learning ASL along with her. The young woman communicates with me by sharing a keyboard, like many I know at Gallaudet, as fluent in written English as I am. She is linked to the rest of the world by webcam in ASL, and by words she reads and eloquently writes, in this way being a full participant in Bébian's commerce of souls. Most Deaf students, because sign language is not their medium of instruction, are taught practically nothing under our teaching systems, and are virtually illiterate. Studies of British "experts" on Deaf education in the late twentieth century write that "developing deaf pupils' ability to communicate, preferably in an oral way, is the central goal of deaf education . . . Language development [*sic*] must be the central facet of the educational program."[9]

A French study published in 2007 stated unabashedly that "the policy regarding the management of profound deafness in childhood in France . . . emphasizes an oral/aural communication mode and mainstreaming."[10] This in the face of a 1998 study of the Deaf in France which found that "of the profoundly deaf 80% are illiterate and only 5% reach university." France reacted to the study by passing a law in 2005 expressly stating that Deaf children have a "right" to be educated in sign language, but the law has not been implemented by decree.[11] The author of the 1998 report recently stated that no funds were available to implement it, and none would be.[12] The educational establishment in the West, which is composed almost exclusively of hearing people, has shown mystifying stubbornness in the face of failure. Fifty years ago a leading educator wrote that insofar as the oral systems in Great Britain and the United States are concerned, "the major conclusion that can be drawn from a thorough investigation of the literature on the education of the deaf is bluntly that it has failed."[13] In the United States today, the average Deaf eighteen-year-old writes on a level comparable to that of a hearing eight-year-old.[14]

Even students considered relative "successes" in oralist programs are failures as communicative human beings. David Wright, a South African raised for the most part in England, profoundly deafened post-lingually by scarlet fever at age seven, graduated from Oxford in 1942. He may have retained some slight residual hearing. He turned to poetry, and announces proudly that "my life after I left Oxford had less and less to do with deafness and deafness less and less to do with my life," but about that later life he tells us nothing. Throughout the life he does tell us about, he has great difficulty understanding people whom he doesn't know. Even those he does know are difficult to understand, including his public school tutor ("one of the many people I could never learn to lipread"), his tutor at Oriel College ("unable to lipread the man, I would not admit it but pretended to understand"), a classmate and fellow poet at Oxford—and probably everyone else ("I have never reached a high standard of lipreading").

Wright, who could speak as a child, retained his speech through years and years of hard work, but did not converse naturally by mouth, because he couldn't hear what others were saying. He had no knowledge of British Sign Language, or of the prelingually Deaf, and he praises what he sees as the victory of oralism in 1880 in startlingly glowing terms. He writes that, after the Congress of Milan, "all countries, with the exception of the United States [*sic*], adopted the oral method as the preferred system of instruction. Governments were spurred into beginning to take on the responsibility of financing and supervising the education of the deaf. In a moment of euphoria, the resolutions passed by the Conference were described by one of the English delegation as 'the deaf child's Magna Carta.' Perhaps it was not an exaggeration."[15]

As we have seen, Milan was rather the oralists' carte blanche, for the Deaf were not welcome at the conference. The sociologist Bernard Mottez notes that in France 95 percent of the Deaf from birth are scholastic failures, and rarely even graduate from high school. He observes that the academic failure of the Deaf is due to the denial, by the hearing, of the right of the Deaf to be taught in their own language by Deaf teachers. France, he emphasizes, has remained faithful to oralist orthodoxy since the Congress of Milan.[16]

It is true that about 5 percent of children born Deaf have Deaf parents and, thanks to them, become fluent in their natural tongue. But the 95 percent born to hearing parents are able to learn sign language only from their peers in the schoolyards of their integrated or mainstream schools or in special courses given by Deaf adults who are not their schoolteachers. Signed languages are not embraced by our schools for the education of our Deaf children.

Today the system remains unchanged, but the argument has shifted substantially. The oral education of the Deaf continues its predominance in Europe and the United States. Bébian's system was broken by Milan and has remained so ever since. But as we are about to see, oral education is now justified no longer for reasons of religion, nation, progress, race, or the other arguments of the past, but on the basis of the development of cochlear implants, which are said to enable Deaf children, to some degree, to hear and speak.

13

Language in Electrons

As we have seen, the system of progressive Deaf education in Europe and the United States, established in the early nineteenth century, was effectively broken several decades later. Moreover, it has stayed broken. The remarkable of work of William Stokoe and others has not fundamentally changed the dramatic educational difficulties that Deaf children still confront today.

Most Deaf children go to mainstream schools, are "educated" orally, and are assisted by interpreters who use manually coded systems. As we have seen, none of these systems is a language. Some Deaf students are educated in ASL at Gallaudet's Kendall School, at Gallaudet University itself, at Rochester Technical Institute, and elsewhere, but they are the few.

At Saint Jacques in Paris, while a number of subjects are still taught in French sign language, few teachers are fluent in LSF. In the high school, the teaching medium also tends to be a mix (cued speech, signed French, LSF), because of the varying linguistic profiles of the older children and the paucity of fluent teachers. The overall direction at the school appears to be oral. The notion is that a Deaf child taught spoken French will have greater access to the French language than will a child taught in LSF. For the earliest classes (roughly, kindergarten or younger through age seven), the linguistic emphasis is emphatically oral. There is an unspoken idea that LSF is more a teacher's tool than an integral, reciprocal method of teaching and learning. This misunderstanding is Bébian upside down, in his own school, the birthplace of Deaf education.

A few years ago, on a cool spring day, I passed through the gates of Saint Jacques as usual, ready to cross its quiet courtyard on my way to the library. But on this day the silence in the courtyard was deafening. It was one of those mornings Dickens describes, common in spring, when the young year courts summer in the sunshine and lingers with winter in the shade.[1] There were more than two hundred people gathered there, all angry, all signing, responding to a speech being given by one of their leaders. He was standing in front of the statue of the abbé de l'Épée and his young bronze charges. The speaker was signing in the sun, condemning the school, the government, and Deaf education. Five of the protesters were engaged in a hunger strike and had been sheltered from the lingering winter in a large room inside the school.

I was approached by one of the young women I recognized, about twenty years old and far more handsome than any painting I've seen of the Duchesse de Berry. She passed me a leaflet setting forth the demands of the hunger strikers: "We the deaf proclaim ourselves to be in the final season of our discontent. With the mainstreaming of the deaf, with our oralization, with the planting of electrodes in our heads, with the mediocrity of our teaching, with our inability to communicate with the signless professionals who confront us . . . We demand the full and unqualified recognition of our language by the Government. In reality, what are these laws that are supposed to have been passed for our benefit? Has the teaching of our language been encouraged and developed? Are more classes given in sign? No. Quite the contrary: Mainstreaming and implants are practiced on a massive scale."[2] These claims were not dissimilar to those asserted by the students at Gallaudet when they demanded, and obtained, their first Deaf president of the university in 1988, and those of Emmanuelle Laborit a few years ago, when she pointed out that the laws supposedly benefiting the Deaf were empty envelopes.

The introduction of the cochlear implant toward the end of the twentieth century has become a critical part of the educational equation, particularly in the context of the breakdown of the nineteenth-century system. Hearing professionals report that the development and improvement of the cochlear implant have led to "a paradigm shift" in the medical treatment of deafness. Today about 80 percent of infants born Deaf in the West are implanted.[3] Whether cochlear implants have brought about a comparable change in the circumstances and lives of these children is a separate question.

The issues are dauntingly complex because the exposure of a Deaf child to sign language and the teaching of speech after implantation are, in the minds of most hearing professionals, mutually exclusive propositions. While a child could become fluent in a signed language naturally and easily, doctors and speech therapists (and anxious hearing parents), as well as the manufacturers of the implants, discourage it because after the device is implanted, it takes a great deal of time and effort to learn to speak and to try to hear and lipread with it.

Juan Pablo Bonet had the same concerns, as we have seen, some four hundred years ago, in 1620. The practice of his art of teaching the Deaf to speak required such concentration on the part of the students, and sign language was such an easy way out for them, that "it was important never to let the mute use it." Similarly, the final resolution adopted by the Congress of Milan in 1880 held that "the simultaneous use of speech and signs has the disadvantage of being prejudicial to speech." The use of a signed language cannot, of course, be prejudicial to itself. But the perception that it is a form of speech has seldom been seriously articulated, from the time of Milan to our own day, and has seldom if ever been the view of the medical community. Indeed, while doctors, psychologists, and speech therapists are, or should be, fully cognizant of the fact that signed languages are the surest and quickest path to the mind of a Deaf child, they remain as indifferent to the reality as were Ponce, Bonet, Pereire, Amman, and Alexander Graham Bell.

As a matter of common policy and practice there may be little or no opportunity left for these children to learn and use a signed language: today "clinicians usually emphasize the importance of spoken language skills for children with cochlear implants, and there are many anecdotal reports of centers refusing to implant children unless their parents agree to provide oral-only educational placements." Nor is it a simple matter to master a signed language in later years. Many pediatric patients have spent much of their childhoods developing oral and aural skills—time that, for at least some, may have come at the cost of developing actual language ability. As these children grow older, their capacity to learn a signed language fluently will diminish, not having been triggered at the critical early age. For those who devised the cochlear implant early-intervention programs in Australia, however, this is not much of a concern. In their view, signing "is anathema" because "it hinders oral skill development."[4]

The overall reaction of the Deaf community, which was originally caught off guard by the promotion of these new devices, has been one of skepticism and fear. Added to their uncertainty is their physical inability to make meaningful judgments about whether or to what extent these devices do, in fact, make children speakers and hearers. As Ferdinand Berthier so aptly observed, the Deaf don't have the ability to compare speech to their own language.[5]

Cochlear implants are not hearing aids, which amplify sound. The implants instead send electronic signals directly to the auditory nerve. A plethora of statistics, studies, and medical and paramedical opinions have been used to attempt to quantify the effectiveness of the implants. Their efficacy is generally measured by a statistical analysis of scores on a variety of word tests performed in a clinic or laboratory.

The first experiment with a cochlear implant was done, suitably enough, in Paris over a half century ago. André Djourno and Charles Eyriès performed the experiment in 1957. Their device directly stimulated the auditory nerve using a single electrode. While the device ultimately failed, for a time their (late-deafened) patient was able to distinguish between tones at high frequency (which he said were like "silk ripping") and low frequency ("burlap tearing"). But he was unable to understand speech.[6]

About twenty years later, in 1978, the Australian Graeme Clark pioneered a significant advance in the technology when he developed the first cochlear implant using multiple electrodes.[7] Since Clark's time, implants have become increasingly sophisticated. The implant is designed to send electrical signals resembling those of speech and other sounds to the extensions or fibers of the hearing nerve located in the center of the cochlea, bypassing the dead or moribund hair cells (see Chapter 2 and Appendix 1 for discussions of the internal ear). Annual industry sales currently amount to over $5 billion. As of early 2013, approximately 324,000 people worldwide had received implants. In the United States, roughly 58,000 adults and 38,000 children had been implanted.[8]

Today's cochlear implant has several components: (1) an outside microphone designed to capture speech (and other sound) and convert it to electric current, (2) an outside speech processor that receives the electric current from the microphone, compresses it into workable levels of electricity, breaks it down or "filters" it into as many as twenty-two separate frequency bands, adjusts or "maps" these filter outputs to the patient's electric current thresholds and noise-comfort levels, and sends the data to (3) an outside headpiece with a radio transmitter that sends the information by radio waves to (4) a receiver-stimulator implanted in the skull, which in turn converts the radio waves back into electric current and sends the current by wire to (5) a bundle of electrodes, which are platinum plates embedded in a silicone coil that is threaded into the upwardly spiraling path of the cochlea. Only items (4) and (5) are implanted inside the head. The headpiece (3) is worn on the head and is held in place, through the skin, by a magnet on the implanted receiver-stimulator. The speech processor (2) is worn behind the ear like a hearing aid or in a larger version on the belt.

In order to implant the electrodes in the cochlea, a section of the mastoid bone behind the ear is removed and a depression is made in the parietal bone behind and above it to make a bed for the receiver-stimulator. The surgeon then pierces the membrane of the round window, and threads the silicone coil containing the electrodes into slightly more than a full turn of the cochlea's lower chamber (scala tympani). In the course of the operation the cochlea's epithelial (hearing) cells are destroyed. The receiver-stimulator, to which the coil of electrodes is attached, is then placed in its bed in the skull.

It had been thought until recently that the number of electrodes in the coil would be substantially increased over time—to thirty or more, in order to multiply the responses of the cochlear nerve fibers. But in fact additional electrodes, beyond twenty-two or so, appear not to help. It is now hoped that the quality of the mapping done by

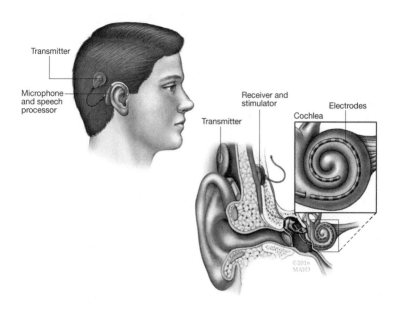

Cochlear implant (Used by permission of Mayo Foundation for Medical Education and Research. All rights reserved.)

the outside speech processor, and the interpretation of the resulting signals by the brain, particularly when the child is young and the language faculty is at its strongest, is what will count. Much, perhaps, like my mind's adaptation to lyricals as a child—though, unlike these children, I had a significant amount of residual hearing to work with.

Cochlear implants afford help to those who have fluently spoken and heard before, and then become deaf without having lost their ability to speak. The Massachusetts Eye and Ear Infirmary states generally that "the improvement in auditory perception (hearing) following cochlear implantation varies widely from patient to patient. Nearly all patients have some perception of sound. Even if this awareness is only the detection of the presence or absence of a sound in the environment, it can be a substantial aid to lipreading. In most cases, implantees have some additional ability to discriminate pitch and loudness, which further enhances the benefit of the device. In a limited number of patients, the implant may even provide good enough hearing to permit use of the telephone."[9]

Though it takes hard work and years of training with speech therapists, the signals sent to the auditory nerve may be sufficient to enable those who have heard before to hear like those who are severely deaf at all frequencies, and at times better to the extent their brains are able to relate the signals they receive to the speech they remember. Even I have difficulty lipreading and deciphering lyricals, though with hearing aids I capture most vowels and at times some consonants.

But a person severely deaf at all frequencies, apart from people like the few whom Bonet found with a sixth sense for it (rare according to the jurists), will have great difficulty lipreading, even with a hearing aid. The detection of a "sound in the environment" will hardly suffice. It is difficult to measure the performance of these implanted people meaningfully because speech therapists tend to focus on discrete one-word or one-sentence-at-a-time tests, in quiet settings, rather than on conversational capability. People who have been speaking all their lives are shown announcing to the camera that they can hear again. Uninitiated observers tend to equate the hearing of these subjects with the quality of their speech, and to assume that both have triumphed. Implanted patients are never shown in an unrehearsed conversational environment.

Many of these patients do welcome the ability to capture sound once more, although they do not again become (as they once were) an integral part of the hearing world. They fare far less well than I do with my hearing aids. Speech is nonetheless their language. They speak well, and it is generally too late in life for them to develop any fluency in sign language. In any event that is usually far from what they want, for to late-deafened adults in general a signed language is a symbol of Deafness, the language of what David Wright in 1989 called "a linguistic ghetto," the language of an alien world.[10]

The implantation of prelingually (usually congenitally) Deaf children, by contrast, raises the critical, far more difficult, and controversial questions. When the first experiments were done in the 1970s, on children who had been born Deaf and had been so for years, the results were disappointing. In an effort to improve outcomes, children were implanted earlier in life. Infants twelve months old and younger are now being implanted. A recent trial at New York University found that implantation in children as young as six months was safe. The notion is that the implants will begin to function at the beginning of the critical age for the child's development of language, which as we have learned, ranges from about six months to three or four years of age and, in diminishing fashion, on to about age twelve.

"Deaf children," according to an article in the *New England Journal of Medicine*, are now developing "language skills similar to those of hearing children." The National Institutes of Health reports: "Studies have . . . shown that eligible children who receive a cochlear implant at a young age develop language skills at a rate comparable to children with normal hearing, and many succeed in mainstream classrooms." A director of research at a California university reports that "results with the cochlear implant are astounding."[11] The inventor Graeme Clark praises the implant as the first major advance for the deaf since sign language was "developed 200 years ago [*sic*] . . . by the abbé de l'Épée at the Paris Deaf School."[12] Clark and two others were awarded the highly regarded Lasker-DeBakey Clinical Medical Research Award in 2013 for their work on cochlear implants. Clark's colleague at the University of Melbourne has observed that "after refining the cochlear device, we see children with just one implant [who] have come to have the same social, educational and vocational opportunities as their normal-hearing peers, an outcome undreamed of in the past."[13]

The Alexander Graham Bell Association states that "current research . . . substantiates that children who receive implant(s) at an early age can demonstrate impressive growth in spoken language and literacy achievement comparable to the levels of their peers with typical hearing." One academic paper asserts that sign language and residential schools for the Deaf (beginning with the Hartford School in 1817) had resulted in "assortative mating" (marrying someone like yourself) and a proliferation of Deaf people. Now, they contend, the introduction of cochlear-implant technology is profoundly altering the "mating structure" of the Deaf population. Because the implants facilitate oral communication and educational mainstreaming, they assert, substantially all the Deaf children of hearing parents will—I imagine like a stray gaggle of geese alighted upon some Great Lake— be redirected into "the hearing mating pool."[14]

A 2011 final summary of a ten-year study of children with implants in France described results that were "clearly more positive" than those of an earlier study of the same children at the end of the first five years (in 2006), "with real progress in the acquisition of language and the production of speech" during the second five years.[15] One report has stated that after six months of implantation, children "reach the same linguistic performance" as normally hearing children. In 1993 a doctor at the University of Southern California claimed that "the cochlear prosthesis on which I have worked for years . . . will inevitably lead to the extinction of the alternative culture of the Deaf, probably within a decade."[16] Similarly, thirteen years later, one writer observed that "technology has decisively shifted the balance of power in the oralists' favor." He added that "the signing deaf community will last another generation or two, but already it is seeing the signs on the wall."[17] Presumably in Roman characters. While the praise for cochlear implants is often fulsome, if not at times ambiguous (what is "linguistic performance"?), these terms of elimination and disappearance, and of "mating" practices, evoke the memory of Bell's observation over a century ago that the oral system of teaching was bringing about the "near extinction" of the system of signs.[18] As well as Frank Sanborn's statement at the time that "there are still [deaf mutes] in Boston, but they are a decreasing class, and it is not expedient to increase them."[19]

The arguments proferred in favor of cochlear implants are numerous. First, the history of the Deaf is admittedly a terrible history, throughout which people who couldn't hear at all were given the virtually impossible tasks of trying to speak and read lips. But that is not the world of today. These children are learning to speak and to hear. Not like normally hearing children, but implant-technology is expected to improve, as it has in the past. Moreover, even if one were to agree with the perception that signed languages are speech, or a form of speech, they are not the speech of the world at large, into which it is the proper goal of medicine, science, and the hearing parents of these Deaf children to integrate them, both in school and in their later personal and professional lives.

Second, the alternative is to embed these children in a minimal society and to give them, in 95 percent of the cases, a language different from that of their parents. Deaf people who use sign language comprise only about 500,000 to one million people in the United

States, less than 0.25 percent of our population of over 320 million. They would not be able to understand teachers who spoke, and there are not enough qualified and available sign language teachers to go around. In the workplace, the same problems will arise, both at the training stage and, if they succeed at being trained, in performing their jobs as well in a society that hears and speaks and whose language is the spoken language of the country they live in.

Third, hearing parents of Deaf children are understandably driven, as they have been in the past, to make their children "normal," "hearing," able to live "in the broader world," and, of course, like themselves. They are reluctant to surrender their child to the world of the Deaf and to sign language—to the more productive side of the classroom, perhaps, but also to the potential control of others, to a language the parents do not know, and to a world of no spoken language, to a life of silence. In several parents' words: "For us the objective is . . . that the implant permit the *normal* inclusion, the *normal* scholarity [of our child] so that he can be integrated with other children, that he be taught in a school that is entirely *normal* . . . that he emerge from it like . . . all the other children." "Our goal was that he not be rejected." "Since we have chosen oralism, we wanted [our child] to be integrated in a *normal* school, that she live like hearing children knowing all the while that she will always be deaf and have a deaf identity." "[We wish] to offer our child a chance to communicate with us. That he be able to live *normally* with others." "[We wanted] our child to communicate with everyone and not just with *people like him.*"[20]

"Most often it is the doctors (60% of the time) or the speech therapists (20%) who are the first to suggest [the implant]," and the implant is usually done.[21] Thus, however difficult and time-consuming the search for articulated speech becomes, the fact is that the parental and medical quest for this outcome will trump the child's fluency in the minority language.

There are, however, numerous studies, statistics, and arguments that point in quite a different direction. Many contend that the efficacy of cochlear implants in bringing these children into the hearing world is a matter of considerable doubt. In the United Kingdom, children with cochlear implants have been found to have the same educational placement profile as same-age severely deaf children with hearing aids. Medical staff at the University of Toronto found in December 2007 that the performance of children using cochlear implants on tests of spoken language "was not different from that of children [using hearing aids] with a hearing threshold of 90 to 100 dB at all frequencies." The Center for Deaf Children at Boston's Children's Hospital reports that "children who use cochlear implants (as with children who use hearing aids) experience significant difficulty listening and learning in classroom environments with background noise and typical classroom commotion."[22] The ten-year French study referred to earlier reported that implanted children had difficulty understanding words in normal environments (in background noise) and great difficulty understanding their teachers in a classroom.[23]

The National Institutes of Health, while praising the "language skills" of implanted children in 2013 as noted earlier, cautions that "an implant does not restore normal hearing. Instead, it can give a deaf person a useful representation of sounds in the environment and help him or her to understand speech." Claire Ramsey of the University of California at San Diego writes that the implanted "congenitally deaf child . . . will still have severely impaired hearing and limited speech proficiency."[24] One study noted in 2010, as a common example, a teacher's report that there must be "realistic expectations that [an implanted child is] still a deaf child with an expensive hearing aid . . . [and] not a hearing child." The University of Toronto observes that with "enriched" spoken language environments and ongoing auditory-verbal therapy, the sound the implanted child will hear will become "meaningful" and "will enhance his or her ability to listen, hear, and speak." They observe, however, that the cochlear implant will *not* provide normal hearing, will *not* guarantee intelligible speech or age appropriate language skills, and will *not* guarantee educational success.[25]

As stated in another report, implanted children show "auditory speech perception levels and language skills comparable to those of severely deaf children without hearing aids." Another study showed that children with implants did not differ from peers with hearing aids in the perception of stress and intonation. Julia Sarant of the University of Melbourne reports that prelingually Deaf children in particular perform significantly less well with implants than do other children, writing that "the majority of published evidence supports a significant influence of degree of hearing loss on outcomes for speech perception abilities and language development."[26]

As to comprehensibility, a 2007 ten-year study done by the cochlear implant center at Montpellier, France, found that only twenty-two of eighty-two children developed connected speech intelligible to an average listener, a figure comparable to the speech of Deaf children with hearing aids and intensive oral training. Of the implanted children, 45 percent were in mainstream schools, even though this required enormous effort on the part of the child and his or her family. Problems included difficulties in communication, an inability to understand instructions, a lack of vocabulary, and the need to ask for frequent help and explanation.[27]

As is almost universally the case in these studies, there is no comparison with the linguistic performance (in reading and writing) of

Deaf children who both sign and read and write. Virtually all studies of the children with implants ignore the comparison. In fact, these children appear to fare much better. One study has found that (1) the spoken and written narrative abilities of implanted children lagged significantly behind those of their hearing peers, and (2) both the signed and written narratives of the signing children were of comparable complexity to those of their hearing peers.[28]

These Deaf children, having benefited from Bébian's legacy and learned their own language first with ease, are better able to make the instant translations and syntactical inversions necessary to demonstrate extensive narrative abilities. For many, comparisons of this kind are reminiscent of the words of W. G. Jenkins of Hartford in 1893: "Right under my eyes are two irreconcilable things. Pupils sign-bound, sign-grained reading Dickens . . . and oral pupils unable to read number one and two of our Hartford Readers."[29] By contrast, many in the Deaf community believe that the medical profession is saying "Don't educate these children in their natural language. Operate on them and give them a semblance of ours."

Some accounts of the progress of the children create problems of their own. One manufacturer's report states that after six months of implantation, impaired children reached "the same linguistic performance" as normally hearing children. The "linguistic performance" tests were based solely on interviews of parents, who of course want to attest to their children's progress. They were asked about their children's "changes in vocalization associated with device use," "alertness to sounds," and their ability to "derive meaning from sound," none of which is a measure of "linguistic performance." The results of the parents' interviews were called a "scale," with little or no examination of the children themselves.

Those who devise and administer these studies are generally psychologists, speech therapists, and researchers, none Deaf or partially deaf, with skills that are neither medical nor scientific nor, quite often, as in the 2011 French study referred to above, particularly helpful.[30] The French study also cited, with approval, a statement of the psychologist Helmer Myklebust that the absence of auditory stimulation may give rise to a change in cognitive organization with adverse effects on other perceptive registers.[31] Myklebust is the American psychologist who, as noted in Chapter 10, wrote that deafness led to "deviant emotional and social behavior."

What are we to make of these contrasting voices of praise and criticism of cochlear implants? Has science introduced a modern, workable version of oralism, and overtaken the language, culture, and history of the Deaf? Or are cochlear implants "an expensive hearing aid," a continuation, in the form of a device, of the oralist theories and practices of the past, an extension of the misguided idea that the very faculty Deaf children lacked should be the instrument of their instruction?

14

Picture a Classroom

The central question for these Deaf children, as for all children, comes down to one of belonging, completeness, and happiness. Where will their minds and hearts, as social, communicative human beings, most comfortably reside, now and in their later lives?

It is clear that implanted congenitally and other prelingually Deaf children are not being exposed to speech as hearing children are. The Deaf children are missing 3,478 out of 3,500 hearing channels; the twenty-two they are given in the implant are artificial and imprecise, and do not reflect the extraordinary intricacies of the sound waves of natural speech and their complex processing in the natural ear. As we have seen in Chapter 2 and in Appendix 1, in a normal ear, speech and other sounds are processed first by the eardrum and its connected, delicate and precise middle ear bones before they even arrive at the cochlea. Sound is then processed by the organ of Corti with its endolymph, basilar membrane, sixteen thousand inner and outer hair cells, two million stereocilia, tip links, shears, synapses, and afferent and efferent signals to and from the brain. The implant's twenty-two electrodes are a primitive device by comparison, sending highly degraded, underspecified, and atypical signals to the brain.[1] The implanted children are hearing only a simulacrum of speech.

It is hoped that these signals—along with the help of audiologists, speech therapists, technicians, and others, as well as the capacity of the children's young brains to interpret the signals—will guide them to what is in effect a second language. One recent piece addresses the effort to reach the child's brain: "Cochlear implants . . . involve a biological interface between technology and the human brain. Not only must we find the right way to encode and deliver interpretable information to the brain, we must then find the right way to train the brain to decode and interpret that information."[2]

Since children were first implanted over thirty years ago, in 1985, "studies [have not been] reporting substantial increases in success rates, especially in language development."[3] Noam Chomsky speaks of the poverty of the input when he compares a hearing or signing child's extraordinarily self-enriched production of grammatically organized speech, but here the problem is the poverty of the signals from the implant compared to those produced by the natural ear. For the partially deaf, like myself, the brain's reorganization of lyricals is difficult enough even with the natural hearing, the hair cells and stereocilia, we have left. But where the clarity of the signal is lacking at all frequencies the task is far more difficult:

> Implants fail to give the deaf child the minimal elements necessary for the normal development of language during the three or four first [critical] years of life, however early the implantation and whatever the rigor of speech therapy. Once again, we find the problem of language deficit in the deaf child . . . too often trivialized by professionals and parents dedicated to the ideals of hearing and speech.
>
> Children don't develop the ultra-rapid capacity to master sign simply in order to annoy or disillusion the professionals . . . [They do so because] function trumps the organ. [T]he language faculty . . . uses [the brain's] substrate most suited to

its deployment . . . One of the great difficulties in teaching oral language to a deaf child is that it puts the emphasis on the *signifiers* rather than on the referent (what is signified).[4]

As Bébian wrote, it is the idea (or referent) that has to give the word meaning before the word can, in turn, become an effective interpreter of the idea. The children are also confronted with the problem of the critical difficulty in understanding what is going on around them. As stated in a Swedish study: "The parents stressed that the children needed to look at the person speaking in order to hear what was said. However, in several classes the children with cochlear implants were seated so that they had a good view of the teacher and the assistant but not of the other children, who were seated beside or behind them. This made it difficult for the children with the implant to see and hear what the other children said and what answers they gave to the teacher's questions, which of course affected their ability to follow the teaching."[5]

We are brought at this point full circle to the problem posed by Jean-Marc Itard almost two hundred years ago. First, these children are being taught during their critical years to pronounce and listen to words they need to search for and, second, in doing so, to focus their eyes and minds intently and solely on speech therapists, audiologists, and parents. Their oral instruction needs to be direct, that is, limited to their perception of words addressed solely to them. As a result, as Itard pointed out, their isolation makes normal conversation inaccessible, leaving them in a passive state whenever they are not solely and directly engaged. Itard was speaking not only of profoundly deaf children, but also of severely deaf children with some residual hearing, analogous to our implanted children today.

In Itard's view, what these children needed was the advantage of general discourse, an awareness and understanding of the discussion about them—what others were saying and how they reacted to what they were being told. No spoken language, amplified or implanted, is more analogous to that of the hearing child than a signed language for the Deaf child. None can offer to that child, Itard believed, as does a signed language, the benefit of free, easy, continuous, direct, and indirect communication, not only between the child and his teachers, but also among classmates.

It is only then, he concluded, that, using their own language, their intelligence would flourish with the various combinations of these diverse relationships, as they acquired with ease the ability to express their ideas clearly in signed languages. His goal was that these children thrive like the Deaf celebrants at Berthier's banquets, where a phrase launched from one end of the table would be grasped at the other, or a thought or sentiment would find an immediate echo in each heart, as people gathered with one group and then another as if all were moved by a single mind: here a crossfire of questions, there a medley of stories and news of the day.

Today many believe that these implanted children, still severely deaf, are not being given that opportunity because they are learning, during the potentially vibrant years of their greatest facility with language, solely how to speak and to hear a language that is not really their own. They have become lost in the very environments in which Itard, who spent his life with them, found active participation to be indispensable to the education of severely deaf children:

> There is a concern that even those deaf or hard-of-hearing children who, with the help of a cochlear implant or hearing aids, successfully acquire spoken language and are able to conduct conversations in optimal conditions may be at a major disadvantage in situations that are difficult for them to hear or

lipread . . . [T]his has been termed "social deafness," [which] is likely to affect not only children's social interactions, such as play and conversations with peers, but also classroom learning, particularly with current teaching practices that incorporate inquiry-based learning involving cooperative learning situations and high levels of student-student dialogue in which there is a division of tasks within a group of students.[6]

Harry Lang of Gallaudet University writes of their struggles not only in overcoming communicative difficulties associated with deafness, "but especially with regard to intellectual functioning and language development." Children growing up with cochlear implants and oral-only language, in his view, "are likely to experience psychological trauma until they are exposed to sign language and Deaf culture."[7] And while the reported (clinical) success rates for spoken language acquisition continue to improve in Australia, "questions remain about the longer term benefits of these devices in education and other areas of the children's personal and social development."[8] If a child improves on a training protocol "in the clinic, laboratory, or even at home, there is little evidence that this training will also improve [his] ability to perceive speech or communicate in everyday real-world conditions in daily life."[9]

No research has yet shown that a Deaf implanted child learns spoken language to the extent that he or she can cope with normal communication outside the laboratory. As reported in the earlier-mentioned Swedish study, "Studies often give a very positive picture of the implant use and tests show that the children make significant progress in production as well as perception of words in laboratory settings. But although pronunciation and discrimination of words is related to development of spoken language . . . it is not the same as being able to hear, understand and communicate in everyday settings."[10] An excellent case in point is the ten-year French study which refers to its tests on "word perception," "identification of simple and complex phrases," and "comprehension of syntax and semantics." Most of the tests given to the implanted children were in clinical settings and asked the children to identify various words and phrases by choosing the correct answer from a series of illustrations.[11] Exercises of this nature bear little resemblance to the real world, and provide a disquieting reminder of the way the twin sisters behind the Pantheon were being taught as l'Épée found them in the eighteenth century.

As many of these children grow older with the implants, they continue to consider themselves Deaf and turn to sign language for fulfillment. As one implanted undergraduate reported: "It is emotionally exhausting to pretend to be a regular, hearing person. It is only when deaf people who are raised with oral exclusive education learn sign language as adults that they develop strong self-esteem and experience the end of the psychological distress caused by the deprivation of their most natural and comfortable form of communication."[12] Few hearing people today, including doctors, psychologists, speech therapists, educators, and others, are aware of or care to contemplate the fact that oralism as a modern policy was never an educational one. It was a doctrine advocated by Bell and others to eliminate the Deaf over time, as a "defective race of human beings," by rendering them incommunicative.[13]

In the course of my own interactions with a significant number of students implanted as infants or as young children, I have found that many who attend mainstream schools today are able to understand the teacher in class only if the teacher wears a microphone that is electronically connected to their implant. Implanted children are learning to speak with varying degrees of clarity and to hear in particular situations: electronically in a quiet environment, when directly addressed, by interpreting speech-like signals from the teacher's microphone or from the implant, and by reading lips. Background noise makes hearing difficult. It is also very difficult for such students to engage in general discussions with more than one person, and to remain aware of the wordplay or conversations going on around them.

Picture a classroom, as Bébian loved to say, for a picture is worth a thousand words, a thousand signs, a thousand clinical surveys of the Deaf, an image that can encapsulate a history. Picture a high school debate about politics, language, history, science—the subject of your choice, led by a hearing teacher. On the right, five unimplanted students are seated, Deaf since birth. On the left, you have five other students, born Deaf, fitted with cochlear implants, and trained orally. Behind each individual is an interpreter, signing what the teacher and the implanted Deaf are saying, or saying what the unimplanted Deaf are signing.

On the right side, you will have thorough and lively conversation, laughter, an understanding of the ideas of the teacher and virtually everyone else in the room, limited only by the imperfect speech of the implanted speakers. On the left, you will see a struggle for the lips of their teacher, their fellow implanted students and the speaking interpreters, an effort to make sense of speech, to capture the rapid and fleeting ideas of everyone as they pass them by. In such a scene, I would be working with what I can hear to find the missing consonants and vowels, the missing ideas to which my lyricals may ultimately lead me. The signing Deaf will return home from the discussion ever engaged, aware of what has gone on, what has been said to and around them, happy and complete. Many fear, however, that the implanted students, like legions of Deaf children over the past 140 years, will go home tentative, uncertain of what they have heard and of the words to come, today, tonight, and tomorrow.

Appendix 1: A Mortal Trinity

The Ear We See

The ear is a wonder of nature, a work of art, an offspring of evolutionary time and change, a mortal trinity. The outer ear is the first constituent of this trinity.

The edges and ridges and hollows of each of our auricles (the ear we see), gather sound waves and channel them into the ear canal. The canal funnels the sound waves to our eardrum, a thin membrane which marks the inner boundary of our outer ear.

The eardrum vibrates back and forth between the middle and inner ear at the same frequencies, and with the same intensity, as those of the arriving sound waves. These waves are oscillations of air traveling to the eardrum through the ear canal. If the incoming sound waves (compressions and rarefactions) arrive at the eardrum at shorter intervals, it oscillates faster. When a higher-intensity sound wave arrives, there is a larger displacement of the eardrum from its resting position. When the compression of a sound wave strikes the eardrum it pushes it in, and when the rarefaction follows, the internal pressure pushes the eardrum back out.

The Middle Ear

The second part of our auditory trinity is the middle ear, which stays generally in a state of equilibrium with the atmosphere around us. That is, the static pressure on the internal side of the eardrum remains equal to the pressure outside. Whenever the ambient pressure decreases or increases (as we gain altitude in a plane, for example, or climb down a mountain), we

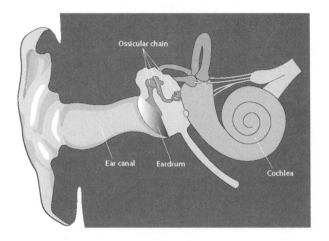

Our external (E), middle (M), and inner (I) ear (Adapted by
Bill Nelson from an image by S. Blatrix, "Journey into the World of
Hearing" www.cochlea.eu/en/, by R. Pujol et al., NeurOreille,
Montpellier, France.)

equalize the pressure on the inner side of the eardrum (the middle ear cavity). We do so by yawning or swallowing, contracting a muscle that opens our Eustachian tubes (named for an Italian anatomist), which leads from the middle ear cavity to the back of our throat, our mouth, and the pressure of the air around us, returning the eardrum to equilibrium.

The middle ear cavity houses the three tiniest bones (ossicles) in our body, called the hammer, the anvil, and the stirrup (named for its shape). The arm of the hammer is attached to the inside of the eardrum and thus vibrates with it, mechanically transmitting the vibrations inward to the anvil, which in turn conveys them to the stirrup. The stirrup's "footplate" slips into the membrane of an oval-shaped window, which is the entry to the liquid-filled cochlea and the outer boundary of our inner ear. The stirrup sends the vibrations passed to it by the hammer and anvil into the oval window.

We take our ears for granted, though their mechanical and electronic structures, and their developmental history, are highly complex. To take just

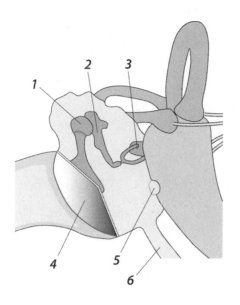

The middle ear, including (1) the hammer, (2) the anvil, (3) the stirrup, (4) the eardrum, (5) the round window, and (6) the Eustachian tube (Adapted by Bill Nelson from an image by S. Blatrix, "Journey into the World of Hearing" www.cochlea.eu/en/, by R. Pujol et al., NeurOreille, Montpellier, France.)

one example, the evolutionary history of our middle ear illustrates how our language emerged from the sea. Our ancient marine ancestors were able to hear sound in water without ossicles. But as they moved to land they developed a need for airborne, higher-frequency hearing, notably to detect insect prey. This produced an evolutionary co-option of structures formerly used for other purposes into the ossicles of the middle ear.[1] First, the ancient fish, *Eusthenopteron,* which lived about 400 million years ago, developed a bone deformity in its hyomandibula, a bone that coordinated the fishes' feeding and breathing movements. That deformity partially obstructed its gill openings (called spiracles). The bone receded in *Eusthenopteron*'s aquatic successors. A wider cavity was also found in *Panderichthys,* a fish, like *Eusthenopteron,* of the Upper Devonian period. That broader space is now widely regarded as a transitional predecessor of our middle ear cavity.

A few million years after *Panderichthys,* the precursor of the ear's stirrup (item 3 in the illustration above) appeared in that broader space, in the ear of

Acanthostega: *the beginnings of our middle-ear ossicles* (Raul Martin, "Acanthostega." Pencil, 2003. For the Museo del Jurásico de Asturias -MUJA (Colunga-Asturias, Spain. Courtesy of Raul Martin.)

another of our predecessors, *Acanthostega*, an early aquatic and extraordinarily versatile tetrapod. He had paddle-like legs and feet, gills and lungs, fins and a tail. *Acanthostega's* stirrup-like structures are thought to have evolved from its marine ancestors' hyomandibula, which had become a structural component of *Acanthostega's* skull. The jaw joint of *Acanthostega's* descendants later developed from an auxiliary joint, and the fixed and jointed bones that had formed the original jaw became crucial elements—the hammer and anvil—of our middle ear bones. Thus as our ancestors moved from sea to land, their gills and jaws transformed themselves to enable the whispers of those insects and, much later in evolutionary time, the voices and words of others, to reach the cochlea and ultimately the brain.

The human middle ear increases the intensity of the airborne sound waves in two ways. First, the area of the eardrum, the entrance to the middle

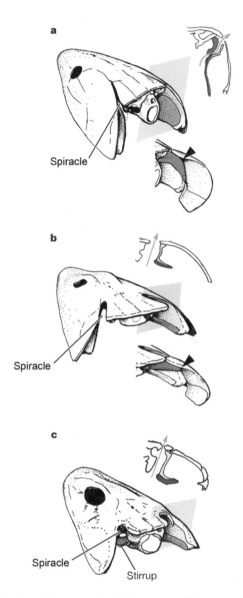

Early evolution of the tetrapod middle ear space. Shown are the respective middle ear spaces of Eusthenopteron (*top*), Panderichthys (*middle*), *and* Acanthostega (*bottom*). (Adapted by permission from Macmillan Publishers Ltd: Nature 439: 318–321 [19 January 2006], copyright 2006.)

ear cavity, is about three-fifths of a square centimeter and thus almost twenty times larger than the area ($3/100$ths of a cm^2) of the footplate of the stirrup and the oval window at the entrance to the cochlea. Since intensity equals force divided by area, this increases the sound pressure at the oval window for a gain of about 25.4 dBs over the sound pressure at the eardrum.

Second, the arm and head of the hammer are longer than the anvil and its extension to the stirrup. The difference raises the sound pressure by an additional 2.3 decibels. The combined effect is a 27.7-decibel increase in pressure from the eardrum to the cochlea, almost enough to make up for all of the loss at the boundary between the air in the middle ear and the fluid in the cochlea.

The Inner Ear

The cochlea, the innermost part of our auditory trinity, is by far the most complex, sensitive, and vulnerable component of our ear. For the hearing, the Deaf, and the partially deaf, it is the principal determinant of the language we speak or sign. Hearing loss caused by cochlear damage is the most common form of deafness, and partial deafness, in the world. It affects about 30 million people in the United States alone. The cochlea is a small snail-like shell that coils upward upon itself in diminishing diameter, with two and a half turns from its base to the top or apex.

The central axis (modiolus) of each cochlea houses the cochlear branch of the eighth (hearing) nerve. Cochlear structures are vulnerable to disease, to damage by certain antibiotics and other drugs, to infection and allergy, and to genetic mutation. They also deteriorate with age. Often the cause of cochlear damage is not known and cannot be reliably determined. There are, to be sure, many other forms of hearing loss. A *conductive* loss is caused by defects in the transmission of sound through the middle ear, caused by damage to the eardrum or ossicles, or by the presence of fluid in the middle ear as a result of infection. Mechanical problems of the middle ear can often be corrected by surgery, and middle ear infections are usually treatable by medication. For most people with hearing loss, however, the incapacitating damage has been done to the cochlea. Its cells and membranes are inaccessible, irreparable, and irreplaceable.

The cochlea evolved in mammals in the late Mesozoic era, about 100 million years ago. The human cochlea's coiled shell houses three winding, liquid-filled duct-like chambers or scalae, separated from each other by two membranes. The oval window leads into the uppermost compartment, the scala vestibuli. The lowest chamber, the scala tympani, winds down from the apex to the round window at the bottom, which leads back into the middle ear.

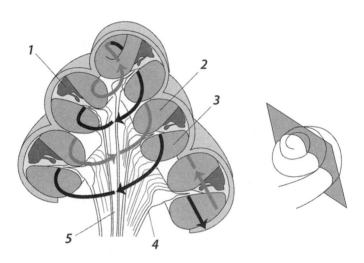

Plan of cross-section of the organ of Corti. This mid-modiolar section shows the coiling of the cochlear duct (1) which contains endolymph, and the scala vestibuli (2) and scala tympani (3) which contain perilymph. The light-colored arrow is from the oval window, the darker arrow points to the round window. Within the modiolus, the spiral ganglion (4) and the auditory nerve fibers (5) are seen. (Adapted by Bill Nelson from an image by S. Blatrix, "Journey into the World of Hearing" www.cochlea.eu/en/, by R. Pujol et al., NeurOreille, Montpellier, France.)

The cochlea's middle compartment (scala media) contains the inner sanctum of our language, our music, all that we hear: the organ of Corti (named after the nineteenth-century Italian anatomist Alfonso Corti). Many now call it the "organ of hearing." No human-made system can equal its performance. It consists of a number of phalanx-like cells that lean against each other and sit upon the basilar (lower) membrane.

When the footplate of the stirrup presses against the oval window, it generates a pressure wave that moves in an upward spiral through scala vestibuli (the lighter-shaded arrow in the above illustration), to the cochlea's apex, and then spirals downward through the lowest chamber, scala tympani (the darker arrow). The wave travels almost instantaneously through the incompressible liquids of the cochlea. The pressure generated by the stirrup's footplate at the oval window at the entrance to scala vestibuli is released by the round window at the exit of scala tympani, which bulges outward as the oval window bends in. During the rarefaction phase of the sound wave the process is reversed as the outward motion of the stirrup pulls the liquid wave in the other direction, toward the oval window, as the round window bends in to scala tympani.

The pressure wave causes the perpendicular displacement of the basilar membrane of the organ of Corti, in transverse waves, up and down like a ripple on a pond, except that each wave is most intense at a particular place. The organ of Corti is tonotopically organized—it is tuned. As the basilar membrane winds upward in scala media from the base of the cochlea to its apex, it responds optimally (with the greatest amplitude, or up and down movement) to sounds of specific frequencies. The higher frequencies cause maximum movement at the bottom (first) turn of the cochlea (20,000 Hertz at the base to 5,000 Hertz at the middle of the turn), where the basilar membrane is stiff and, unlike the cochlear shell itself, relatively narrow. The membrane responds optimally to decreasing frequencies as it climbs toward the apex. It responds to frequencies of about 1,000 Hertz just after the start of the second turn, 500 Hertz just after the middle of that turn, and only 20 Hertz at the apex, where it is broader and much less rigid.

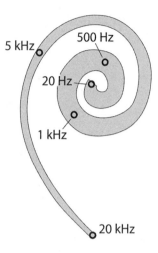

Some characteristic frequencies from the base (20,000 Hz) to the apex (20 Hz) of the cochlea's basilar membrane. Note the progressive enlargement of the membrane as it ascends. (Adapted by Bill Nelson from an image by S. Blatrix, "Journey into the World of Hearing" www.cochlea.eu/en/, by R. Pujol et al., NeurOreille, Montpellier, France)

Hair Cells

The critical cells leaning against each other in the organ of Corti are known as hair cells, a name derived not from the body of the cell but from the fine "feelers" (stereocilia) that project like tufts of hair from the cell body into the endolymph of scala media. Endolymph is a potassium-laden liquid found nowhere else in the body. A single row of hair cells runs up the modiolar (inner) side of each ear's organ of Corti as it coils from base to apex. There are about 3,500 of these "inner" hair cells, each containing about 40 stereocilia. Running along the outer side of the coil are three parallel rows of "outer" hair cells, about 12,500 of them in all, each with about 150 stereocilia. Thus there are 16,000 hair cells in a human cochlea.

We acquire all our inner and outer hair cells early in fetal development. They do not proliferate and are not replaceable. Their stereocilia, while plentiful (about two million in all) are a vulnerable population—highly susceptible to damage or destruction by loud sounds, disease, life-saving medicines (aminoglycosides for serious infections and cisplatin for testicular and ovarian cancer), genetic mutations, and aging. Their days are numbered, for many of us, while we are still young. This is why, in general, many who have

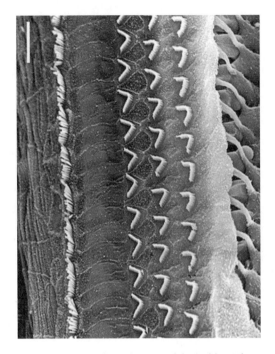

Looking down from the apex of the cochlea: The single row of cells (left) is on the inner side of the cochlea and is composed of the inner hair cells; the outer three rows are the outer hair cells. (Photograph by M. Lenoir, "Journey into the World of Hearing," www.cochlea.eu/en/, by R. Pujol et al., NeurOreille, Montpellier, France.)

heard well when they were young become hard of hearing as they grow older. The stereocilia do not regenerate, they are lost with aging, and over a period of decades that adds up to meaningful hearing loss.

The movements of the basilar membrane, most pronounced at the place of optimal frequency, cause the stereocilia of both the inner and outer hair cell bodies to move sideways, back and forth, in the endolymphatic fluid of scala media, like waving wheat in a crosswind, first toward the outside of the

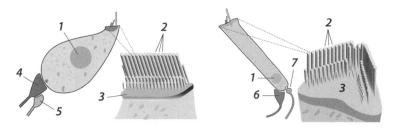

The inner (IHC) and outer (OHC) hair cells of the organ of Corti. The inner hair cells appear on the left in the image, the outer hair cells are shown on the right. 1. Nucleus, 2. Stereocilia, 3. Cuticular plate, 4. Radial afferent ending, 5. Lateral efferent ending, 6. Medial efferent ending, 7. Spiral afferent ending
(Adapted by Bill Nelson from an image by S. Blatrix, "Journey into the World of Hearing," www.cochlea.eu/en/, by R. Pujol et al., NeurOreille, Montpellier, France.)

cochlea and then back toward its central axis. The hair cells themselves, like the basilar membrane, are also independently frequency-sensitive or tuned. Our inner hair cells, far fewer in number than their outer counterparts, are heavily innervated by auditory nerve fibers that reach into the organ of Corti from a set of openings (called habenula perforata) in the thin shell of the modiolus all along the basilar membrane as it winds upward to the apex of the cochlea.

Our Ears Are Electric

The stereocilia grow from shorter on the medial (internal) side to taller on the lateral (outer) side of the top of the hair cell, like the bars that measure signal strength on a computer or a GPS. Their tips are connected to each other by thin filaments called tip links. These tip links are attached at their lower end to one or more (probably two) transduction channels embedded in the cellular membrane on the tip of the stereocilium. The pumping of ions in the cells lining the outer wall of scala media give it a positive resting charge of about +80 millivolts (mV), the highest positive resting electrical potential within the body. The hair cell itself has a negative resting potential of -60 mV throughout, for a total difference in potential energy of 140 mV. When the hair bundle moves, shear causes the tip links to tighten; that pulls open the molecular gates of apical channels attached to the tip links, and a potassium current then flows. Those channels admit calcium ions, which depolarize the cell—make its interior more positive. The depolarization is "felt" rapidly (at the speed of light in that medium) by voltage-sensitive calcium channels at the cell's base. Those channels open, admitting calcium ions that trigger the release of neurotransmitter from synaptic vesicles.

The "synapse" is the minute gap that separates the base and the lower sides of each hair cell body from the endings (dendrites) of the auditory nerve fibers that reach out from the modiolus. The neurotransmitter from the synaptic vesicles causes the nerve fibers' receiving dendrites to open their own ion channels on the other side of the synapse and to "fire" by admitting the flow of positive ions from the hair cell. Successive neurons follow suit, setting the charge's path from neuron to neuron all along the auditory nerve. The current that is generated by the hair cell is a graded signal. That is, the strength of the flow of current varies directly (lower to higher) with the shearing force on the stereocilia caused by the movement of the basilar membrane. Consequently, the changes over time in receptor current mirror the shape of the mechanical input signal, that is, of the sound wave.

The central auditory nervous system conveys information from the inner hair cells in the cochlea to the auditory cortex in the brain. Each inner hair cell is innervated by an average of eight nerve fibers. The outer hair cells are principally under the control of efferent nerve fibers that carry information in reverse—they are messengers from the brain stem to the cochlea. They appear to have a motor (or electromotile) function, changing their length, shape, and stiffness in response to electrical stimulation. Their stereocilia (unlike those of the inner hair cells) are embedded in a gelatinous "roof" above the organ of Corti called the tectorial membrane. They perform an amplificatory function by changing their shape in response to efferent signals from the brainstem that are themselves triggered by information provided by the afferent fibers, that is, the messengers to the brain from the inner hair cells. There are substantially fewer efferent fibers, each innervating about ten outer hair cells (versus eight afferent fibers for *each* inner hair cell). The nerve fibers gather in the twisted bundle within the modiolus and are then joined by nerves from our vestibular (balance) system to form the entire auditory nerve tract of the eighth nerve.

Thus when we hear, the information sent to the brain returns in a kind of feedback cycle. The movements of the outer hair cells intensify the motion of the basilar membrane at the places of optimal frequency and thus of the motion of the related inner hair cells as well, improving substantially the ear's frequency selectivity (discrimination). Therefore even in the earliest stages of our ear's transmission of auditory signals, our higher nerve centers appear to be playing a contributing role in a fraction of twenty thousandths of a second, and all of this seamlessly forms a part of our recognition of sound—the mechanics of hearing require no voluntary thought, despite the complexity of the overall process.

On to the Brain

The discharge patterns of the neurons or cell bodies of the auditory nerve electronically encode the frequency and intensity of sound registered in the mechanical movements of the basilar membrane. Like the place-coded organ of Corti, the auditory nerve's receptive fibers are also tuned to respond best to particular frequencies. Nerve fibers innervating the hair cells near the base of the cochlea are most receptive to high frequencies. Those innervating hair cells closer to the apex respond optimally to low frequencies. There is therefore a close correlation between the frequency selectivity in the cochlea and that of the auditory nerve, and we perceive frequency as a function of the manner in which particular neurons are firing.

Unfortunately, even with our highly developed understanding of the ear itself, we do not yet know exactly how the auditory nerve and the brain manage to record the electrical mirror of the sound wave recorded by the corresponding current flows in the hair cells in the cochlea. While the hair cells are able to produce a graded spectrum by varying current flow, our neurons operate on an on/off basis. That is, either they fire or they do not. But they are most sensitive to the characteristic frequencies of the hair cells they innervate, and there are a number of theories (pulse rate, intervals, synchrony), none of them certain, as to how the auditory neurons encode and transmit the graded signal to the brain.

The higher levels in the auditory system are even more complex. The neural charges follow labyrinthine patterns through various nuclei (nerve bundles) in the brain stem and on to the auditory cortex (and back to the cochlea). Little is known about these neural pathways and about the auditory cortex itself. Some cortical neurons respond only to complex sounds, for example the sound of a kiss, or a broken egg. Some respond only if the frequency of the tone is modulating, others only to the onset of a stimulus, still others solely to its termination.

The passage of our spoken languages through the air, to the ear, and on to our neural pathways is a complex and enchanting one. It is mirrored only by the journey of signed languages, as given by hand and expression and seen by the eye in the medium of light, to the same pathways of understanding in the brain.

Appendix 2: The Handshapes of American Sign Language

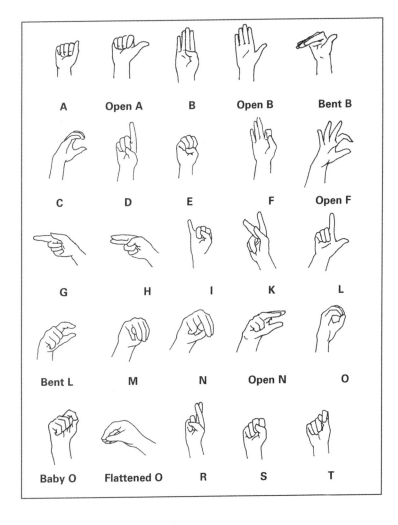

A   Open A   B   Open B   Bent B

C   D   E   F   Open F

G   H   I   K   L

Bent L   M   N   Open N   O

Baby O   Flattened O   R   S   T

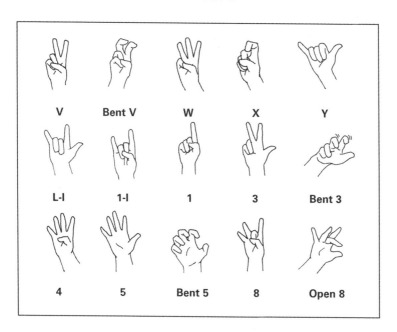

V	Bent V	W	X	Y
L-I	1-I	1	3	Bent 3
4	5	Bent 5	8	Open 8

Modern American manual alphabet and related handshapes. These conventional signs are used to approximate the configuration of the hands in expressing phonemic elements of American Sign Language. (American Sign Language handshapes from *The American Sign Language Handshape Dictionary*, 2nd ed., by Richard A. Tennant and Marianne Gluszak Brown, illustrated by Valerie Nelson-Metlay (Washington, DC: Gallaudet University Press, 2010): 26–27. Reprinted by permission of the publisher. Copyright 2010 by Gallaudet University.)

Notes

Except where otherwise expressly indicated, all translations of works quoted from the French are by the author. All Internet links were active as of December 21, 2016.

Chapter 1. In the Beginning Was the Word

1. As noted in the Preface, the capitalized term *Deaf* in this book generally means profoundly deaf people whose tongue is a signed language. The term may be said to include as well all those born deaf, or become so soon thereafter, notably because sign is the only language that comes immediately, fully, and naturally to them. The term also encompasses those who embrace the culture and values of the modern signing Deaf community. In all quotations the terms (*Deaf* or *deaf*) remain as in the original source.

2. See Polich, *Emergence of the Deaf Community in Nicaragua.*

3. Plato, *Cratylus,* XXXIV, 444d–423b; Aristotle, *De Sensu,* 437B.

4. Presneau, "Le son 'à la lettre,' " 20; Augustine, *De quantitate animae,* chapter 18; Bertin, *Auguste Bébian,* 30–31.

5. Presneau, "Le son 'à la lettre,' " 21.

6. Saint-Loup, "Les sourds-muets au moyen-age," 13; Mark 7:31–37.

7. Bertin, *Auguste Bébian,* 30.

8. Montaigne, *Essais,* book 2, chapter 12; Diderot, *Lettre sur les sourds,* 113.

9. Berthier, *Les sourds-muets,* 47.

10. Diderot, *Lettre sur les sourds,* 113.

11. Desloges, *Observations,* 13–14.

Chapter 2. Language in Air, Language of Light

1. For a superb animated illustration of the workings of the entire ear, and a helpful visual guide to the discussion in this chapter and in Appendix 1, see *Promenade 'Round the Cochlea,* http://www.neuroreille.com/promenade/english/ear/fear.htm.

Chapter 3. The Age of Darkness

1. Lane, *When the Mind Hears,* 91.
2. Bonet, *Réduction de las letras,* xxii, 40–41. I have done the translations from the work in Spanish with the help of the French edition.
3. Ibid., 73–103.
4. Ibid., 139.
5. Ibid., 127, 153.
6. Ibid., 161.
7. Ibid., 274.
8. Ibid., 124, 130.
9. Lane, *When the Mind Hears,* 103.
10. Desloges, *Observations d'un sourd et muèt,* 32–33, translated by Franklin Philip in Lane, *Deaf Experience,* 209.
11. Saint-Loup, "Les sourds-muets au moyen-age," 15.
12. Geoffroy, *Dissertation sur l'organe de l'ouïe,* 18–19, 26–27.
13. Lane, *When the Mind Hears,* 134.

Chapter 4. The Enlightenment

1. It is important to emphasize, notwithstanding some of the descriptive examples given here, that signed languages are neither obvious nor iconic. A controlled study has shown that non-signers do no better than random chance when interpreting actual signs, even under multiple-choice conditions, and indeed speakers of one signed language do not do much better in interpreting the signs of another. Signs may have an origin in an iconic representation, but it is an evanescent one, language-specific, generally not transparent, and in any event tends to be effaced as a signed language develops over time. See Klima and Bellugi, *Signs of Language,* 21–34.
2. The signer's dominant hand (right or left) is the more active in signed languages. Thus, for a right-handed person, in the sign for "on" the right hand falls on the left.
3. Bébian, *Essai sur les sourds-muets,* 25.
4. Berthier, *Les sourds-muets,* 51.
5. Ibid., 45; l'Épée, *La véritable manière,* 18; Bertin, *Auguste Bébian,* 44.
6. Bébian, *Mimographie,* 27–28.
7. Berthier, *Les sourds-muets,* 39.
8. Lane, *When the Mind Hears,* 33.
9. Lane, *Deaf Experience,* 77.

10. Ibid., 78–79, translation by Franklin Philip; Roch-Ambroise Sicard, "Notice sur l'enfance de Massieu," in Sicard, *Théorie des signes*, 626.

11. Bébian, *Journal de l'instruction*, vol. 2, 24–26.

12. Berthier, *Les sourds-muets*, 51.

13. Bernard, *Approche de la gestualité*, 143.

14. Bertin, *Auguste Bébian*, 93, 175.

15. Ibid., 75.

16. Ibid., 154; Berthier, "Lettre supplique."

17. Bertin, *Auguste Bébian*, 122.

18. Locke, *The Works of John Locke (Essay Concerning Human Understanding)*, book 3, chapter 2, section 1.

19. Bébian, *Éloge*, 3, 15–16.

20. Bébian, *Journal de l'instruction*, vol. 2, 26–27.

21. Ibid., 24–25 ; Berthier, *Les sourds-muets*, 12.

22. "Lettres closes" in Bébian, *Journal de l'instruction*, vol. 2, 25.

23. Bébian, *Essai sur les sourds-muets*, 13–14.

24. Bébian, *Journal de l'instruction*, vol. 1, 137, 150, n. 1.

25. Bébian, *Journal d'enseignement*, vol. 2, 30.

26. Ibid., 42–43 ; Sicard, *Cours d'instruction*, 36, 77.

27. Bébian, *Journal de l'instruction*, vol. 1, 160.

28. Bébian, *Essai sur les sourds-muets*, 65; Bébian, *Manuel d'enseignement*, vol. 2, 7–15; ibid., 25.

29. Bébian, *Journal de l'instruction*, vol. 1, 137–138.

30. Bébian, *Manuel d'enseignement*, vol. 2, 93–94.

31. Ibid., 180.

32. Bertin, *Auguste Bébian,* 48.

33. Itard essay in Bébian, *Journal de l'instruction*, vol. 1, 255. See also Lane, *When the Mind Hears*, 138–141.

34. Bébian, *Examen critique*, 58.

35. Encrevé, *Sourds et société*, 201, 247–248.

36. Bertin, *Auguste Bébian*, 155; Lane, *When the Mind Hears,* 119.

37. Encrevé, *Sourds et société*, 154, 254.

Chapter 5. France Comes to America

1. Quartararo, *Deaf Identity*, 50.

2. Lane, *When the Mind Hears*, 183.

3. Bertin, *Auguste Bébian*, 283.

4. Thomas Gallaudet to Ward Woodbridge, March 14, 1818, in Humphrey, *Life and Labors of the Rev. T. H. Gallaudet*, 60, 61–62.

5. Clerc, "Autobiographical Sketch," in Barnard, *Tribute to Gallaudet*, 106–116.

6. Originally called the "Connecticut Asylum for the Education and Instruction of Deaf and Dumb Persons."

7. Padden and Humphries, *Deaf in America*, 17; Buchanan, *Illusions of Equality*, 4; Lane, *Mask*, 113.

8. Berthier, *Discours*, 22.

Chapter 6. The Banquets of the Deaf

1. Berthier, *Notice sur la vie*, 23; Bertin, *Auguste Bébian*, 52, n. 143; Itard, "Constat médical." The sagittal suture is the connective tissue between the two parietal bones of the skull.

2. Bertin, *Auguste Bébian*, 127–128.

3. The term *sourds-muets* or *deaf-mute* (and sometimes *deaf and dumb*) was used well before and throughout most of the nineteenth century, and was dropped after the Congress of Milan in 1880 to reinforce the illusion that the Deaf could be taught to speak and to read lips. The term was retained thereafter (until well into the twentieth century) to denote those who were not "intelligent" enough to learn to speak, and thus given its deprecatory connotation.

4. Société Centrale, *Banquets*, vol. 1, 32.

5. Ibid., 31.

6. Encrevé, *Sourds et société*, 173.

7. Société Centrale, *Banquets*, vol. 1, 13–14.

8. Note from F. Encrevé to the author, July 6, 2016. See also Encrevé, *Sourds et société*, 170–171, 209, 342. The first two bound volumes of the proceedings at the banquets were published in the late 1840s and in 1864, respectively, in the name of the committee's incorporated successor, the "Société Centrale des Sourds-Muets de Paris." The Société changed its name in 1867 to the Société Universelle des Sourds-Muets and published the third volume under that name in 1870.

9. Société Centrale, *Banquets*, vol. 1, 1, 11, 14, 17, 26, 61, 56, 79, 128, 138; vol. 2, 122, 141; Société Universelle, *Banquets*, vol. 3, 57–58.

10. Société Centrale, *Banquets*, vol. 1, 148. Harlan Lane used Hugo's phrase for the title of his monumental history of the Deaf, *When the Mind Hears*.

11. There are, however, material similarities between French and American sign language due to the teaching and influence of Laurent Clerc in America as discussed in Chapter 5.

12. Société Centrale, *Banquets*, vol. 1, 87.

13. Ibid., 70–71.

14. Ibid., 64.

15. Ibid., 8; Bébian, *Examen critique*, 36.

16. Pélissier, *Poésies d'un sourd-muet*, 89, 91, 93. Lamartine's first six lines for Pélissier read in French as follows: C'est par les sens en nous que descend la lumière; / Mais, je le reconnais à vos touchants accents, / Dans votre âme captive elle entre la première, / Suppléer à la nature et se donne des sens.

17. Berthier, *Les sourds-muets*, 29.

18. Société Centrale, *Banquets*, vol. 1, 25–26. The Phoenician alphabet (about 1000 B.C.E.) is the source of virtually all modern alphabets. Some nineteen of our letters can be traced directly to their Phoenician counterparts in shape, alphabetical sequence, and, for the most part, sound. See D. Sacks, *Letter Perfect*, ix–xv, 11–17.

19. Société Centrale, *Banquets*, vol. 1, 80–81.

20. Ibid., 34.

21. Ibid., 46–47.

22. Ibid., 12.

23. Ibid., 85–86.

24. Ibid., 104.

25. Ibid., 127.

26. Société Universelle, *Banquets*, vol. 3, 90.

27. Société Centrale, *Banquets*, vol. 1, 86–87.

28. Encrevé, *Sourds et société*, 103.

29. Bébian, *Essai sur le sourds-muets*, 16–17.

30. Encrevé, *Sourds et société*, 169.

31. Ibid., 180, 216.

32. Société Centrale, *Banquets*, vol. 1, 95.

33. Encrevé, *Sourds et société*, 233–234, 242–243.

34. Ibid., 124.

35. Ibid., 273.

36. Société Centrale, *Banquets*, vol. 2, 81.

37. Encrevé, *Sourds et société*, 285.

38. Ibid., 333 (quoting the sermon of Le Courtier).

39. Ibid., 335–338 (quoting the sermon of Charles Freppel, Bishop of Angers).

40. Ibid., 329.

41. Société Universelle, *Banquets*, vol. 3, 57–58.

42. Encrevé, *Sourds et société*, 353.

43. Société Central, *Banquets*, vol. 1, 79; *Discours*, 22; Bébian, *Examen critique*, 36.

Chapter 7. The Congress of Milan

1. O. Sacks, *Seeing Voices*, 24, citing Harlan Lane; Moody, *La langue des signes*, vol. 1, 29.

2. Encrevé, *Sourds et société*, 396.

3. Ibid., 273.

4. Lane, *When the Mind Hears*, 380–381.

5. Encrevé, *Sourds et société*, 402.

6. Ibid., 400, 404.

7. Ibid., 415–416.

8. Ibid., 416.

9. Ibid., 425.

10. Lane, *When the Mind Hears*, 392.

11. Encrevé, *Sourds et société*, 438.

12. Ibid., 439.

13. Lane, *When the Mind Hears*, 389.

14. Ibid., 409.

15. Encrevé, *Sourds et société*, 445–446.

16. Lane, *When the Mind Hears*, 393.

17. Encrevé, *Sourds et société*, 457.

18. Woodward, *Signs of Sexual Behavior*, 35–37.

19. Lane, *Mask*, 113; Encrevé, *Sourds et société*, 474.

20. Encrevé, *Sourds et société*, 475, 492.

21. Cuxac, "Le Congrès de Milan," 100.

Chapter 8. The Debate in England

1. Baynton, *Forbidden Signs*, 85.

2. Several years after Gallaudet was founded, when a member of the House Committee on Appropriations suggested that funding for the college be withheld, "shoulders shook with laughter" at the reply of another Congressman: "May any

gentleman who undertakes to open his mouth in opposition to this appropriation . . . be struck dumb." Gallaudet, *History of the College for the Deaf*, 77.

3. Van Cleve et al., *A Place of Their Own*, 74, 83.

4. Munro (Saki), *Short Stories*, 119, 122; Lane, *When the Mind Hears*, 344.

5. Dodd and Campbell, *Hearing by Eye*, 192.

6. Lane, *Mask*, 98.

7. Coudon, *Le silence apprivoisé*, 47, 103, 109, 250, 252, 261.

8. Ibid., 69, 257–258, 260, 273.

9. Stokoe, "Sign Language Structure," 17.

10. *Royal Commission Report*, 18, para. 31246; 68.

11. Ibid., 32, paras. 13444–13445; 39, paras. 21707–21709; 31, para. 13425.

12. Berthier, *Notice sur la vie*, 27. Bébian was also offered the directorship of the School for the Deaf in Saint Petersburg.

13. *Royal Commission Report*, 27, para. 21570. The critical word "quickest" appears to have vanished in (inaccurate) accounts of Bell's testimony that have been put forward since the nineteenth century. See, for example, Kyle et al., *Sign Language*, 56; Kerr Love and Addison, *Deaf Mutism*, 297; O. Sacks, *Seeing Voices*, 27n. Bell's words "without reference to language" in the quote appear to mean "without reference to [learning] *speech.*" He used the words interchangeably.

14. *Royal Commission Report*, 39, paras. 21707–21709.

15. Ibid., 39, para. 21705.

16. Ibid., 39, para. 21707.

17. Jenkins, "Question of Signs," 217.

18. Ibid., 218.

19. Bell, "Question of Sign-Language," 8; Bell, "Growth of the Oral Method."

20. *Royal Commission Report*, 28, para. 21579.

21. Ibid., 40, para. 21718.

22. Ibid., 48, para. 21748; 7–8, para. 21399.

23. Ibid., 27, para. 21570.

24. Bébian, *Examen critique*, 16.

25. *Royal Commission Report*, 65, para. 21985.

26. Ibid., 24, para. 21548.

27. Ibid., 28, para. 21579.

28. Ibid., 50–51, paras. 21835–21837.

29. Ibid., 57–59, paras. 21901–21925.

30. Ibid., 29, para. 21585.

31. Bell, *Deaf Variety,* 56.

32. *Royal Commission Report,* 19, para. 21502; 13, para. 21450.

33. Ibid., 19, para. 21503; 21, para. 21517 (emphasis added).

34. Bébian, *Éloge,* 3; Bonet, *Réduction de las letras,* xxii; Société Centrale, *Banquets,* vol. 1, 85–87.

35. Ibid., 23, para. 21540. Clerc's name sign was not even close to the sign for *false,* either in French sign language, where a Y-shaped dominant hand (see Appendix 2) is brought down upon the other in neutral space, or in American Sign Language, where a 1-shaped hand moves (closely) past the nose and down to the breast. The sign for *deaf* in both languages was and is an index finger (1-shaped hand) touched to the cheek just before the ear and then to the chin (or vice versa). Bell did not know sign language well, and may have speculated (erroneously) that the line drawn down the cheek signifying Clerc's scar negated any congenital deafness.

36. Lane, *When the Mind Hears,* 360–361.

37. *Royal Commission Report,* 55, para. 21879.

38. Ibid., 54, para. 21868; 56, para. 21887.

39. Baynton, *Forbidden Signs,* 103.

40. Société Centrale, *Banquets,* vol. 2, 30.

41. Quartararo, *Deaf Identity,* 95.

42. Encrevé, *Sourds et société,* 466.

43. List, "Heinicke et l'oralisme," 55, 57; Quartararo, *Deaf Identity,* 86; Cuxac, "Le Congrès de Milan," 100, 102–105.

44. Bell, *Deaf Variety,* 41.

45. Encrevé, *Sourds et société,* 459.

46. Ibid., 488–489.

47. World's Congress of the Deaf, 177.

Chapter 9. Helen Keller

1. Lash, *Helen and Teacher,* 154.

2. See, e.g., her early correspondence published as "Helen Keller's Letters" in Keller, *Story of My Life.*

3. As John Macy (who was also Helen's co-amanuensis and editor for a time) wrote, "Read[ing] the lips with her fingers . . . is a clumsy and unsatisfactory way of receiving communication, useless when Miss Sullivan or someone else who knows

the manual alphabet is present to give Miss Keller the spoken words of others." "John Macy's Account" in Keller, *Story of My Life*, 245–246.

4. Lash, *Helen and Teacher*, 631.

5. Shattuck essay in Keller, *Story of My Life*, 446–447. Shattuck believed that "for the most part" Keller's writings in *The Story of My Life* and elsewhere were not ghostwritten, based on his reading of her letters after the age of twelve, her personality, her independence of mind, and the onerous work methods she used.

6. Canby, "The Frost Fairies," in her *Birdie and His Fairy Friends*.

7. Both stories are printed in "John Macy's Account" in Keller, *Story of My Life*, 262–266.

8. Arthur Keller to Anagnos, February 5, 1892: "When Miss Annie first read it to us I questioned her closely about it and told her I did not think the dear child could have written it without suggestion from some older person, when she assured me that it was original, as she now claims." See A. Keller, Letter.

9. Sullivan to Anagnos, November 4, 1891. See Sullivan, Letter.

10. Keller to Anagnos, November 4, 1891, *Perkins Annual Report (1891)*, 94.

11. "John Macy's Account" in Keller, *Story of My Life*, 256.

12. "King Frost Again."

13. Keller, *Story of My Life*, 59.

14. Anagnos, "Note."

15. Ibid., 94.

16. "Miss Sullivan's Methods," anonymous manuscript, 141–143; see Lash, *Helen and Teacher*, 134. Lash suggests the manuscript was written in 1906 by David Hall, a lawyer (and the brother-in-law of Anagnos's wife), in defense of the Perkins School's finally distancing itself from Helen and Anne after these events.

17. A panel was formed consisting of four blind and four sighted teachers and officials at Perkins, plus Anagnos. No record of these proceedings, held in early 1892, can be found at Perkins.

18. Lash, *Helen and Teacher*, 141.

19. "John Macy's Account," in Keller, *Story of My Life*, 133.

20. Anagnos, Letter, June 22, 189[2?] (duplicate handwritten copy in Perkins Archives, in which the month and day, but not the year, appear). The date of the letter may be June 22, 1894. In *Story of My Life*, 62, Helen wrote that "For two years [after the inquiry, Anagnos] seems to have held the belief that Miss Sullivan and I were innocent. Then he evidently retracted his favorable judgment, why I do not know."

The Perkins archivists confirm that it was Perkins's practice to retain duplicate handwritten copies of outgoing correspondence.

21. The August letter, critical because of both its similarities to Canby's other story and its timing, was not included among Helen's letters published in *Story of My Life* in 1905 ("John Macy's Account," in Keller, *Story of My Life*, 328). Macy attributes the hiatus in the correspondence to the depressing effect of the charges of plagiarism. But the letter, of course, was sent to Anagnos just *before* Anne sent him "The Frost King."

22. Anagnos, Letter.

23. Lash, *Helen and Teacher*, 143.

24. Ozick, "What Helen Keller Saw."

25. Keller to Sanborn, September 28, 1906. See H. Keller, Letter. The statement is based on hearsay ("one of our friends reported the matter direct to us [Helen and Anne]"). The letter adds that when Anagnos was later asked by another friend "who went straight to him from us" whether those were his words, Anagnos replied that "[Helen's] teacher had taught [her] to deceive," words that mirror those of his earlier letter concluding that Helen "was induced" to assert repeatedly that she had not been familiar with Canby's book.

26. "Squarehand" was written in script on paper fitted over a grooved writing board.

27. Sanborn, Letter.

28. Bell, "Question of Sign-Language," 4.

29. Keller, *Story of My Life*, 247.

30. Keller, *Midstream*, 132–133.

31. Keller, *Story of My Life*, xiv, 242, 246, 240, 450.

32. Lash, *Helen and Teacher*, 489.

33. Herrmann, *Helen Keller*, 77; Gitter, *Imprisoned Guest*, 291.

34. Keller to William Wade, in Keller, *Story of My Life*, 366.

35. Keller, *Story of My Life*, 217, 173.

36. Ibid., 22, 35, 38–40, 47–48.

37. Herrmann, *Helen Keller*, 252.

38. Ibid., 248–249; Helen's short quotation on the "purple peaks" of Killarney is from William Allingham's *The Abbot of Inisfallen*.

39. Lash, *Helen and Teacher*, 264.

40. Coates, "Profile of Helen Keller."

41. Cutsforth, *The Blind*, 51, 52–56.

42. Ibid., 51.

43. Herrmann, *Helen Keller*, 299.

44. Laborit, *Le cri de la mouette*, 73.

45. Lash, *Helen and Teacher*, 47; "Anne Sullivan's Account" in Keller, *Story of My Life*, 243–244.

46. "John Macy's Account" in Keller, *Story of My Life*, 237.

47. "Anne Sullivan's Account" in Keller, *Story of My Life*, 145.

48. Keller, *Story of My Life*, 137, 138, 144–145, 153–154.

49. Bébian, *Journal de l'instruction*, 156–157.

50. Lash, *Helen and Teacher*, 46.

51. "Anne Sullivan's Account" in Keller, *Story of My Life*, 138, 146, 148, 153.

52. Lane, *When the Mind Hears*, 159.

Chapter 10. Bébian Reborn

1. Myklebust, *Psychology of Deafness*, 144; Maher, *Seeing Language in Sign*, 20.

2. Maher, *Seeing Language in Sign*, 17–18, 42.

3. Bébian, *Mimographie*, vi.

4. Maher, *Seeing Language in Sign*, 41.

5. Ibid., 30–33.

6. Stokoe, *Language in Hand*, 53; Baker and Battison, eds., *Sign Language and the Deaf Community*, 32.

7. Stokoe, *Language in Hand*, 54.

8. Conversation with Harlan Lane, fall 2007.

9. Maher, *Seeing Language in Sign*, 52.

10. Stokoe, "Sign Language Structure," 5.

11. Stokoe is not alone here. Other modern American experts have confused (1) l'Épée's convoluted methodical sign (e.g., striking a desk with the index finger for emphasis to indicate the suffix *-able*, meaning [as in English] capable of being "-ed " [manag*ed*, manage*able*; ador*é*, ador*able*]) with (2) the eighteenth-century French sign for the word *able* itself. Compare Klima and Bellugi, *Signs of Language*, 71, with l'Épée, *La véritable manière*, 23–25. That sign in LSF (for the equivalent French word, *capable*) is the inflection of the open hands inward to a (closed) S shape at breast level (not an index finger tapping on the table); in ASL both hands are held at breast level, side by side in an S shape, palms down, and then quickly moved down together. In fact, the space constraints and absence of "props" are, in general, the same for LSF, ASL, and other sign languages for reasons of visibility and economy of time and space. See Frères de Saint-Gabriel, *Iconographie des signes*, 125.

12. Edwards, *Words Made Flesh*, 27, 40, 42, 44; Lane and Grosjean, *Recent Perspectives*, 127–129.

13. Oliver Sacks made a similar error almost thirty years later when he described Bébian, who was never Sicard's student and regarded him as something of a buffoon, as "Sicard's pupil." See O. Sacks, *Seeing Voices*, 20.

14. In Bébian's terms, *caractères indicatifs du mouvement, caractères de la main, caractères des diverses parties du corps,* and *points physionomiques.*

15. Maher, *Seeing Language in Sign*, 66.

16. Stokoe, "Sign Language Structure," 6.

17. Note from Humphries to the author, July 22, 2016.

18. Maher, *Seeing Language in Sign*, 66.

19. Nagourney, "Stokoe Dies at 80." Nagourney seemed to have had only the faintest idea about whom he was writing.

20. Maher, *Seeing Language in Sign*, 57.

21. Searle, "Chomsky's Revolution."

22. Stokoe, "Sign Language Structure," 16; Fox, *Talking Hands,* 93.

23. He does show it phonetically for us as *kehreem*. Stokoe explains that *chereme* is the most practical of terms: "The combining form, <u>cher</u>-, 'handy,' as old as Homeric Greek, has been preferred to the learned <u>chir</u>- or <u>cheir</u>-," though only a classicist would have a clue as to what Stokoe was talking about. He also uses the term loosely since he does not discuss the *chereme's* (signed *phoneme's*) role in change of meaning. He really considers the specific place, shape, and motion components of a sign as *phones*, though it is clear that a change in one (and not the other) of the components in a sign will often wholly change its meaning and will thus be a true phoneme.

24. Stokoe makes this point in characteristically awkward prose: "If this non-congruence of configuration cheremes and alphabetic configurations is kept in mind, we may for convenience still make use of letter symbols to represent the cheremes of the sign language." See Stokoe, "Sign Language Structure," 22.

25. Compare Bébian, *Mimographie* (plates 1 and 2) with ibid., 34–35.

26. Bébian, *Éloge*, 53–54, and *Manuel d'enseignement*, vol. 2, 143–144.

27. Bertin, *Auguste Bébian*, 54.

Chapter 11. To Sign Is to Speak

1. Chomsky, *Language and Mind*, 81; Lorenz, "Kant's Doctrine of the A Priori," 234.

2. There are, however, neural aphasias in which grammatical competence—and only grammatical competence—is impaired. Ibid., 81.

3. See, for example, Searle, "End of the Revolution;" Berwick and Chomsky, *Why Only Us*; and Tattersall, "At the Birth of Language."

4. Bébian, *Journal de l'instruction*, vol. 1, 160–161.

5. See Goldin-Meadow and Mylander, "Spontaneous Sign Systems."

6. Stokoe, *Language in Hand*, 33–34.

7. Stokoe to Maher, January 1, 1991, in Maher, *Seeing Language in Sign*, 63.

8. Berthier, *Les sourds-muets*, 32, translated by Franklin Philip in Lane, *Deaf Experience*, 176.

9. Rowe and Levine, *Concise Introduction to Linguistics*, 258; O. Sacks, *Seeing Voices*, 90; Neidle et al., *Syntax of American Sign Language*, 30.

10. Klima and Bellugi, *Signs of Language*, 35.

11. Société Centrale, *Banquets,* vol. 1, 100.

12. Laborit, *Le cri de la mouette*, 73.

Chapter 12. Milan Is Still, and Always, Today

1. Fant to Maher, May 1, 1991, quoted in Maher, *Seeing Language in Sign*, 171–172.

2. Bertin, *Auguste Bébian*, 43.

3. Livingston, *Rethinking the Education of Deaf Students*, 3.

4. Virgil, *The Aeneid*, book 2, line 1: *Conticuere omnes intentique ora tenebant* (Everyone now became still and attentive), and book 1, lines 1–3: *Arma virumque cano Troiae qui primus ab oris Italiam, fato profugus, Laviniaque venit littora* (I sing of arms and of a man who, driven by fate, was the first to come to the Italian shore from the coast of Troy).

5. Proust, *Du côté de chez Swann*, 1. *Longtemps, je me suis couché de bonne heure. Parfois, à peine ma bougie éteinte, mes yeux se fermaient si vite que je n'avais pas le temps de me dire: "Je m'endors."* (For a long time, I went to bed early. At times, with my candle barely out, my eyes closed so quickly that I hadn't the time to tell myself: "I'm going to sleep").

6. Laborit, *Le cri de la mouette,* 49, 53–54, 55–56, 73, 87–88. Quotations from Laborit in the subsequent three paragraphs of the text are all from this work.

7. For another common account of orally trained, isolated Deaf children expecting an early death, see, for example, the 1992 documentary film written and directed by Nicolas Philibert, *Le pays des sourds*.

8. Shakespeare, *King Lear*, act 1, scene 1, lines 96–102.

9. Lane, *Mask of Benevolence*, 215.

10. Uziel et al., "Ten-Year Follow-up," 626.

11. Gillot, *Le droit des sourds*.

12. Gillot, "Le droit des sourds: Où en est-on?"

13. Kohl, *Language and Education of the Deaf*, 13.

14. Marschark, *Raising and Educating a Deaf Child*, 178.

15. Wright, *Deafness*, 43, 89, 103, 110, 178.

16. Mottez, *Les sourds existent-ils?*, 284–285, 314.

Chapter 13. Language in Electrons

1. Dickens, *Barnaby Rudge*, 790.

2. Five Deaf Individuals, *Grève de la faim*.

3. Waltzman and Roland, *Cochlear Implants*, 1; Humphries et al., "Language Acquisition for Deaf Children."

4. Marschark et al., "Will Cochlear Implants Close the Reading Achievement Gap?," 20; Hu, "Silenced Voice"; Power, "Models of Deafness."

5. Berthier, *Discours* (1857).

6. Waltzman and Roland, *Cochlear Implants*, 2–4.

7. See Clark, *Sounds from Silence*.

8. Kirkwood, "Research Firm Analyzes Market Share"; National Institutes of Health, "Cochlear Implants."

9. Massachusetts Eye and Ear Infirmary, *Cochlear Implants*.

10. Wright, *Deafness*, xv.

11. Papsin and Gordon, "Cochlear Implants"; National Institutes of Health, "Cochlear Implants"; Sherman, "Closing the Gap."

12. Clark, *Sounds from Silence*, 203.

13. Scott, "Inventor of Bionic Ear Wins Prestigious Award."

14. Alexander Graham Bell Association, "Position Statement"; Arnos et al., "Comparative Analysis of the Genetic Epidemiology of Deafness."

15. Centre Technique National, *Rapport final* (covering the full ten years of the study), 2.

16. Quoted in Lane et al., *People of the Eye*, 167.

17. Chorost, *Rebuilt*, 133, 137.

18. Bell, "Growth of the Oral Method."

19. Sanborn, Letter.

20. Centre Technique National, *Premier rapport* (on the first five years of the ten-year study), 147–148.

21. Ibid., 147.

22. Punch and Hyde, "Children with Cochlear Implants," 406; Papsin and Gordon, "Cochlear Implants for Children," 2381; Boston Children's Hospital, *Program Considerations*, 7.

23. Centre Technique National, *Rapport final*, 150.

24. Quoted in Ouellette, "Hearing the Deaf," 1259.

25. Punch and Hyde, "Children with Cochlear Implants," 414; Hospital for Sick Children, University of Toronto, "Cochlear Implant Program, Information for Parents" (emphasis in original).

26. Marschark et al., "Will Cochlear Implants Close the Reading Achievement Gap?"; Sarant, "Cochlear Implants in Children," 352.

27. Uziel et al., "Ten-Year Follow-up," 615, 619.

28. Marschark et al., "Will Cochlear Implants Close the Reading Achievement Gap?"

29. Jenkins, "Question of Signs," 217.

30. Centre Technique National, *Rapport final*, 5–7. The introduction to the *Rapport final* offers the following tautological sentences: "In oral communication, perception and production play a very important role. They permit the acquisition and production of language, which is, in its oral form, one of the means of generating exchanges through a sophisticated system of linguistic communication" (47).

31. Ibid., 161.

Chapter 14. Picture a Classroom

1. Faulkner and Pisoni, "Some Observations about Cochlear Implants."

2. Humphries et al., "Language Acquisition for Deaf Children."

3. Ibid.

4. Gorouben and Virole, *Le bilinguisme*, 178–180; Power, *Models of Deafness*.

5. Tvingstedt and Preisler, "A Psychosocial Follow-up Study of Children with Cochlear Implants," 14.

6. Punch and Hyde, "Children with Cochlear Implants," 406.

7. Lang, "Cochlear Implants in Children," 2; Ouelette, "Hearing the Deaf," 1270.

8. Punch and Hyde, "Children with Cochlear Implants," 405.

9. Faulkner and Pisoni, "Some Observations about Cochlear Implants."

10. Humphries et al., "Language Acquisition for Deaf Children." The statement is based on a 2001 Council of Europe report, though the authors note that "the findings of that report are still largely true: cochlear implant 'stars' are visible, but they are few and far between." See also Tvingstedt and Preisler, "A Psychosocial Follow-up Study of Children with Cochlear Implants," 9.

11. Centre Technique National, *Rapport final*, 58–69.

12. Ouelette, "Hearing the Deaf," 1260.

13. Bell, *Deaf Variety*, 41.

Appendix 1. A Mortal Trinity

1. The study of the evolutionary transition of our predecessors from fish to tetrapod is a field in which information and interpretation have grown substantially in recent years. See generally Clack, "The Fish-Tetrapod Transition," and "Getting a Leg Up."

Bibliography

Alard, Jean. *Controverse entre l'abée de l'Épée et Samuel Heinicke* (Controversy between the abée de l'Épée and Samuel Heinicke). Paris: G. Pelluard, 1881.

Alexander Graham Bell Association for the Deaf and Hard of Hearing. "Position Statement: Cochlear Implants in Children." http://www.agbell. org/Document.aspx?id=386.

Amman, Johann Conrad. *Surdus Loquens* (Deaf man talking). Amsterdam: Apud Henricum Wetstenium, 1692.

Anagnos, Michael. Letter, June 22, 189[2?] [1894?]. Archives of the Perkins School for the Blind, Watertown, MA.

———. "Note." Sixtieth Annual Report of the Trustees of the Perkins Institution and Massachusetts School for the Blind for the Year Ending September 30, 1891. Boston: Wright & Potter Printing Co., State Printers, 1892. https://archive.org/stream/annualreportoftr5860perk#page/n577/mode/2up.

Anderson, Stephen R. *Languages: A Very Short Introduction.* Oxford, Eng.: Oxford University Press, 2012.

Aristotle. *De Sensu.* Cambridge, Eng.: Cambridge University Press, 1906.

Arnos, Kathleen S., et al. "A Comparative Analysis of the Genetic Epidemiology of Deafness in the United States in Two Sets of Pedigrees Collected More Than a Century Apart." *American Journal of Human Genetics* 83, no. 2 (2008): 200. http://www.ncbi.nlm.nih.gov/pmc/articles/PMC2495057/.

Augustine, *De quantitate animae* (The measure of the soul). Philadelphia: Peter Reilly Co., 1933.

Autin, Jean. *Les Frères Pereire.* Paris: Perrin, 1984.

Baker, Charlotte, and Robin Battison, eds. *Sign Language and the Deaf Community: Essays in Honor of William C. Stokoe*. Silver Spring, MD: National Association of the Deaf, 1980.

Barnard, Henry. *Tribute to Gallaudet*. Hartford, CT: Brockett & Hutchinson, 1852. https://archive.org/details/tributetogallaud00barn2.

Bauby, Jean-Dominique. *Le scaphandre et le papillon* (The diving bell and the butterfly). Paris: Robert Laffont, 1997.

Bauman, H. Dirksen, ed. *Open Your Eyes: Deaf Studies Talking*. Minneapolis: University of Minnesota Press, 2008.

Baynton, Douglas C. *Forbidden Signs*. Chicago: University of Chicago Press, 1996.

Bébian, Roch-Ambroise Auguste. *Éloge de Charles-Michel de l'Épée, fondateur de l'Institution des Sourds-Muets* (In praise of Charles-Michel de l'Épée, founder of the Institution of the Deaf). Paris: J.G. Dentu, 1819.

———. *Essai sur les sourds-muets et sur le langage naturel, ou introduction à une classification naturelle des idées avec leurs signes propres* (An essay on the deaf and their natural language, or an introduction to the natural relationship between ideas and the signs that express them). Paris: J.G. Dentu, 1817.

———. *Examen critique de la nouvelle organisation de l'enseignement dans l'Institution Royale des Sourds-Muets de Paris* (A critical examination of the new teaching system at the Royal Institute of the Deaf in Paris). Paris: Treuttel et Wurtz, Hachette, 1834.

———. *Journal de l'instruction des sourds-muets et des aveugles* (Journal of the instruction of the deaf and the blind), vols. 1 and 2 (in a single volume). Paris: Hachette, 1826–1827.

———. *Manuel d'enseignement pratique des sourds-muets* (A practical manual for teaching the deaf), vols. 1 and 2. Paris: Mequignon l'aîné, 1827.

———. *Mimographie, ou Essai d'écriture mimique, propre à régulariser le langage des sourds-muets* (Mimography, or An essay on the writing of signs in order to standardize the language of the deaf). Paris: Chez Louis Colas, 1825.

Bekesy (von), Georg. *Experiments in Hearing.* New York: McGraw Hill, 1960.

Bell, Alexander Graham. "Growth of the Oral Method of Instructing the Deaf." Address to the Horace Mann School for the Deaf, Boston, 1894. https://archive.org/details/cihm_24571.

——. *Memoir upon the Formation of a Deaf Variety of the Human Race.* Paper presented to the National Academy of Sciences in New Haven, Connecticut, on November 13, 1883. http://www.biodiversitylibrary.org/item/86278#page/8/mode/1up.

——. "The Question of Sign-Language." *The Educator* 5, no. 3 (1894): 3.

Bernard, Yves. *Approche de la gestualité à l'institution des sourds-muets de Paris au XVIIIe et au XIXe siècle* (The approach to sign language at the Paris institute of the deaf in the eighteenth and nineteenth centuries). Ph.D. diss., Université de Paris, 1999.

Berthier, Ferdinand. *Discours prononcé en langage mimique le 8 août 1857 à la distribution des prix de l'Institution des Sourds Muets de Paris* (Prize day speech given in sign language at the Institution of the Deaf in Paris, August 8, 1857). Paris: Boucquin, 1857.

——. "Lettre supplique" (Letter in support of Auguste Bébian). Archives of the Institut national de jeunes sourds, Paris, 1831.

——. *Notice sur la vie et les ouvrages de Auguste Bébian, ancien censeur des études de l'Institut Royal des sourds-muets de Paris* (An account of the life and works of Auguste Bébian, former director of studies at the Royal Institute of the deaf in Paris). Paris: J. Ledoyen, 1839.

——. *Les sourds-muets avant et depuis l'abbé de l'Épée* (The deaf before and after the abbé de l'Épée). Paris: Ledoyen, 1840.

Bertin, Fabrice. *Auguste Bébian et les sourds: Le chemin de l'émancipation* (Auguste Bébian and the deaf: The path of emancipation). Ph.D. diss., Université de Poitiers, 2015.

Berwick, Robert C., and Noam Chomsky. *Why Only Us: Language and Evolution.* Cambridge, MA: MIT Press, 2015.

Bézagu-Deluy, Maryse. *L'Abée de l'Épée.* Paris: Éditions Seghers, 1990.

Biesold, Horst. *Crying Hands: Eugenics and Deaf People in Nazi Germany.* Washington, DC: Gallaudet University Press, 1999.

Bonet, Juan Pablo. *Réduction [or Reduccion] de las letras y arte para enseñar a ablar los mudos* (The simplification of letters and the art of teaching the deaf to speak). Madrid: Francisco Abarca de Angulo, 1620.

———. *Réduction des lettres à leurs éléments primitifs et art d'enseigner à parler aux muets.* French translation from the Spanish by E. Bassouls and A. Boyer. Paris: Chez les Traducteurs, 1891.

Boston Children's Hospital. *About Cochlear Implants.* Boston: Children's Hospital, 2005–2007.

Buchanan, Robert M. *Illusions of Equality, Deaf Americans in School and Factory, 1850–1950.* Washington, DC: Gallaudet University Press, 1999.

Campbell, Ruth, et al. "Activation of Auditory Cortex during Silent Lipreading." *Science* 276, no. 5312 (1997): 593.

Canby, Margaret T. *Birdie and His Fairy Friends: A Book for Little Children.* Philadelphia: Claxton, Remsen & Haffelfinger, 1873.

Center for Deaf and Hard of Hearing Children, Boston Children's Hospital. *Program Considerations for a Child with a Cochlear Implant in the Oral/ Mainstream Classroom.* Boston: Children's Hospital, 2003.

Centre Technique National d'Études et de Recherches sur les Handicaps et les Inadaptations (CTNERHI). *Premier rapport global à 5 ans* (Interim five-year global report). Paris, 2006. http://acfos.org/wp-content/uploads/base_doc/sciences_techniques/rapport_ctnerhi_suivilongitudinal.pdf.

———. *Rapport final sur le suivi longitudinal sur 10 ans d'enfants sourds pré-linguaux implantés* (Final report on the ten-year longitudinal study of implanted prelingually deaf children). Paris, 2011. Conclusions available at http://acfos.org/wp-content/uploads/base_doc/societe/revue37_conclusion_ctnerhi.pdf.

Chomsky, Noam. *Language and Mind,* 3rd ed. Cambridge, Eng.: Cambridge University Press, 2006.

———. *Syntactic Structures.* Berlin: Mouton de Gruyter, 1957, 2002.

Chorost, Michael. *Rebuilt.* New York: Mariner, 2006.

Clack, Jennifer A. "The Fish-Tetrapod Transition: New Fossils and Interpretations." *Evolution: Education and Outreach* 284, no. 2 (2009): 213. http://link.springer.com/article/10.1007/s12052-009-0119-2.

———. "Getting a Leg Up on Land." *Scientific American* 293, no. 100 (2005): 7.

Clark, Graeme. *Sounds from Silence*. St. Leonards, New South Wales: Allen & Unwin, 2000.

Coates, Robert. "Profile of Helen Keller." *New Yorker*, January 25, 1930.

Cohen, Leah Hager. *Train Go Sorry*. New York: Houghton Mifflin, 1994.

Commission of the United Kingdom on the Condition of the Blind, the Deaf and Dumb, etc. *Report*. Washington, DC: Volta Bureau, 1892. https://archive.org/stream/gu_educationdeafoogall#page/n7/mode/2up.

Coudon, Jean-Max. *Le silence apprivoisé* (Silence tamed). Paris: Éditions Anne Carrière, 2005.

Cutsforth, Thomas D. *The Blind in School and Society*. New York: American Foundation for the Blind, 1951, 1972.

Cuxac, Christian. "Le Congrès de Milan" (The Congress of Milan). In *Le pouvoir des signes* (The power of signs). Paris: Institut national de jeunes sourds, 1990.

Davis, Susan. *Our Forgotten Children in the Schools*. Bethesda, MD: SHHH Publications, 2001.

Desloges, Pierre. *Observations d'un sourd et muèt, sur un cours élémentaire d'éducation des sourds et muèts* (Observations of a deaf man on an elementary course of education for the deaf). Paris: B. Morin, 1779.

Dickens, Charles. *Barnaby Rudge*. In *The Works of Charles Dickens*, vol. 6. New York: P.F. Collier, 1880.

Diderot, Denis. *Lettre sur les sourds et muets* (Letter concerning the deaf). Paris: G.F. Flammarion, 2000.

Dodd, Barbara, and Ruth Campbell. *Hearing by Eye: The Psychology of Lip-Reading*. London: Erlbaum Associates, 1987.

Edwards, Rebecca A. R. *Words Made Flesh*. New York: New York University Press, 2012.

Encrevé, Florence. *Sourds et société française au XIXe siècle* (The deaf and French society in the nineteenth century). Ph.D. diss., Université de Paris, 2008.

Engstrom, Hans, Harlow W. Ades, and Anton Andersson. *Structural Pattern of the Organ of Corti*. Stockholm: Almqvist & Wiksell, 1966.

l'Épée (de), Charles-Michel. *La véritable manière d'instruire les sourds et muets, confirmée par une longue expérience* (The real way to teach the deaf, proved through long experience). Paris: Chez Nyon l'Aîné, 1784.

Fain, Gérald. *De la parole au chant, qu'est-ce que la voix?* (From speech to song, what is the voice?). Paris: Édition le Pommier, 2007.

Faulkner, Kathleen F., and David B. Pisoni. "Some Observations about Cochlear Implants: Challenges and Future Directions." *Neuroscience Discovery* 1, no. 9 (2013). http://dx.doi.org/10.7243/2052-6946-1-9.

Five Deaf Individuals. *Grève de la faim des Cinq Sourds* (Hunger strike of the Deaf Five). Paris: Communiqué, 2008.

Fox, Margalit. *Talking Hands.* New York: Simon & Schuster, 2007.

Frères de Saint-Gabriel, Les. *Iconographie des signes, 1853–1854* (The iconography of signs, 1853–1854). Limoges: Éditions Lambert-Lucas, 2006.

Gallaudet, Edward Miner. *History of the College for the Deaf.* Washington, DC: Gallaudet University Press, 1983.

Geisler, C. Daniel. *From Sound to Synapse.* New York: Oxford University Press, 1998.

Geoffroy, Étienne-Louis. *Dissertation sur l'organe de l'ouïe* (Dissertation on the organ of hearing). Paris: Cavelier, 1778.

Gérando, Joseph-Marie. *De l'éducation des sourds-muets de naissance* (On the education of the deaf from birth). Paris: Mequignon l'Ainé Père, 1827.

Gillot, Dominique. *Le droit des sourds* (The rights of the deaf). Paris: Parliamentary Report, 1998.

———. "Le droit des sourds: Où en est-on?" (The rights of the deaf: Where are we?). Lecture, October 1, 2015, Institut national de jeunes sourds, Paris.

Gitter, Elisabeth. *The Imprisoned Guest: Samuel Howe and Laura Bridgman, the Original Deaf-Blind Girl.* New York: Farrar, Straus and Giroux, 2001.

Golan, Lew. *Reading between the Lips.* Chicago: Bonus Books, 1995.

Goldin-Meadow, Susan, and Carolyn Mylander. "Spontaneous Sign Systems Created by Deaf Children in Two Cultures." *Nature* 391 (1998): 279.

Gorouben, Annette, and Benoît Virole, eds. *Le bilinguisme aujourd'hui et demain* (Bilingualism today and tomorrow). Paris: Centre Technique National d'Études et de Recherches sur les Handicaps et les Inadaptations, 2004.

Grahame, Kenneth. *The Wind in the Willows.* London: Methuen and Co., 1908.

Gray, Charlotte. *Reluctant Genius: Alexander Graham Bell and the Passion for Invention.* New York: Arcade Publishing, 2006.

Groce, Nora Ellen. *Everyone Here Spoke Sign Language: Hereditary Deafness on Martha's Vineyard.* Cambridge, MA: Harvard University Press, 1988.

Habets, Bill. *The Tinnitus Handbook.* Encinitas, CA: United Research Publishers, 2002.

Hall, David P. (attrib.). "Miss Sullivan's Methods: A Comparison between Her Reports to the Perkins Institution and the Statements Made in the Volume Entitled 'The Story of My Life' by Helen Keller." Archives of the Perkins School for the Blind, Watertown, MA, unpublished manuscript, 1905(?).

Herrmann, Dorothy. *Helen Keller: A Life.* Chicago: University of Chicago Press, 1998.

Hickok, Gregory, Ursula Bellugi, and Edward S. Klima. "Sign Language in the Brain." *Scientific American* 284, no. 6 (2001): 57.

Hillenbrand, James M. *Auditory Physiology.* Unpublished manuscript, Western Michigan University, Kalamazoo, 2009.

Hospital for Sick Children, University of Toronto. "Cochlear Implant Program, Information for Parents," 2014. http://www.sickkids.ca/Cochlear-Implant/Information-for-parents/Expectations/index.html.

Hu, Jennifer. "The Silenced Voice: Examining the Evolving Debate on Pediatric Cochlear Implantation." *Business Ethics* (2014). http://business-ethics.com/2014/09/30/1852-the-silenced-voice-examining-the-evolving-debate-on-pediatric-cochlear-implantation/.

Hudspeth, A. James. "How the Ear's Works Work." *Nature* 341 (1989): 397.

Humphrey, Heman. *The Life and Labors of the Rev. T.H. Gallaudet, LL.D.* New York: Robert Carter & Brothers, 1857.

Humphries, Tom L., et al. "Language Acquisition for Deaf Children: Reducing the Harms of Zero Tolerance to the Use of Alternative Approaches." *Harm Reduction Journal* 9, no. 16 (2012). http://harmreductionjournal. biomedcentral.com/articles/10.1186/1477-7517-9-16.

Itard, Jean-Marc. "Constat médical relatif à la blessure de Paulmier, daté du 3 janvier 1821" (Medical report relating to Paulmier's injury, dated January 3, 1821). Archives of the Institut national de jeunes sourds, 1821.

Jenkins, W. G. "The Question of Signs." *The Educator* 4, no. 8 (1893): 216.

Keller, Arthur H. Letter, February 5, 1892. Archives of the Perkins School for the Blind, Watertown, MA.

Keller, Helen. Letter, September 28, 1906. Helen Keller Archives of the American Foundation for the Blind, New York.

———. *Midstream: My Later Life.* Garden City, NJ: Sun Dial Press, 1929.

———. *The Story of My Life, with Supplementary Accounts by Anne Sullivan, Her Teacher, and John Albert Macy.* New York: W.W. Norton, 1903, 2003, 2004.

Kerr Love, James, and William Hall Addison. *Deaf Mutism.* Glasgow: James MacLehose & Sons, 1896.

"King Frost Again." *The Goodson Gazette, Virginia School for the Deaf,* January 16, 1892.

Kirkwood, David H. "Research Firm Analyzes Market Share, Retail Activity, and Prospects of Major Hearing Aid Manufacturers." *Hearing Health and Technology Matters* (2013). http://hearinghealthmatters.org/hearing-newswatch/2013/research-firm-analyzes-market-share-retail-stores-prospects-of-major-hearing-aid-makers/.

Kisor, Henry. *What's That Pig Outdoors? A Memoir of Deafness.* New York: Penguin Books, 1990.

Klima, Edward S., and Ursula Bellugi. *The Signs of Language.* Cambridge, MA: Harvard University Press, 1979.

Knaebel, Georges. *Brouhaha: Analyse d'une surdité* (Brouhaha: Analysis of a particular deafness). Paris: la Chambre d'Échos, 2000.

Kohl, Herbert R. *Language and Education of the Deaf.* New York: Center for Urban Education, 1966.

Kyle, Jim G., Bencie Woll, G. Pullen, and F. Maddix. *Sign Language: The Study of Deaf People and Their Language.* Cambridge, Eng.: Cambridge University Press, 1988.

Laborit, Emmanuelle. *Le cri de la mouette* (The cry of the seagull). Paris: Robert Laffont, 1993.

Ladd, Paddy. *Understanding Deaf Culture: In Search of Deafhood.* Clevedon, Eng.: Multilingual Matters, 2003.

Lane, Harlan. *The Mask of Benevolence.* 1992; New York: Vintage Books, 1993.

———. *When the Mind Hears.* New York: Vintage Books, 1989.

Lane, Harlan, ed. *The Deaf Experience.* Washington, DC: Gallaudet University Press, 1984, 2006.

Lane, Harlan, and François Grosjean. *Recent Perspectives on American Sign Language.* Hillsdale, NJ: Lawrence Erlbaum, 1980.

Lane, Harlan, Richard C. Pillard, and Ulf Hedberg. *The People of the Eye: Deaf Ethnicity and Ancestry.* New York: Oxford University Press, 2011.

Lang, Harry G. "Cochlear Implants in Children: Ethics and Choices." *Sign Language Studies* 3, no. 1 (2002): 90. http://scholarworks.rit.edu/article/1646.

Lash, Joseph P. *Helen and Teacher.* Reading, MA: Addison-Wesley, 1980.

List, Gunther. "Heinicke et l'oralisme: Un exemple de modernisation" (Heinicke and oralism: An example of modernization). In *Le pouvoir des signes* (The power of signs). Paris: Institut national de jeunes sourds, 1990.

Livingston, Sue. *Rethinking the Education of Deaf Students.* Portsmouth, NH: Heinemann, 1997.

Locke, John. *The Works of John Locke.* London: C. and L. Rivington, 1824. http://enlightenment.supersaturated.com/johnlocke/BOOKIIIChapterII.html#BOOKIIIChapterII2.

Lorenz, Konrad. "Kant's Doctrine of the A Priori in the Light of Contemporary Biology." In Michael Ruse, ed., *Philosophy after Darwin: Contemporary and Classical Readings.* Princeton, NJ: Princeton University Press, 2009.

Maher, Jane. *Seeing Language in Sign: The Work of William C. Stokoe.* Washington, DC: Gallaudet University Press, 1996.

Marschark, Marc. *Raising and Educating a Deaf Child.* New York: Oxford University Press, 2007.

Marschark, Marc, et al. "Will Cochlear Implants Close the Reading Achievement Gap for Deaf Students?" Oxford Handbooks Online, 2012. http://www.oxfordhandbooks.com/view/10.1093/oxfordhb/9780195390032.001.0001/oxfordhb-9780195390032-e-009.

Massachusetts Eye and Ear Infirmary. *Cochlear Implants.* Boston: Massachusetts Eye and Ear Infirmary, 2009.

McConkey Robbins, Amy, et al. "Effect of Age at Cochlear Implantation on Auditory Skill Development in Infants and Toddlers." *Archives of Otolaryngology and Head and Neck Surgery* 130 (2004): 570.

Medoff, Mark. *Children of a Lesser God.* New York: Dramatists Play Service, 1980.

Mirzoeff, Nicholas. *Silent Poetry: Deafness, Sign, and Visual Culture in Modern France.* Princeton, NJ: Princeton University Press, 1995.

Montaigne, Michel de. *Les Essais.* Paris: Christophile Journel, 1659. http://www.bribes.org/trismegiste/montable.htm.

Moody, Bill, et al. *La langue des signes* (Sign language). Paris: Éditions IVT, vol. 1: *Histoire et grammaire* (History and grammar), 1998; vols. 2 and 3: *Dictionnaire bilingue LSF/Français* (Bilingual dictionary LSF/French), 1997.

Moore, Brian C. *Cochlear Hearing Loss.* London: Whurr Publishers, 1998.

——. *An Introduction to the Psychology of Hearing.* London: Elsevier, 2004.

Mottez, Bernard. *Les sourds existent-ils?* (Do the deaf exist?). Paris: l'Harmattan, 2006.

Munro, H. H. *The Short Stories of Saki.* New York: The Modern Library, 1958.

Myklebust, Helmer R. *The Psychology of Deafness.* New York: Grune & Stratton, 1960.

Nagourney, Eric. "William Stokoe Jr., Sign Language Advocate, Dies at 80." *New York Times,* April 11, 2000. http://www.nytimes.com/2000/04/11/us/william-stokoe-jr-sign-language-advocate-dies-at-80.html.

National Institutes of Health, National Institute on Deafness and Other Communicative Disorders. "Cochlear Implants." http://www.nidcd. nih.gov/health/hearing/pages/coch.aspx.

Neidle, Carol, et al. *The Syntax of American Sign Language: Functional Categories and Hierarchical Structure (Language, Speech, and Communication)*. Cambridge, MA: MIT Press, 2000.

Ouelette, Alicia. "Hearing the Deaf: Cochlear Implants, the Deaf Community, and Bioethical Analysis." *Valparaiso Law Review* 45, no. 3 (2011): 1247. http://scholar.valpo.edu/cgi/viewcontent.cgi?article= 1840&context=vulr.

Ozick, Cynthia. "What Helen Keller Saw." *New Yorker,* June 16, 2003. http:// www.newyorker.com/magazine/2003/06/16/what-helen-keller-saw.

Padden, Carol, and Tom Humphries. *Deaf in America: Voices from a Culture*. Cambridge, MA: Harvard University Press, 1988.

———. *Inside Deaf Culture*. Cambridge, MA: Harvard University Press, 2005.

Papsin, Blake C., and Karen A. Gordon. "Cochlear Implants for Children with Severe-to-Profound Hearing Loss." *New England Journal of Medicine* 357, no. 23 (2007): 2380. https://mcb.berkeley.edu/courses/mcb61/ NEJM_CochlearImplants.pdf.

Pélissier, Pierre. *Poésies d'un sourd-muet* (Poetry of a deaf man). Paris: Gosselin, 1844.

Petitto, Laura Ann, et al. "Speech-like Cerebral Activity in Profoundly Deaf People Processing Signed Languages: Implications for the Neural Basis of Human Language." *Proceedings of the National Academy of Sciences* 97, no. 25 (2000): 13961.

Philibert, Nicolas. *Le pays des sourds* (The land of the deaf). Documentary film. Paris, 1992.

Pinker, Steven. *How the Mind Works*. New York: W.W. Norton, 1997.

———. *The Language Instinct*. New York: William Morrow, 1994.

Plann, Susan. *A Silent Minority: Deaf Education in Spain, 1550–1835*. Oakland: University of California Press, 1997.

Plato. *Cratylus*. Trans. C. D. C. Reeve. Indianapolis: Hackett Publishing, 1998.

Polich, Laura. *The Emergence of the Deaf Community in Nicaragua.* Washington, DC: Gallaudet University Press, 2005.

Power, Des. "Models of Deafness: Cochlear Implants in the Australian Daily Press." *Journal of Deaf Studies and Deaf Education* 10, no. 4 (2005): 451. http://jdsde.oxfordjournals.org/content/10/4/451.full.

Preisler, Gunilla. *Cochlear Implants in Deaf Children.* Strasbourg: Council of Europe Publishing, 2001.

Presneau, Jean-René. "Le son 'à la lettre,' l'éducation des enfants sourds et muets avant l'abbé de l'Épée" (Sound 'letter by letter,' the education of deaf children before the abbé de l'Épée). In *Le pouvoir des signes* (The power of signs). Paris: Institut national de jeunes sourds, 1990.

Proust, Marcel. *Du côté de chez Swann* (Swann's way). Paris: Éditions Gallimard, 1987.

Punch, Renée, and Merv Hyde. "Children with Cochlear Implants in Australia: Educational Settings, Supports, and Outcomes." *Journal of Deaf Studies and Deaf Education* 15, no. 4 (2010): 405. http://jdsde.oxfordjournals.org/content/15/4/405.full.pdf+html.

Quartararo, Anne T. *Deaf Identity and Social Images in Nineteenth-Century France.* Washington, DC: Gallaudet University Press, 2008.

Rée, Jonathan. *I See a Voice: Deafness, Language and the Senses—A Philosophical History.* New York: Henry Holt, 1999.

Romoff, Arlene. *Hear Again.* New York: League for the Hard of Hearing Publications, 1999.

Rosenfeld, Sophia. *A Revolution in Language: The Problem of Signs in Late Eighteenth-Century France.* Stanford, CA: Stanford University Press, 2002.

Rowe, Bruce M., and Diane P. Levine. *A Concise Introduction to Linguistics.* Boston: Pearson, 2006.

Sacks, David. *Letter Perfect.* New York: Random House, 2003.

Sacks, Oliver. *Seeing Voices.* Berkeley: University of California Press, 1989, 1990.

Saint-Loup (de), Aude. "Les sourds-muets au moyen-age: Mille ans de signes oubliés" (The deaf in the middle ages: A thousand years of forgotten signs). In *Le pouvoir des signes* (The power of signs). Paris: Institut national de jeunes sourds, 1990.

Sanborn, Frank B. Letter, *Boston Daily Advertiser*, April 18, 1892. Archives of the Perkins School for the Blind, Watertown, MA.

Sarant, Julia. "Cochlear Implants in Children: A Review." *In Tech* (2012): 352. http://www.intechopen.com/books/hearing-loss/cochlear-implants-in-children-a-review.

Scott, Rebecca. "Inventor of Bionic Ear Wins Prestigious Award and Inspires New Field of Endeavour." In *The Age National* (2013). http://www.theage.com.au/national/education/voice/inventor-of-bionic-ear-wins-prestigious-award-and-inspires-new-field-of-endeavour-20131008-2v5bd.html.

Searle, John R. "End of the Revolution." *New York Review of Books* (2002). http://www.nybooks.com/articles/2002/02/28/end-of-the-revolution/.

———. "A Special Supplement: Chomsky's Revolution in Linguistics." *New York Review of Books* (1972). http://www.nybooks.com/articles/1972/06/29/a-special-supplement-chomskys-revolution-in-lingui/.

Seth, Vikram. *An Equal Music.* London: Phoenix House, 1999.

Sherman, Carl. "Closing the Gap between Cochlear Implants and Natural Hearing." *Brainfacts.org* (2014). http://www.brainfacts.org/about-neuroscience/technologies/articles/2014/closing-the-gap-between-cochlear-implants-and-natural-hearing/.

Sicard, Roch-Ambroise. *Cours d'instruction d'un sourd-muet de naissance* (Course of instruction for a child born deaf). Paris: Le Clere, 1799–1800.

———. *Théorie des signes, ou Introduction à l'étude des langues* (Theory of signs, or Introduction to the study of languages). Paris: J.G. Dentu, 1808.

Société Centrale des Sourds-Muets de Paris. *Banquets des sourds-muets réunis pour fêter les anniversaires de la naissance de l'abbé de l'Épée* (Banquets of the deaf assembled to celebrate the birthday anniversaries of the abbé de l'Épée), vol. 1 (1834–1848). Paris: J. Ledoyen, 1842 [*sic*]; vol. 2 (1849–1863), Paris: L. Hachette, 1864.

Société Universelle des Sourds-Muets. *Banquets des sourds-muets réunis pour fêter les anniversaires de la naissance de l'abbé de l'Épée* (Banquets of the deaf assembled to celebrate the birthday anniversaries of the abbé de l'Épée), vol. 3 (1864–1869). Poissy, France: Arbieu, Lejay et Cie, 1870.

Solomon, Maynard. *Beethoven.* New York: Schirmer Trade Books, 1977, 2001.

Stenross, Barbara. *Missed Connections.* Philadelphia: Temple University Press, 1999.

Stokoe, William C. *Language in Hand.* Washington, DC: Gallaudet University Press, 2001.

———. "Sign Language Structure: An Outline of the Visual Communication Systems of the American Deaf." University of Buffalo: Studies in Linguistics Occasional Papers no. 8, 1960. Reprinted in *Journal of Deaf Studies and Deaf Education* 10, no. 1 (2005). http://jdsde.oxfordjournals. org/content/10/1/3.full.pdf+html.

Stokoe, William C., Dorothy C. Casterline, and Carl G. Croneberg. *A Dictionary of American Sign Language on Linguistic Principles.* Silver Spring, MD: Linstok Press, 1965, 1976.

Stremlau, Tonya M., ed. *The Deaf Way: Anthology II.* Washington, DC: Gallaudet University Press, 2002.

Sullivan, Anne. Letter, November 4, 1891. Archives of the Perkins School for the Blind, Watertown, MA, and *The Mentor* 2, no. 1 (1892): 13.

Swiller, Josh. *the unheard.* New York: Henry Holt, 2007.

Tattersall, Ian. "At the Birth of Language." *New York Review of Books*, August 18, 2016. http://www.nybooks.com/articles/2016/08/18/noam-chomsky-robert-berwick-birth-of-language/.

Tucker, Bonnie P. *Cochlear Implants.* Jefferson, NC: McFarland & Company, 1998.

———. *The Feel of Silence.* Philadelphia: Temple University Press, 1995.

Tvingstedt, Anna-Lena, and Gunilla Preisler. "A Psychosocial Follow-up Study of Children with Cochlear Implants in Different School Settings," 2006. https://dspace.mah.se/bitstream/handle/2043/8147/Psychosocial%20Follow%20up%20Study.pdf;sequence=1.

Uziel, Alain S., et al. "Ten-Year Follow-up of a Consecutive Series of Children with Multichannel Cochlear Implants." *Otology & Neurotology* 28, no. 5 (2007): 615.

Van Cleve, John, John Vickrey, and Barry A. Crouch. *A Place of Their Own: Creating the Deaf Community in America.* Washington, DC: Gallaudet University Press, 1989.

Virgil. *The Aeneid.* Trans. Robert Fitzgerald. New York: Vintage Books, 1990.

Waltzman, Susan P., and J. Thomas Roland Jr., eds. *Cochlear Implants.* New York: Thieme Medical Publishers, 2006.

Winefield, Richard. *Never the Twain Shall Meet: Bell, Gallaudet, and the Communications Debate.* Washington, DC: Gallaudet University Press, 1987.

Woodward, James. *Signs of Sexual Behavior.* Carrollton, TX: T.J. Publishers, 1979.

World's Congress of the Deaf. *Proceedings.* Published in a single volume along with National Association of the Deaf, *Report of the Seventh Convention.* St. Louis, MO, 1904.

Wright, David. *Deafness.* London: Faber and Faber, 1969, 1990.

Yost, William A., and Donald W. Nielsen. *Fundamentals of Hearing.* New York: Holt, Rinehart and Winston, 1977.

Index

Italicized page numbers indicate illustrations and photographs.

Abstract ideas, expression of, 37–39, 75, 88–90, 136, 138, 161, 198

Acanthostega, 204–205, *205, 206*

Air: as the medium of spoken language (and all other sound), 7–8; range of displacement based on intensity of sound, 8–11

Alexander Graham Bell Association, 188

Alphabet: Bonet's theory concerning the shapes of the Roman alphabet (1620), 13, 109; origins of, 223n18. *See also* Manual alphabets

American Annals of the Deaf, 122

American Association to Promote the Teaching of Speech to the Deaf, 117, 125, *128,* 144. *See also* Alexander Graham Bell Association

American School for the Deaf (Hartford), 56, 92

American Sign Language (ASL): Deaf schools (in addition to Gallaudet University using) 110, 179; as formal language, 147, 152; Gallaudet University using for instruction, 93, 145, 170, 179; handshapes of, 18, 156, *216–217*; methodical signs claimed to be incorporated in, 149–150; phonemes (or cheremes) of, 155 (*see also* Phonemes); sexual intercourse, sign for, 89–90; shared signs with other signed languages, 134–135, 140, 229n11; Signed English using root signs from, 171; Stokoe's introduction to, 147; Stokoe's recognition of as formal language, 152, 154–161; tactile (TASL), 133, 134, 141; word order in, 147

Amman, Conrad, 12, 19, 105, 182; *Surdus loquens,* 17

Anagnos, Michael, 118–124, 127, 227n20, 228n25

Anatomy of the ear, 9, 195, 202–212, *203,* 219n1

Andover Theological Seminary, 51–52

Aristotle, vii, 2

Articulation. *See* Oralism

ASL. *See* American Sign Language

Assortative mating. *See* Intermarriage among the Deaf

Augustine, Saint: existence of signed languages recognized by, 2, 45; belief that the Deaf could never learn to read, 2, 49; writes that both

Augustine, Saint (*continued*)
spoken and signed languages "pertain to the soul," 2, 167. *See also* Chomsky, Noam
Auricle (outer ear), 202

Background noise. *See* Real-world communication
Balestra, Serafino, 84, 85, 86, 88, 89
Baptism of the Deaf, 2
Battison, Robin, 149
Bébian, Auguste, vii, 34–44, *35*; words and signs as expressions of preexisting ideas, 37–39, 197; writing as the "painting" of our speech, defined by, 38–39, 136, 138, 156,; as advocate for Deaf education using signed languages, 75–76, 97, 100, 102, 103, 111, 145; Clerc influenced by, 50, 56; views Sicard as "completely ignorant" of signed languages, 38; cochlea recognized as organ of speech by, 103; as director at Saint Jacques, 55; strikes Paulmier on the head with a set of keys, 58–59; dismissed from Saint Jacques, 58; end of life of, 71; declared by Berthier to be "an honorary deaf man," 35; praised by Lenoir as "deaf at heart," 103; "Essay on the Deaf and Their Natural Language," 150; French sign language notation developed by, 157–158, 160, 230n14; Berthier annual banquets of the Deaf in honor of l'Épée and, 66; on methodical signs vs. natural sign language, 149–150; "Mimography: An Essay on the Writing of Sign in Order to Standardize the Language of the Deaf," 151, 157–158, *159*; "picture a classroom" for Deaf instruction, 48, 201; praise for, after his death, 71–72; on principle of first language within each of us, xi, 136, 137, 150, 165; "the thought, born in the brain, bursts forth [in our first language] like a flame sparkling in crystal," 41; running other schools for the Deaf after dismissal from Saint Jacques, 70–71, 225n12; Stokoe compared to, 158; as an example of Isaiah Berlin's *fox,* Stokoe his *hedgehog,* 159; teaching others on the instruction of the Deaf, 49; working with Clerc and Massieu, 54–55
Behavioral linguistics, 164–165
Bel, as measurement of sound, 8
Bell, Alexander Graham, viii, *95, 128*; as advocate of oralism and rejection of signed languages, 92, 105, 112, 116, 144, 182, 189; but viewing them as the quickest way to reach the minds of the Deaf, 100; considers the signing Deaf to be "glory[ing] in their defect," 103; background of, 94–97; "bel" named for, 8; compared to Bonet and Amman, 105; characterizes the use of signed languages as comparable to the exhibition of one's false teeth in public, 103; claims to teach the Deaf to pronounce "foreign sounds," 105; as a eugenicist with a goal to "breed" the Deaf out of existence, 106–107; associating deafness with dwarfism, six-fingered persons, and sexual

abnormalities, 106; *Deaf Variety*,
106–109, 129; view of the
congenitally Deaf as "a defective
race of human beings," 112; Keller
and, 116–117, 120, 125–126; scientific
display by, at Paris World's Fair, 84;
testifying before Royal Commission
on teaching the Deaf, 100–106,
225n13; on underclass of Deaf who
use signed languages, 97, 103–104;
wife's and mother's deafness, 94–97,
100–101, 109

Bell, Mabel, 94–96, would have no
friends among the Deaf, 96; Bell's
inability to improve her speech,
109

Bellugi, Ursula, 168, 169

Berlin, Isaiah, 159

Berry, Duchesse de, 58

Berthier, Ferdinand, vii, *44*; as
advocate for signed languages in
Deaf instruction, 56–57, 82, 115,
147, 152; background of, 44; Central
Society of the Deaf-Mutes of Paris
and, 76; on Diderot's opinion of
the Deaf, 5; on future research on
language and understanding, 168;
honoring Bébian, 35; on inability of
Deaf to compare speech to signed
languages, 182; compares writing to
signed languages, calling the latter
the Deaf's "Art of Phoenicia," vii,
68, 223; Legion of Honor conferred
upon, 61–75; his annual banquets
of the Deaf in honor of l'Épée,
61–76, 81–82; on l'Épée's lack of
teaching skill, 34; loss of influence
of, 81; politics and, 75; seeking to
reinstate Bébian at Saint Jacques,

59–60; teaching Deaf instruction to
others , 48–49

Bertin, Fabrice, 36–37, 160

Blanchet, Alexandre, 77

Blind and Deaf. *See* Deafblind persons

Bonaventure, Saint, 18, 155

Bonet, Juan Pablo, vii; claims Roman
letters reflect the shapes of the
mouth in speaking, 13, 109; use of
leather tongue by, 13–16; Bell
compared to, 105; cochlea
recognized as organ of speech by,
103; on inferiority of Deaf, 13, 107;
on impossibility of teaching
lipreading to the Deaf, 15, 186;
refusing to recognize benefits of
signed languages, 182; use of Saint
Bonaventure's manual alphabet by,
156; on teaching the Deaf to speak,
12, 13–17, 126–127, 181

Braidwood family, 53, 56

Brain's role in hearing and developing
language, 10, 195, 214–215;
comparable regions of the brain
used for expressing and
understanding both speech and
signed languages, xii, 168; efforts to
train the brain to decode and
interpret information from the
cochlear implant, 196

Britain: cochlear implants, efficacy of,
191; experts on Deaf education in,
176; oralism in, 53, 177–178; schools
for the Deaf in, 53. *See also* Royal
Commission on teaching the Deaf

British Sign Language (BSL), 147, 171;
word order in, 147; tactile BSL
(TBSL), 141

Bürgers, Hendricus Jacobus, *113*

Canby, Margaret: "The Frost Fairies," 118–123, 228n21, 228n25

Carlin, John, 65, 93, 107

Caruso, Enrico, 7

Casterline, Dorothy Sueoka, 154

Catholic Emancipation Act (Britain, 1829), 65

Catholicism, association with signed language, 78–79

Center for Deaf Children at Boston's Children's Hospital, 191

Central Society for the Education and Assistance of the Deaf, 76, 77, 80–82

Central Society of the Deaf-Mutes of Paris, 76

Chambellan, Victor-Gomer, 111

Cheremes, 155, 230nn23–24

Child development and language acquisition, 162–165; cochlear implants and, 185; Deaf children acquiring oral and aural skills at expense of signed language mastery, 182, 199; "home" signs, development of by Deaf children, 165–166

Children of a Lesser God (play), 132

Chomsky, Noam: language faculty,162–165, 196; definition of language by, 168–169; richness of a child's language compared to the poverty of the stimulus, 163; Stokoe and, 165–168; Syntactic Structures, 162–165, 167

Chorost, Michael, viii, 189

Christ: curing a Deaf man, 3, 4; and The Word, in Christian teaching, 3–4, 86, 91

Civil Code of 1804, 74

Clark, Graeme, 183, 187–188

Clarke Institution (Northampton, Massachusetts), 84, 126

Clerc, Laurent, 51; on Bébian's role in Deaf teaching, 35; Bell's criticism of, 104, 108, 226n35; early life of, 50; French sign language used by, 48; l'Épée's techniques and, 150; Gallaudet studying French sign language with, 50–51, 54–55; improving Deaf lives, 107; in London with Sicard, 54; methodical signs and, 137, 150; name sign for, 108, 226n35; at Saint Jacques, 55; similarities between French and American sign languages due to, 223n11; teaching of sign language by, 48–49; in United States, 55–56, 65

Coates, Robert, 130–131

Cochlea: converts mechanical to electrical energy, 9–10; as an organ of speech, 18–19, 195; the inner sanctum of all that we hear, 207; three winding chambers (compartments, ducts, scalae), 208–209; organ of Corti contained in its middle compartment, 209; evolution of, 208; characteristic frequencies (of hair cells within), 203, 208, 210, 211, 212

Cochlear implants, 11, 181–194; arguments against, 191–194, 198; arguments in favor of, 189–191; children with implants learning signed languages later in life, 200; compared to hearing aids, 183, 186–187, 191–192; compared to signing children's reading and writing skills, 193; components of, 183–185, *185*; Deaf culture, effect on, 188–189; efficacy of, 183; global use of, 183; hearing parents reporting on their Deaf child's progress with, 193; infants receiving, 187; multiple electrodes, use of, 183, 195; as paradigm shift in treatment of deafness, 181; prelingually Deaf persons and, 187–191; teaching speech vs. signed languages, after implanting, 181–182; emphasis on the signifier (the word) rather than the referent (the idea), 196; comparison of Itard's (later) views with, 197; failure to offer what signed languages can, 197-198; clinical and laboratory settings versus real-world experience, 198–200

CODA (hearing children of Deaf adults), 35

Cogswell, Alice, 52–53

Cogswell, Mason, 52–53

Committee of Deaf-Mutes (France), 60–62

Configurations and movements, of molecules of air to convey spoken languages, and of shapes in light for signed languages, xii, 8, 136, 155, 169

Congenitally Deaf persons: children born Deaf, xi–xii; inability to lipread, 20; need to flourish intellectually, 47; ability to speak, 127; age of implant, 187; born of hearing parents, 104, 108; cochlea functioning of, 10; cochlear implants and, 181, 187–191; goal to reduce number of, 106–109

Congress of Milan (1880), 83–91, 222n3 (Ch. 6); background and earlier congresses, 83–86; Deaf persons at, 86; final resolution adopted, 88–89, 181–182; harm perpetrated by, 91; Italian control of, 86; organizers of, 86; praise for, 177–178; as breaking Bébian's teaching system, 178, 179; suppression of signed languages in Deaf education after, 90–91; Tarra presenting students from oral schools at, 87–88

Connecticut Asylum for the Education and Instruction of Deaf and Dumb Persons, 222n6

Copeland, Charles, 130

Corrado, Alfredo, 172–173, 175

Coudon, Jean-Max, 96–97

Council of Europe report (2001), 234n10

Council of Orange (6th century), 2

Croneberg, Carl, 154

Cures for deafness in Middle Ages, 21

Cutsforth, Thomas, 130–131, 133, 136

Cuxac, Christian, 91

Daguerre, Louis, 63

Deafblind persons, 132; at University of Paris at Saint Denis, 139–143. See *also* Keller, Helen

Deaf children of Deaf parents, 178

Deaf communities' reaction to cochlear implants, 182

Deaf culture, effect of cochlear implants on, 188–189

Deaf education: Deaf teachers, 48, 56, 114, 144, 171; sign-educated European children reading Racine,

Deaf education: (*continued*)
Molière, Voltaire, Cervantes, Goethe, and Pushkin, 49; sign-educated American Deaf children reading Dickens, Scott and Alcott; all others far behind, 40, 102; French influence on, 43, 49; Laborit's education as a Deaf child, 172–173; low educational attainment of orally educated Deaf children, 144–145, 178; 80% of French Deaf children said to be illiterate, 176; 95% of such children scholastic failures, 178; seen as a failure in Great Britain and the United States, 177; mainstream schools, 179, 188, 192, 200; no schooling for Deaf children, 114; segregation of Deaf during education, 106; signed languages' use in, 48–49, 178. *See also* American Sign Language (ASL); Congress of Milan (1880); Oralism; Royal Commission on teaching the Deaf; *experiences of Deaf individuals by name of person (e.g., Helen Keller)*; *specific schools and educators by name*

"Deaf-mute" terminology, 222n3 (Ch. 6)

Deaf persons: capitalized term *Deaf,* xii, 219n1; change of paradigm making the deaf into the Deaf, 36; classification of, by Justinian, 2–3; medical experiments with, 21; intermarriage among, 106–109, 188; late-deafened adults' rejection of signed languages, 187. *See also* Inferiority of Deaf

Deaf President Now (Gallaudet University), 59, 181

"Deaf variety" of the human race, 106–109, 129

Decibel as unit of measurement of sound, 8

Denison, James, 86

Desloges, Pierre, 6

Detmold, George, 146, 152

Dez (designator), *tab* (tablet), and *sig* (signation), Stokoe's respective terms for shape, place, and motion, the formative elements of signs, 155

Dickens, Charles, read by sign-educated Deaf students in Hartford, 102, 114, 193; description of early spring by, 180

Diderot, Denis, compares the Deaf to primitive man, 5; regards French as "the most exact" of all languages, 5, 165

Djourno, André, 183

Dubois, Benjamin 82

Dupin, André, 66

Ear anatomy, 9, 195, 202–212, *203*, 219n1

Ear canal, 202

Eardrum, 8–9, 10, 21, 194; as inspiring Bell's study of the telephone, 94; Bell's fanciful strengthening of (by shouting), 103; sound's vibrations transmitted by, to anvil, hammer, and stirrup, 202-203, 207

Early death, as expectation of isolated Deaf children, 173, 231n7 (Ch. 12)

Edison, Thomas, 127

Education of the Deaf. *See* Deaf education; Gallaudet University; Oralism; Saint Jacques

Electric charge, 212–214

Encrevé, Florence, xv, 74, 110

Enlightenment, 36, 53

Epithelial cells. *See* Hair cells

Etcheverry, Martin, 84

Eugenics, 106–107

Europe: aristocratic families, speaking ability required in order to inherit, 12, 15; popularity of oralism in, 90, 99, 102, 112, 178

Eustachian tubes, and the equilibrium of the middle ear, 203

Eusthenopteron, 204, *206*

Evolutionary history, 234; of cochlea, 208; of middle ear, 204–205, *206*

Expression of ideas, signed languages used to convey, 38–39

Eye gaze, importance of, 156–157

Eyriès, Charles, 183

Facial expression, 29, 134; Bébian's observation that signs express the objective world around us, *physionomie* how the world affects us, 157–158; Stokoe's failure to provide symbols for, 158

Family learning signed language simultaneously with Deaf child, 174, 176

Fant, Louie J. Jr., 147, 152, 170

Faure, Félix, *113*

Fay, Étienne de, 19

Fingerspelling, 19, 28, 38, 42, 53, 148; ASL handshapes distinguished from, 156; Keller using fingerspelling by touch, 117, 118, 136, 156

Forestier, Claudius, 59, 61, 69, 77, 86, 90

Fowler, Sophia, 92

Français signé (signed French), 60, 171–172, 179

France: cochlear implants, study of, 188, 191, 194; Committee of Deaf-Mutes, 60–62; Deaf education in, 22–49, 179–181; illiteracy and lack of schooling for Deaf children in, 114, 176–177; manual alphabet, nineteenth century, *18*; oralism in, 178, 179; right of Deaf children to education in signed languages, 176; schools for the Deaf, 22, 48–49, 83, 90; voting rights for the Deaf in, 75. *See also* Saint Jacques

Freedom of association among the Deaf, 106–109

French sign language. *See* Langue des Signes Française (LSF)

Gallaudet, Edward, *93*; as advocate of signed languages, 92; background of, 92–93; at Milan Congress (1880), 86, 88; mother's deafness, 92, 97–98; testifying before Royal Commission on teaching the Deaf, 97–100, 152

Gallaudet, Thomas (brother of Edward), 86

Gallaudet, Thomas (father of Edward), *52*; Clerc and Massieu as sign language instructors of, 150; Clerc brought to United States by, 55–56, 92; early life of, 50–53; founding American School for the Deaf (Hartford), 56; improving Deaf lives, 107; learning French sign language at Saint Jacques, 54–55; in Paris, 54–55; Stokoe on, 150

Gallaudet University (formerly College): accreditation, 152; ASL as teaching medium at, 93, 145, 151, 179; congressional appropriation for, 224–225n2; Deaf President Now (1988), 59, 181; Detmold as dean, 146; discouraging Deaf students from becoming teachers, 144; Edward Gallaudet as first president of, 93; failure to appreciate Stokoe, 170–171; graduates of, 93–94, 97, 147; hearing administrators at, 145; l'Épée's obscurity at, 151; Visitors Center's pictorial history of Deaf people, 170. *See also* Stokoe, William C.

Genetic predisposition to deafness, 108

Geneviève, Sainte, 22

Gérando, Joseph-Marie de, 45–46, 56, 60, 61, 144

Germany, 111

Goldin-Meadow, Susan, 165–166

Guérin, abbé, 85, 87–88, 89–90, 106

Hair cells, 9–10, 183, 195–196, 210–214, *211–212*

Hall, David, 227n16

Handshapes, 18, *18*, 134, 155; of ASL, *216–217*; manual alphabets and, 155–156; Stokoe's recognition of, 156

Hartford School. *See* American School for the Deaf

Haydn's *Creation*, 4

Hearing aids, 171, 183, 186–187, 191–192

Hearing children of Deaf adults (CODA), 35, 108

Hearing teachers, 60, 77, 81, 83; failure to learn signed languages or their syntax, 171–172; at Gallaudet, 146; motivation for banning signed languages, 111, 148. *See also* Saint Jacques

Hebrew, study of, 162

Heinicke, Samuel, 12, 19–20, 56

Henney, Nella, 117, 130

Herrmann, Dorothy, 127, 129, 131–132

Hildegarde of Bingen, Saint, 3, *4*, 89

Home signs, 1, 53, 133–135

Hopkins, Sophia, 120–123

Howe, Samuel Gridley, 56, 127

Hugo, Victor, vii, 110–111, 167

Humphries, Tom, 152

Inferiority of Deaf: Bell on, 97, 103–104, 129, 200; Bonet on, 13, 107; Diderot on, 5; Gérando on, 45; hearing people's view of signed languages and, 146–147; idiots, use of term, 90; Lacharrière on, 77–78; Sicard on, 45; Tarra on, 114

Inner ear, 9, *203*, 207–209

Intellectual ability. *See* Child development and language acquisition

Intermarriage among the Deaf, 106–109, 188

Itard, Jean-Marc, 45–48, *46*, 58–59, 103, 197–198

Jenkins, W. G., 101–102, 193; reports that sign-educated children far ahead of the orally educated, 102

Jerome, Saint, declares that, by signs and gestures, the Deaf can understand "the whole gospel," 2

Joyce, James, xiii; and lyricals: *berginsoff, bergamoors, bergagambols, bergincellies*, xiii. See Lyricals

J. R. Pereire Society, 79

Justinian Code, 2–3, 6

Keller, Arthur (father of Helen), 119, 227n8

Keller, Helen, 109, 116–143, *121, 128*; Anagnos's opinion of, 118–124, 227n20, 228n25; autobiography by, 117, 126, 227n5, 228n21; Bell and, 116–117, 120, 125–126; developing "home" signs prior to Anne Sullivan's arrival, 52, 133–138, 166; education of, 116–117; as emblematic figure for oralism, 117, 124–125; "The Frost King," 118–123, 228n21, 228n25; lipreading by, 117, 118; loss of own voice (of sign as her natural language), 135–138, 143, 175; non-congenital deafness and blindness of, 116, 118; publications and writings by, 117–118, 129–130; speaking ability of, 118, 126, 129; *The Story of My Life*, 117, 126, 227n5, 227n20, 228n21; Sullivan as aide for, 116–118; Polly Thomson as aide for, 117, 126, 131–132; on vaudeville circuit with Sullivan and Thomson, 138; writing of "The Frost King," 118–123; ultimate break with Anagnos and Perkins, 123–124

Kendall School (Gallaudet), 179

Kinesic movements (natural gestures accompanying speech), 166

Klima, Edward, 168–169

Laborit, Emmanuelle, *174;* conversation in tactile sign language with a Deafblind woman, 132–133, 169, raised orally in early childhood, 172, 175; taught French sign language by Corrado and Moody, 172–175; in the role of Cordelia (in *King Lear)*,175–176

Lacharrière, Jules Ladreit de, 77–78, 81, 84

Lamartine, Alphonse de, 65, 66–67, 167, 223n16; writes that light, for the Deaf, "makes [a] sense of itself," 66

Lane, Harlan, xv, 148, 222n10

Lang, Harry, 199

Language: brain's neural activity and, 10, 168; central importance of, 90–91; child development and language acquisition, 162–165; definition of, 168–169; unique human capacity for, xi, 39. *See also* Signed languages; *specific names of signed languages*

Language Faculty, as an organic structure in the brain, 162; as giving man a soul in the modern age, xi, 165; as Bébian's principle of first language, 165; as an echo of Augustine's view that both speech and signed languages "pertain to the soul," 167

Langue des Signes Française (LSF), 26–27, 34–37, 46, 48, 50, 61; Bébian's system of French sign language symbols, 157–158; Clerc's and Massieu's knowledge of, 138; development of, 150–151; French teachers of the Deaf choosing

Langue des Signes Française (*continued*)
signed French over, 171–172; God,
sign for, 90; Laborit learning,
172–176; Saint Jacques's use of,
179–180; shared signs with other
signed languages, 134–135, 140,
229n11; Tactile LSF (LSFT), 141;
word order in, 147

Lash, Joseph, 127, 227n16

Lasker-DeBakey Clinical Medical
Research Award to developers of
cochlear implants, 188

Le Courtier, François, 79–80

Ledru-Rollin, Alexandre, 64

Lenoir, Alphonse, 59, 60, 61, 71, 81,
103, 107

L'Épée, Charles-Michel de (abbé):
Berthier annual banquets of the
Deaf in honor of, 61–75, 222n8
(Ch. 6); attempt to learn French
sign language, 26, 43; Berthier's
biography of, 44; Berthier's desire
to designate as national symbol for
the French Deaf, 62; celebration of
birthday at Saint Jacques, 81;
cochlea recognized as organ of
speech by, 103; on cochlea's role, 18;
discovery of signed language and,
23–31; Gallaudet University's lack of
knowledge about, 151; methodical
signs of, 26–30, 38, 39, 40, 229n11;
opposition to speech teaching and
lipreading, 79; school for the Deaf
established in Paris by, 24; Stokoe
on, 149

Lincoln, Abraham, 93

Linguistics, 153; Chomsky's revolution
in, 162–165. *See also* Phonemes;
Syntax

Lipreading: Bell's arguments for, 95,
101, 104–105; Bonet on, 15, 186;
Keller using touch for, 117, 118; Paris
resolution on, 84; reliance on, 98,
157; severely deaf persons, difficulty
of, 186; shortcomings of, 19–20, 39,
98; in sixteenth and seventeenth
century Europe, 12; in the movies,
16; by students at Milan school, 88

Location where sign is made, 134, 155,
156

Locke, John, 37, 136, 158

Loudest sounds, 8–11

Louis XV, 22

Louis XVI, 24

Louis-Napoleon Bonaparte, 75

Louis-Philippe, 59, 75

LSF. *See* Langue des Signes Française

Lupo, Lorenzo del, 86

Lyons Congress (1879), 85–86, 87,
106

Lyricals: definition of, xi; as contours
of an elusive language, xi; common
grace with poetry, xiii; Joyce's
lyricals, xiii; as "second tongue" of
partially deaf, xiii; and lipreading,
10, 15; as leading to understanding,
25; compared to electronic signals
from the cochlear implant, 185–186,
196; in the classroom, 201

Macy, John, 117, 118, 125, 126, 133,
226–227n3, 228n21; views the Deaf
who sign as "alien[s] from all races,"
129

Magnat, Marius, 79, 84, 86

Maher, Jane, 145–146

Mainstreaming, 179–180, 188, 192, 200

Mann, Horace, 56

Manual alphabets, 17–18; French manual, nineteenth century, *18*; handshapes using, 155–156

Manually coded systems, 147, 172, 179. *See also* Manual alphabets

Marriage ban on the Deaf, 3–4, 107

Massachusetts Eye and Ear Infirmary, 185

Massachusetts Institute of Technology (MIT), 162

Massieu, Jean, *30*, 31–35; background of, 31; and prayer, 31; first Deaf instructor at Saint Jacques, 32; Gallaudet (Thomas) studying French sign language with, 50, 54–55; methodical signs and, 54, 130, 150; French sign language and, 48–49, 52, 102; as star pupil of Sicard, 33–34, 40, 54

Maurice, Bernard, 70

Mende, Guillaume de, 3

Menière, Prosper, 77

Methodical signs: in ASL usage, 149–150; cessation of use in Deaf education, 150; *français signé* (signed French) and, 60; of l'Épée, 26–30, 38–40, 229n11; Massieu and Clerc using, 33, 54, 130, 150; resurfacing in 1960s and 1970s, 171; shortcomings of, 26–30, 32, 34, 36, 39, 49; Sicard displaying his students' ability to use, 33, 40–41, 138

Middle Ages, 3, 12–21, 86

Middle ear, 9, 195, 202–207, *203–204, 206*

Middle English, 145

Milan Congress. *See* Congress of Milan (1880)

Monglave, Eugène de, 63

Montagne Sainte Geneviève, 22

Montaigne, Michel de, 5

Moody, William, 172, 175

Morphemes, 153, 155

Motion of hands, 134, 155, 156, 158

Mottez, Bernard, 178

Myklebust, Helmer, views Deaf students as having "limited language," 144; writes that deafness "feminizes the male and masculinizes the female," 145, cited favorably in a French study of cochlear implants, 194

National Institute for Deaf Children. *See* Saint Jacques

National Institutes of Health on cochlear implanting of young children, 187, 191

Nationalism in nineteenth century, 112

Neural aphasias, 231n2 (Ch. 11)

New England Journal of Medicine on cochlear implanting of young children, 187

New York Institution for the Instruction of the Deaf and Dumb, 92–93, 100

New York University study on cochlear implants of infants, 187

Nicaragua, emergence of signed language in, 1

O'Connell, John, 65

Old English, 145–146

Oralism, 12–21; abolishing signed languages as teaching medium, 83–91; Bonet's attempts to teach Deaf students to speak, 13–17;

Oralism (*continued*)
British siding with, 53, 177–178; cochlear implants and, 189; continued use, despite failure of, 179–180; continuing fights against, 76–77, 82, 110–111; as doctrine to eliminate the Deaf, 200; early efforts to impose, 19–21; French study (1907) finding ineffectiveness of, 114; goal of articulation method, 84–85, 99; hearing parents choosing for their Deaf child, 190, 196; l'Épée and, 26; Berthier annual banquets of the Deaf in honor of l'Épée referring to, 76; Lyons Congress (1879), 85–86; normal conversation and, 197; Paris Congress (1878), 83–85; Paulmier and, 58; progress as motivation for advocating, 110–111; rise in second half of 1800s, 78–79; Royal Commission siding with, 109–115; Saint Jacques and Bébian's ouster, 58–60; shortcomings of, 18–19, 39, 45–48, 89, 98, 109, 177, 197–198; truce with signed language advocates, 152. *See also* Bell, Alexander Graham; Congress of Milan (1880)

Ordinaire, Désiré, 45, 47, 56, 144

Organ of Corti, 9, 195, *208*, 209, *212*

Orosius: *Historiae*, 146

Ossicles: hammer, anvil, and stirrup of the middle ear, 203, *204*

Outer ear, 9

Oval window (of the cochlea), 203, 206, *208*–209

Ozick, Cynthia, 123, 135

Panara, Robert, 148–149

Panderichthys, 204, *206*

Paris conference (1900), 88

Paris Congress (1878), 83–85

Partially deaf persons, 15; author's experience as, 10; lyricals of, *see* Lyricals; cochlear implants and, 185–186, 196; as students at Milan school used to demonstrate oralism, 88

Paulmier, Louis, 58

Pélissier, Pierre, 66–68, 72–73; writes of a Deaf infant, "never his voice enhanced his grace," 72

Pereire, Émile and Isaac, 78–79, 82; congress held by, 83–85; Milan Congress and, 86; motivation for banning signed languages, 111

Pereire, Jacob-Rodrigues, 12, 19–20, 46, 78, 117, 171, 182

Perkins Institute for the Blind (Boston), 116, 123, 124, 227nn16–17

Peyson, Frédéric, 61, 71–72

Phoenician alphabet, vii, 68, 223n18

Phonemes, 153, 155, 230n23

Pidgin sign language, 147

Place, shape and motion, as formative elements of both spoken and signed languages, xii, 8, 155

Plato, 1–2

Ponce de Leon, Pedro, 12, 155–156, 171, 182

Post-lingually deaf persons: attitude toward signed languages, 96; Bell's mother and wife as, 94–96; as students at Milan school used to demonstrate oralism, 88; Wright's experience as, 177

Prejudice, 38, 112. *See also* Inferiority of Deaf

Prelingually Deaf persons. *See*
  Congenitally Deaf persons
Progress as motivation to ban signed
  languages, 110–111
Proust, Marcel, 172, 231n5 (Ch. 12)
Puybonnieux, Jean-Baptiste, 78

Radcliffe College, 117, 118, 125, 130
Ramsey, Claire, 191
Real-world communication, 97,
  191–192, 199–201
Religious concepts, 89–90
Residual hearing. *See* Partially deaf
  persons
Rochester Technical Institute, 179
Round window (of the cochlea), 21,
  184, 208–209
Royal Commission on teaching the
  Deaf, 92; Bell testifying before,
  100–106, 225n13; decision siding
  with Bell, 109–115; Gallaudet
  (Edward) testifying before, 97–100,
  152

Sacks, Oliver, 225n13, 230n13
Saint Jacques (French National
  Institute for Deaf Children):
  Bébian as preeminent teacher at, 35,
  41–42; Bébian's removal from, 59;
  Berthier as advocate of French sign
  language at, 44, 56–57, 60–61;
  establishment of, 22, 24, 24–25;
  Gallaudet (Thomas) visiting, 54–55;
  hunger strike at (2005), 59, 180;
  influence of, on teaching of Deaf in
  Europe, 49; LSF, use of, 179;
  Massieu as first Deaf instructor at,
  32; oralists and hearing teachers vs.
  Deaf teachers at, 45, 60, 77, 81, 90,

114–115; other names for, 75;
  painting by Hendricus Jacobus
  Bürgers at, *113*
Saki (H. H. Munro), 94, 225
Sanborn, Frank, 124–125, 127, 189
Sanders, George, 109
Schwartz, Sandrine, 140–141
Shattuck, Roger, 118, 126, 227n5
Shea, Gerald: *Song Without Words*, xi;
  lyricals as "language" of the
  partially deaf, xi, xiii, 10, 15, 25, 185,
  186, 196, 201. *See also* Lyricals
Shouting, 103
Sicard, Roch-Ambroise, *32*;
  background of, 32–34; Bébian's
  criticism of, 42; as "never
  under[standing] the language of his
  [Deaf] students, 34"; Berthier's
  biography of, 44; on Clerc's trip to
  United States, 55–56; on Deaf
  charges as wild animals, 137;
  displaying his students' ability to
  use methodical signs, 33, 40–41, 138;
  on inferiority of Deaf, 45; in
  London, 50, 53–54; methodical
  signs and, 27, 38–40, 130, 138, 150;
  at Saint Jacques, 31, 55; Stokoe on,
  150
Signation. *See* Motion of hands; *Dez*
  (designator)
Signed English, 171
Signed French. *See Français signé*
Signed languages: as language of
  children born Deaf, xi; immediacy
  of, 11; as the indispensable
  instrument of Deaf education, 82;
  147; benefits of learning as a child,
  197–199; cheremes in, 155, 230nn23–
  24; cochlear implants, children

Signed languages: (*continued*)
with, still wanting to learn, 200;
Deaf children's ability to learn, 11;
distinctive to each country, 65,
220n1; dominant hand in, 155,
220n2; expression of ideas conveyed
by, 37–39; as formal languages,
154–161, 169; handshapes in, 134,
155; hearing people's view of, 147,
190; history of, 1–6, 45; iconic signs,
65, 133–134, 220n1, 229n11;
interfering with learning spoken
language, 103–104, 111; as speech
itself, 169; l'Épée and, 18, 23–31, 34;
location where sign is made, 134,
155; as manual-visual delivery
system for language, 168; Massieu
and, 32; morphemes, 155; motion of
hands in, 134, 155, 156, 158;
phonological-like elements in, 134;
similarities between French and
American sign languages, 134,
223n11; sophistication of, xii;
suppression of, 45, 88–90, 102–103,
110; teachers of the Deaf relying on
handshapes, 17–18; truce with
oralists, 152; U.S. preference for
oralism over, 83–84, 144; U.S.
schools for the Deaf teaching, 56;
U.S. use of, 189–190; use of term,
xii. *See also* American Sign
Language (ASL); British Sign
Language (BSL); Langue des Signes
Française (LSF); Methodical signs
Simultaneity of circumstances, 136
Sin, describing in signed languages,
89–90
Sleight, W. Blomefield, 98
Smith, Henry Lee, 153

Social deafness, 199
Société Universelle des Sourds-Muets,
222n8 (Ch. 6)
Society for Education. *See* Central
Society for the Education and
Assistance of the Deaf
Softest sounds, 8–11
Sound and speaking ability: cochlear
implants and perception of sound,
185–186, 191–192, 195–196; getting
Deaf to develop sounds pleasant to
the hearing, 13–14, 105; internal
ability to learn language with native
fluency, 162; of Keller, 118, 126, 129;
of prelingually Deaf persons, 127;
range of intensity of, 8–11. *See also*
Oralism
Spain, teaching Deaf to speak in,
12–15, 156
Speaking. *See* Sound and speaking
ability
Speech teaching. *See* Oralism
Speech therapy, 171, 172, 186, 190
Squarehand writing, 124, 228n26
Stereocilia. *See* Hair cells
Stokoe, William C., viii, 69, 133,
145–161; as Chaucerian scholar, 145;
as advocate for signed languages in
Deaf instruction, 147–149, 151; ASL
recognized as formal language by,
152, 154–161; as an example of Isaiah
Berlin's *hedgehog,* Bébian his *fox,*
159; background of, 145–146;
Chomsky and, 165–168; *A
Dictionary of American Sign
Language* (with Casterline &
Croneberg), 157, 160, 161; on facial
expressions, 158; fingerspelling and
handshapes identified by, 156;

Gallaudet University's failure to appreciate, 170–171; as historian of signed languages, 149; learning ASL, 149; linguistics study by, 153; locations of signs identified by, 156; motions identified by, 156, 158 (see *Dez* (designator); as new Bébian, 145; "Sign Language Structure," 154–157, 160–161, 167; system of sign-language symbols developed by, 157–158

Sullivan, Anne, *121*, *128*; on Helen Keller as "wild animal" when they first met, 137; as Keller's aide, 116–117, 125, 129; on Keller's speaking ability, 126; leading Keller to speak in language of others instead of her own "internal voice," 137; manual alphabet used in fingerspelling by, 156; on vaudeville circuit with Keller and Polly Thomson, 138; writing of Keller's "The Frost King" and, 118–123

Synapse, 213

Syntax, differences in, between signed and spoken languages, 36–37, 42; failure of hearing teachers to understand, 171–172; in contemporary linguistics,163–167; postulated as the heart of the language faculty, 163; recursive devices, 164

Tablet. *See* Place; *Dez* (designator)

Tactile sign languages, 141. *See also specific sign languages*

Tarra, Giulio, 86–90, *87*, 111, 114, 129

Teachers for the Deaf: Deaf persons as, 32, 48, 56, 114, 144, 171; hearing

persons as, 60, 77, 81, 83, 111, 146, 171

Telephone, invention of, 94

Théobald, Joseph, 86

Thomson, Polly, 117, 126, 131–132, 138

Tinnitus, 52

Trager, George L., 153

Unheard speech and unspoken speech, 10–11

United Kingdom. *See* Britain

United States: cochlear implants, use of, 183; Deaf education in, 50, 56, 177; Deaf people using sign language in, 189–190; Gallaudet's (Thomas) role in bringing sign language as mode to educate the Deaf to, 50–57; oralism in, 83–84, 144, 178. *See also specific schools*

University of Melbourne study on efficacy of cochlear implants, 192

University of Paris at Saint Denis, 139–143

University of Southern California on effect of cochlear implants on Deaf culture, 188–189

University of Toronto study on efficacy of cochlear implants, 191, 192

Vaïsse, Léon, 81, 82, 84, 86

Valade-Gabel, Jean-Jacques, 77

Vigny, Alfred de, 64

Virgil, 172, 231n4 (Ch. 12)

Voting rights for the French Deaf, 75

Wallis, John, 12

Wells College (Aurora, NY), 145–146

Widerkehr, Joseph de (Deaf painter), 73–74

Wind in the Willows, 7-8

Women's rights in nineteenth century, 73–75

The Word, in Christian teaching, 3–4, 86, 91

Word order of spoken vs. signed languages, 42, 147, 171–172

World's Congress of the Deaf (St. Louis, 1904), 115

Wright, David, 177, 187

Wright Oral School (Pennsylvania), 110

Yale University, 51–52, 92–93